Bringing Learning to Life:
The Reggio Approach to Early Childhood Education
LOUISE BOYD CADWELL

The Power of Projects:
Meeting Contemporary Challenges in Early
Childhood Classrooms—Strategies and Solutions
JUDY HARRIS HELM & SALLEE BENEKE, Eds.

Young Children Reinvent Arithmetic:
Implications of Piaget's Theory, 2nd Edition
CONSTANCE KAMII

Supervision in Early Childhood Education, 2nd Ed.:
A Developmental Perspective
JOSEPH J. CARUSO & M. TEMPLE FAWCETT

The Early Childhood Curriculum:
A Review of Current Research, 3rd Edition
CAROL SEEFELDT, Ed.

Leadership in Early Childhood, 2nd Ed.:
The Pathway to Professionalism
JILLIAN RODD

Inside a Head Start Center:
Developing Policies from Practice
DEBORAH CEGLOWSKI

Uncommon Caring:
Learning from Men Who Teach Young Children
JAMES R. KING

Teaching and Learning in a Diverse World:
Multicultural Education for Young Children, 2nd Ed.
PATRICIA G. RAMSEY

Windows on Learning:
Documenting Young Children's Work
JUDY HARRIS HELM, SALLEE BENEKE, & KATHY STEINHEIMER

Bringing Reggio Emilia Home: An Innovative
Approach to Early Childhood Education
LOUISE BOYD CADWELL

Major Trends and Issues in Early Childhood
Education: Challenges Controversies, and Insights
JOAN P. ISENBERG & MARY RENCK JALONGO, Eds.

Master Players:
Learning from Children at Play
GRETCHEN REYNOLDS & ELIZABETH JONES

Understanding Young Children's Behavior:
A Guide for Early Childhood Professionals
JILLIAN RODD

Understanding Quantitative and Qualitative Research
in Early Childhood Education
WILLIAM L. GOODWIN & LAURA D. GOODWIN

Diversity in the Classroom:
New Approaches to the Education of Young Children,
2nd Ed.
FRANCES E. KENDALL

Developmentally Appropriate Practice in "Real Life"
CAROL ANNE WIEN

Quality in Family Child Care and Relative Care
SUSAN KONTOS, CAROLLEE HOWES,
MARYBETH SHINN, & ELLEN GALINSKY

Using the Supportive Play Model:
Individualized Intervention in Early Childhood
Practice
MARGARET K. SHERIDAN,
GILBERT M. FOLEY, & SARA H. RADLINSKI

The Full-Day Kindergarten:
A Dynamic Themes Curriculum, 2nd Ed.
DORIS PRONIN FROMBERG

Experimenting with the World:
John Dewey and the Early Childhood Classroom
HARRIET K. CUFFARO

New Perspectives in Early Childhood
Teacher Education:
Bringing Practitioners into the Debate
STACIE G. GOFFIN & DAVID E. DAY, Eds.

Assessment Methods for Infants and Toddlers:
Transdisciplinary Team Approaches
DORIS BERGEN

The Emotional Development of Young Children:
Building an Emotion-Centered Curriculum
MARION C. HYSON

Moral Classrooms, Moral Children:
Creating a Constructivist Atmosphere in
Early Education
RHETA DeVRIES & BETTY ZAN

Diversity and Developmentally Appropriate Practices
BRUCE L. MALLORY & REBECCA S. NEW, Eds.

Understanding Assessment and Evaluation in Early
Childhood Education
DOMINIC F. GULLO

Changing Teaching, Changing Schools:
Bringing Early Childhood Practice into Public
Education—Case Studies from the Kindergarten
FRANCES O'CONNELL RUST

Physical Knowledge in Preschool Education:
Implications of Piaget's Theory
CONSTANCE KAMII & RHETA DeVRIES

Caring for Other People's Children:
A Complete Guide to Family Day Care
FRANCES KEMPER ALSTON

Family Day Care:
Current Research for Informed Public Policy
DONALD L. PETERS & ALAN R. PENCE, Eds.

Reconceptualizing the Early Childhood Curriculum:
Beginning the Dialogue
SHIRLEY A. KESSLER & BETH BLUE SWADENER, Eds.

Ways of Assessing Children and Curriculum:
Stories of Early Childhood Practice
CELIA GENISHI, Ed.

(Continued)

Early Childhood Education Series titles, continued

The Play's the Thing:
Teachers' Roles in Children's Play
ELIZABETH JONES & GRETCHEN REYNOLDS

Scenes from Day Care
ELIZABETH BALLIETT PLATT

Raised in East Urban
CAROLINE ZINSSER

Play and the Social Context of Development in Early
Care and Education
BARBARA SCALES, MILLIE ALMY, AGELIKI NICOLOPOULOU,
& SUSAN ERVIN-TRIPP, Eds.

The Whole Language Kindergarten
SHIRLEY RAINES & ROBERT CANADY

Children's Play and Learning
EDGAR KLUGMAN & SARA SMILANSKY

Serious Players in the Primary Classroom
SELMA WASSERMANN

Young Children Continue to Reinvent Arithmetic—
2nd Grade
CONSTANCE KAMII

The Good Preschool Teacher
WILLIAM AYERS

A Child's Play Life: An Ethnographic Study
DIANA KELLY-BYRNE

The War Play Dilemma
NANCY CARLSSON-PAIGE & DIANE E. LEVIN

The Piaget Handbook for Teachers and Parents
ROSEMARY PETERSON &VICTORIA FELTON-COLLINS

Promoting Social and Moral Development in Young
Children
CAROLYN POPE EDWARDS

Today's Kindergarten
BERNARD SPODEK, Ed.

Visions of Childhood
JOHN CLEVERLEY & D. C. PHILLIPS

Starting School
NANCY BALABAN

Ideas Influencing Early Childhood Education
EVELYN WEBER

The Joy of Movement in Early Childhood
SANDRA R. CURTIS

Bringing Learning to Life

*THE REGGIO APPROACH TO
EARLY CHILDHOOD EDUCATION*

LOUISE BOYD CADWELL

FOREWORD BY CARLINA RINALDI

Teachers College
Columbia University
New York and London

Cover design by Pam Bliss. Cover artwork a composite drawing by members of the 2002 Kindergarten Class, The College School.

Chapter opening artwork by Louise Boyd Cadwell.

Figures 3.1, 3.2, 3.3, 6.3, 6.5, 6.6, and Plate 10 are copyright © Municipality of Reggio Emilia—Infant–Toddler Centers and Preschools, published by Reggio Children.

All other photography by Louise Boyd Cadwell, Chuck Schwall, and other members of the St. Louis–Reggio Collaborative.

Published by Teachers College Press, 1234 Amsterdam Avenue, New York, NY 10027

Library of Congress Cataloging-in-Publication Data

Cadwell, Louise Boyd.
    Bringing learning to life : the Reggio approach to early childhood education / Louise Boyd Cadwell ; foreword by Carlina Rinaldi.
        p.   cm. — (Early childhood education series)
    Includes bibliographical references and index.
    ISBN 0-8077-4296-1 (pbk. : alk. paper) — ISBN 0-8077-4297-X (cloth : alk. paper)
    1. Education, Preschool—Philosophy.   2. Early childhood education—Philosophy.   3. Education, Preschool—Italy—Reggio Emilia.   I. Title.   II. Early childhood education series (Teachers College Press)
    LB1140.3 .C225   2003
    372.21—dc21   2002026794

ISBN 0-8077-4296-1 (paper)
ISBN 0-8077-4297-X (cloth)

Printed on acid-free paper
Manufactured in the United States of America

10   09   08   07   06   05   04   03   8   7   6   5   4   3   2   1

For all my colleagues
in Reggio Emilia and in St. Louis
with great love, admiration, and gratitude

Contents

Foreword *by Carlina Rinaldi*   ix

Acknowledgments   xii

Prologue   1

    A Brief History of Reggio Emilia, Italy   2
    Ideas Integral to the Reggio Approach   4
    The Context for Our Work and This Book   6
    The Fall of 2001: A Turning Point   8

1. January—The Arc of a Day   11

    The Start of the Day   12
    Beginning with the Kindergarten   23
    Moving to the Newport Room   31
    Midday   39
    The Afternoon   40

2. February—The Power of Partnership with Parents   42

    Building Relationships: The Parents and the School 44
    Forms and Structures for Parent Participation   46
    Parents Speak to Visiting Educators   59
    Reflections on Our Lives with Parents   66

3. March—Teachers Living in Collaboration   67

    Learning Together Away from Home   67
    Looking at Ourselves Through Amelia's Eyes   79
    Organizing Our Work and Making It Visible   85
    Growing and Changing over Time   97

4. April—Living in a Place That Is Alive   101

    Roots: Developing a Sense of Place   *102*

    Transforming Our Spaces: Transforming Ourselves   *106*

    Atelier *Room Parents*   *118*

    Atelier *Metaphors*   *126*

5. May—What Are the Children Learning?   128

    "The Pattern That Connects"   *129*

    World-Making   *131*

    The Scent Project   *146*

6. June—Returning to Italy   160

    Day 1: Meeting the Town and the Group   *161*

    Day 2: A New View of School   *162*

    Day 3: Theory and Practice   *167*

    Day 4: Going Deeper   *172*

    Day 5: A Day of Rest and Reflection   *188*

    Day 6: Nostalgia for the Future   *192*

Epilogue   195

References   205

Index   208

About the Author   212

Foreword

Dear reader,

This foreword is obviously written for you. However, it is not easy for me to imagine what you are like nor to know your reasons for choosing this book. Maybe you would like to learn more about the Reggio Approach. Or maybe you would like to know how this innovative approach has come to the United States. Perhaps you would like to change your way of teaching or your idea of what school can be. Or maybe you would like to share in this approach and these ideas. Perhaps you think that life and school move in two different arenas and that they are too separate, and you are trying to embrace the excitement in learning and to see life itself as learning. It is difficult for me to respond to your expectations, so I think it would be better if I speak for myself as a reader and share with you what struck me while reading this book. Rather than speak of my expectations, I would like to share with you what I unexpectedly found.

There is, in fact, a pervasive theme in this book that is embedded in the very way that Louise Boyd Cadwell considers the reality that she describes. One could call it *wonder*. The book speaks of a fresh, new perspective that the protagonists of this fascinating story have brought to the classroom and indeed to their lives. In my opinion, to be capable of wonder is to be fully human. Our innate drive to know and the joy that we find in learning is founded in this capacity. The capacity to be amazed opens one to the unknown and to the beauty and poetry found within the act of seeking knowledge. It is awe and wonder that informs this book and the experiences described here.

Unfortunately, it is increasingly rare that school is a place where we are amazed, but the educational journey can be one in which it is possible, among other things, to uphold wonder as fundamental and necessary. This is the wonder that can be seen in the eyes of children, through whom we ourselves must find the courage to see things afresh. If we don't allow ourselves to lapse into routines that keep us from seeing things as new and different, then we can be open to the wonder and the richness that everyday events offer.

I hold that there is nothing worse for us as educators than to fall into a routine, because as events unfold, more often than not, routines lead us to repeat ourselves over and over, and finally, we have nothing left to offer. Falling into a routine, we risk losing the stimulation that our work can give us, and we cease caring about what we are actually offering children. We should pause more often to reflect on what we are doing in school and especially to think about daily life as a series of unexpected opportunities.

Therefore, we must ask the question, Are teachers and adults today still capable of experiencing wonder? We live in a scientific era convinced that we know almost everything, or, at the very least, that it is possible to know everything. Yet, I think we cannot avoid ignorance simply by possessing information and by using the Internet. There are still and there always will be those who are convinced that, beyond what we know, there is still much to discover and to know, and especially that experiences of wonder can actually lead some to learn even as they consider ethical choices.

I believe that the limits of our ignorance lie in our ability and willingness to question ourselves, to go beyond the boundaries of what is known and recognizable, and to seek meaning throughout the whole course of our lives. As Louise tells us of what she and the teachers discovered, of their trials and triumphs, she also shows what this research gave to the teachers and the children on a daily basis. It was not easy, especially for the teachers, to understand and practice this new concept of research as a way to relate to the children everyday and to the experiences that they chose and realized together.

Often in our work, and in our lives, we tend to look for confirmation of what we think and what we believe. We identify our selves with our ideas and our theories. To change our minds, to reconsider our basic theories and beliefs so as to see their limitations, is often perceived as a personal defeat. Often the ensuing crisis is experienced as a loss rather than as the beginning of something new. The fact is that we are too firmly attached to our theories and to our ideas and thus we often close the door to new ways of seeing and understanding. But new ideas spring forth everywhere, particularly if we live among children. The children themselves stand for what is new for us and what is asking for acceptance. We can never predict the way in which the new will appear, but often it has the eyes of a child. We must, therefore, expect the new to appear, help it come forth, follow it, and nurture it.

In fact, this is what the teachers within the stories in this book have done, sustaining their shared effort with the children through attentive and timely documentation. These efforts have given these teachers the possibility of building a sense of something new; they witness this "newness" emerge and know that it needs to be recognized and built upon everyday.

All of this proves once again that school does not renew itself only with rules and regulations, nor does a sense of belonging emerge through tests that measure individual performances to determine whether students conform to the system that produced them. A true innovation, one capable of producing new ways of thinking and of giving school the possibility of becoming a true educational community, in my opinion, is one that changes the movements and the thoughts surrounding daily life, such as those described in Louise's detailed and moving account.

In fact, this book is full of emotions. The author's emotions are evident every time she witnesses an act of understanding, of discovery, of creation. We feel the emotions that the adults and children share when they find the beauty of thinking, building, and creating together. There is a feeling that the voices in this book are singing together, as in a chorus. This "chorality" is something that the protagonists search for consciously and persistently: Having discovered it through experience, it is something that both children and adults seek again and again. The "intellectual pleasure" of altruism flows through much of this book, a pleasure that some American researchers have recently suggested may have biological roots. The capacity to work in groups and to learn to listen to others' reasoning, feelings, and emotions is documented many times in this book. This shows, once again, how altruism is not only generated by the context: It is a completely natural way of being for a community that is committed to learning together.

The German philosopher Schopenhauer recognized that in every one of us there are two kinds of subjectivity. One of these is the "I," which does projects, reaches goals, searches for the conditions for survival, even at the expense of others. Add to this "I" another subjectivity called the "we." This is the "we" that drives a mother without thinking and out of pure instinct to sacrifice herself and her body, her days and nights, her dreams, and, for a time, to suspend her life for the life of her child. We are all born out of a relationship, and we are all born into a relationship: We are born out of the sacrifice of one being for another. Children still hold powerful memories of this loving relationship that generated them, received them, and nourished them.

Do we really think, then, that a society and its schools can continue to suspend relationships, altruism, and cooperation to teach only in the interest of this egotistical "I"? For a response to this (and much more) please read through the following pages, dear reader. But more important, reading this book will give you the chance to reflect on how much change and transformation—as well as curiosity, love, and relationships—are vital for a school. A school that cares not just about learning to read, write, add, and use the computer correctly, but more than anything wants to open itself to life, to generate life because it is capable of generating curiosity, pleasure in research, and new constructs in friendship and solidarity.

Jerome Bruner wrote, "School is not a preparation for life, but is life itself." This is an objective, a hope, a utopia for many of us—a reality for Louise's school, her colleagues, the parents, and the children.

—Carlina Rinaldi
(Translated from Italian by Louise Boyd Cadwell and Ugo Skubikowski)

Acknowledgments

To thank all those who have made it possible for this book to come to life is an enormous responsibility. So many people have cheered me on, read pieces and parts of the manuscript, offered me suggestions and solutions when I was stuck. So many authors have given me inspiration, so many teachers have offered me encouragement, so many children have given me the gift of wonder and discovery. It would be impossible to mention them all here. For all of you I offer my heartfelt gratitude.

First and foremost I want to thank all of my colleagues in St. Louis; it is our story. This time, I am the scribe and the ethnographer; together, we are a team of researchers and dedicated educators who live this work. In the same breath, I thank all of our colleagues and friends in Reggio Emilia, Italy, who are our inspiration—who give the world hope and real dreams for a future worth giving our lives to work for.

I am forever grateful to those authors who have demonstrated for me the stamina, discipline, and craft of writing: John Elder, Julia Alvarez, Karen Gallas, and Carol Flinders, to name only a few. I am deeply thankful for the authors who are breaking ground for the birth of a new worldview. They give us all new insight with which to understand the depth of the educational practice in Reggio Emilia. Among them are Peter Senge and his colleagues, who have written extensively on systems thinking, William Isaacs on dialogue, Fritjof Capra on the concept of an ecological worldview, Johanna Macy on deep ecology, and Thich Nhat Hanh on mindfulness and "interbeing."

I feel deep gratitude for my readers of this manuscript, who gave me not only countless valuable suggestions but also immeasurable support along the way: Carlina Rinaldi, Amelia Gambetti, Vea Vecchi, Carol Anne Wien, Rena Diana, Jeanne Goldhaber, Lori Geismar Ryan, and Ashley Cadwell. My editor, Susan Liddicoat, worked miracles on the first version of the manuscript, giving it new clarity and greater organization. Throughout the process of writing this book, Susan has been an invaluable partner. I thank all those at Teachers College Press for their belief in me and their generous and expert skill in bringing this book to its final form.

Finally, I thank my family, who have, day by day, supported my writing practice and helped me clarify my thoughts—Ashley, Alden, Christopher, and my parents, who are always with me. Today, as I write the final lines of this book here, the sun is shining, the windows are open wide, and the cardinal is singing his indomitable song. It is a day to celebrate.

Prologue

The year has turned, and we have once again arrived in January. This morning my family awoke to frosty light warming its way through layers of ice coating the new storm windows. The thermometer outside reads 18 degrees. I bundle myself in extra sweaters. I realize that something about this particular season calls me to reflect and to write. Perhaps this is true for many of us as the old year ends and we anticipate the new. Maybe this time of year beckons me to slow down and compose my thoughts, because I wrote the first lines of my first book, *Bringing Reggio Emilia Home,* in January of 1995, looking out the windows of this house at softly falling snow. And then, in January of 2000, I began to write this book.

During this month, January 2002, I have been given some days off from teaching to write—a month of days in which to finish the book that I started to write 2 years ago and have otherwise attended to mostly during the summers. The administration and board of the College School, where I teach, have established the tradition of celebrating teachers and staff members who have worked at the school for 10 years. The tenth-year teacher is honored with a gift that will also benefit the school in some way. When asked what I wanted for my tenth year gift, I requested time to bring this book over the finish line.

My first book describes my family's journey to the small northern Italian city of Reggio Emilia in 1991–1992 and my year-long adventure there as an intern in two of its internationally acclaimed, municipally funded preschools. The story continues with my return to teach at the College School in my hometown of St. Louis, Missouri. In 1992, the College School became the lead institution in a consortium of schools where educators were supported with a 3-year Danforth Foundation grant to study and begin to adapt in their own schools the fundamental principles and practices of what is known worldwide as the "Reggio Approach." Three of these schools—the College School, the St. Michael School, and Clayton Schools' Family Center—now form the St. Louis–Reggio Collaborative.

In many ways, this book is a sequel to *Bringing Reggio Emilia Home,* offering continuing stories of change and transformation in the lives of children, teachers, and parents in the three schools of the St. Louis–Reggio Collaborative. Our serious encounter with the Reggio Approach has set us in motion, and there is no going back. I hope this book will reveal our growth, make clear what we have learned, and share it generously. I also hope this book will reach an even wider audience than the first. Most of us who are touched by this approach to education—and to life—feel its power and its relevance far beyond early childhood education. Though we will return to Reggio Emilia for an extended tour in Chapter 6 of this book, in order to get to the heart of the matter, let me take you for a moment into one of the schools in the center of that city.

If you have been there, you may identify with the following description. If you have never heard of Reggio Emilia, try to imagine following a group of first-time visitors into a preschool. Be they teachers or administrators, journalists or politicians, parents or grandparents, during their first moments in one of the schools in Reggio Emilia, most adults feel awestruck, speechless, often moved to tears. Why is this? I think the answer may be that in the schools of Reggio Emilia we see our own great potential reflected in everything that we lay our eyes on. It is as if we recognize our deepest selves in the glistening murals and the robust clay figures made by children; in the tile-floored, sun-filled spaces; and in the way the adults and the children are alive with respect and knowledge of one another. We immediately sense the extraordinary meaning and beauty of everyday life in a school for the youngest citizens—a school that mirrors both who they truly are and who they will become.

The Italian educators challenge us. In every way, they place the child and the particular group of children and their families at center stage. The Italian educators call the children "protagonists," a word meaning the leading characters in a story or drama. With this word and its definition comes a shift in thinking about school. School becomes the place where stories are lived out and life dramas enacted with a particular cast of characters playing the leads. The stories are yet to be written. They will come to life through the collaboration of the three groups of protagonists who play central roles: the children, the parents, and the teachers.

These schools pulse with the energy of stories that trace the search for meaning by children and adults, the joy of the journey, and an abundance of children's fresh ideas in clay and paint, pen and words, numbers and theories. When we are surrounded with this energy, we understand that we are meant to live like this, true to our nature and our birthright as creative thinkers within a close community, not only as children but as human beings. Many of us may have caught glimmers of this truth before, but to walk into the schools in Reggio Emilia is to witness a great flash of insight. Perhaps we weep in these schools because we long for the meaning and beauty of life as it can be lived, not only in school but everywhere. Perhaps we mourn because we see what we have missed. Perhaps we feel a fervent hope that school as we know it, life as we know it, might be transported toward the possible.

In the preschools of Reggio Emilia we come face to face with our potential to live our lives as creative beings participating fully in the midst of a wildly creative and diverse universe. These schools are living testimony to the possible. They stand for the possible. They demonstrate the possible. The educators, parents, community, and young children live the possible. It is not just talk or a dream. The schools are real and alive.

It is this vision of the possible that has captivated educators from all over the globe. We of the St. Louis–Reggio Collaborative are part of a worldwide network working to understand this approach and imagine how the work of the Reggio educators might deeply inspire our own. In order to place the Reggio Approach within a historical, political, and educational perspective, I offer a brief history of Reggio Emilia, Italy, and an outline of ideas and terms that are integral to the Reggio Approach, revised and updated from *Bringing Reggio Emilia Home.*

A BRIEF HISTORY OF REGGIO EMILIA, ITALY

The town of Reggio Emilia is in the hub of a territory influenced by Etruscans and Gauls and founded by the Romans in the 2nd century B.C. During the Renaissance it was the hometown of poets Matteo Maria Boiardo and Ludovico Ariosto. Important episodes in the history of the town are the birth of the Italian republic and the national flag in 1797 and the role the citizens of Reggio Emilia played in the movement against Naziism-Fascism, for which they received Italy's highest gold medal for military valor.

The town is located on the ancient Roman road, the Via Emilia, which crosses the entire region of Emilia Romagna from east to west. The Po River flows through the center of the region, which is bordered by the Apennine Mountains to the south and the Alps to the north. This region of 4 million inhabitants is the largest and richest region in Italy. It is rich in art and architecture, agriculture, industry, and tourism. It is also the region with the most highly developed and subsidized social services in Italy, especially in the area of child welfare (Department of Education, City of Reggio Emilia, 1990).

The history of efforts throughout Italy to provide services and support for families and young children through private, parochial, and federal means began as early as 1820. In 1945-1946, for a short period after the war, strong local initiatives arose, especially in locations that had a tradition of supporting them. It was such an initiative that gave birth to the parent-run schools that were the beginnings of the Reggio Emilia preschools (Edwards, Gandini, & Forman, 1993).

In the 1950s, as educators and parents became aware of the importance of and need for early childhood education, the new ideas about progressive education of Celestin Freinet and John Dewey provoked a debate about the need to change education. In 1951, the Movement of Cooperative Education was formed, led by a strong educator named Bruno Ciari, who was appointed by the liberal administration of Bologna to direct their city school system (Edwards et al., 1993). Loris Malaguzzi, the founder of the preschools in Reggio Emilia, was a close friend and colleague of Bruno Ciari, whose writings have become classics in Italy.

Ciari and his followers believed that "education should liberate childhood energy and capacities" (Edwards et al., 1993, pp. 15-16) and promote the harmonious development of the whole child in communicative, social, and affective domains. Ciari encouraged educators to invite families and other citizen to participate in schools, to provide two teachers in each classroom of 20 children, to enable the staff to work collectively, and to attend carefully to the physical setting of schools (Edwards et al., 1993).

Over the past 30 years, many different scholars from different fields have contributed to the ever-evolving practice of the Reggio Approach. Among them are Susan Issacs, Maria Montessori, Lev Vygotsky, Jean Piaget, Erik Erikson, John Dewey, David Hawkins, Humberto Maturana, Francisco Varela, Gregory Bateson, and Jerome Bruner.

Many regions of Italy, such as Tuscany, Lombardy, Trentino, Piedmont, Veneto, and Liguria, have established high-quality municipal early childhood systems. Emilia Romagna remains one of the most innovative, within which the town of Reggio Emilia is particularly noteworthy. The distinguishing features of the Reggio Emilia schools include the *atelier,* or studio, and *atelierista,* or studio teacher; the importance of the pedagogical team; the participation of parents; the involvement and participation of elected officials in the development of the early childhood system; and a commitment to research, experimentation, communication, and documentation (Edwards et al., 1993).

Today, the municipality of Reggio Emilia supports 21 preschools and 13 infant-toddler centers. The preschools serve a total of 1,508 children between the ages of 3 and 6, and the infant-toddler centers serve 835 children between the ages of 3 months and 3 years. The city also supports 5 infant-toddler centers and 1 early childhood center for children from age 1 to 6 that are managed by cooperatives. There is also 1 infant-toddler center run by parents. The presence of other early childhood services makes it possible to serve 94.6% of all children between ages 3 and 6 and 38% of all children between the ages of 3 months and 3 years (*Municipal Infant-Toddler Centers and Preschools of Reggio Emilia,* 2000).

When children leave these schools at age 6, they enter a state-run public school or a parochial school. The curriculum in these schools is prescribed by the sponsoring institution and follows a traditional model. The teachers in the preschool meet with the first-grade teachers to give them helpful information about the children whom they will receive in their classes in the fall.

Reggio Children, the International Center for the Defense and Promotion of the Rights and Potential of All Children, was established on March 11, 1994. Based on an idea of Loris Malaguzzi, the foundation's mission is "to protect and disseminate the wealth of knowledge and experience accumulated over many years of work in the field of early childhood education by the Infant-toddler Centers and Preschools run by the Municipality of Reggio Emilia" and to create opportunities for exchange and research on the topic of "a new culture of childhood that places real value on the potential and creativity of children" (Giudici, Rinaldi, & Krechevsky, 2001, Appendix E).

IDEAS INTEGRAL TO THE REGGIO APPROACH

In *Bringing Reggio Emilia Home* I distilled the fundamentals of the Reggio Approach into a list of essential elements. Although it seems an inadequate way to describe a whole, complex way of living in school, I quote the list here, and add to it, to provide an orientation to the terms and ideas that are integral to the way the approach works. In Reggio Emilia the educators view:

- *The child as protagonist.* Children are strong, rich, and capable. All children have preparedness, potential, curiosity, and interest in constructing their learning, negotiating with everything their environment brings to them. Children, teachers, and parents are considered the three central protagonists in the educational process (Gandini, 1993).
- *The child as collaborator.* Education has to focus on each child in relation to other children, the family, the teachers, and the community rather than on each child in isolation (Gandini, 1993). There is an emphasis on work in small groups. This practice is based on the social constructivist model that supports the idea that we form ourselves through our interaction with peers, adults, things in the world, and symbols (Lewin, 1995).
- *The child as communicator.* This approach fosters children's intellectual development through a systematic focus on symbolic representation, including words, movement, drawing, painting, building, sculpture, shadow play, collage, dramatic play, and music, which leads children to surprising levels of communication, symbolic skills, and creativity (Edwards et al., 1993). Children have the right to use many materials in order to discover and to communicate what they know, understand, wonder about, question, feel, and imagine. In this way, they make their thinking visible through their many natural "languages." A studio teacher, trained in the visual arts, works closely with children and teachers in each school to enable children to explore many materials and to use a great number of languages to make their thinking visible.
- *The environment as third teacher.* The design and use of space encourages encounters, communication, and relationships (Gandini, 1993). There is an underlying order and beauty in the design and organization of all the space in a school

and the equipment and materials within it (Lewin, 1995). Every corner of every space has an identity and a purpose, is rich in potential to engage and to communicate, and is valued and cared for by children and adults.

- *The teacher as partner, nurturer, and guide* (Edwards, 1993). Teachers facilitate children's exploration of themes, work on short- and long-term projects, and guide experiences of joint, open-ended discovery and problem solving (Edwards et al., 1993). To know how to plan and proceed with their work, teachers listen and observe children closely. Teachers ask questions; discover children's ideas, hypotheses, and theories; and provide occasions for discovery and learning (Gandini, 1993).

- *The teacher as researcher.* Teachers work in pairs and maintain strong, collegial relationships with all other teachers and staff; they engage in continuous discussion and interpretation of their work and the work of children. These exchanges provide ongoing training and theoretical enrichment. Teachers see themselves as researchers preparing documentation of their work with children, whom they also consider researchers. The team is further supported by a *pedagogista* (pedagogical coordinator) who serves a group of schools (Gandini, 1993).

- *The documentation as communication.* Careful consideration and attention is given to the presentation of the thinking of the children and the adults who work with them. Teachers' commentary on the purposes of the study and the children's learning process, transcriptions of children's verbal language (i.e., words and dialogue), photographs of their activity, and representations of their thinking in many media are composed in carefully designed panels or books to present the process of learning in the schools. The documentation serves many purposes. It makes parents aware of their children's experiences. It allows teachers to better understand children, to evaluate their own work, and to exchange with other educators. Documentation also shows children that their work is valued. Finally, it creates an archive that traces the history of the school and the pleasure in the process of learning experienced by many children and their teachers (Gandini, 1993).

- *The parent as partner.* Parent participation is considered essential and takes many forms. Parents play an active part in their children's learning experience and help ensure the welfare of all the children in the school. The ideas and skills that the families bring to the school and, even more important, the exchange of ideas between parents and teachers, favor the development of a new way of educating, which helps teachers to view the participation of families not as a threat but as an intrinsic element of collegiality and as the integration of different wisdoms (Spaggiari, 1993).

I realize now that there is an important point missing from this list—that the essential nature of the organization is at the heart of this approach. I have added it here.

- *Organization as foundational.* Intricate and complex organization appears at every level and within every context in the municipal schools of Reggio Emilia—from the collections, arrangements, and care of collage materials on a shelf, to the daily preparation and serving of a nutritious meal for children and teachers, to the thoughtful selection of small groups of children by a group of adults who consider multiple perspectives, to the layered agenda and inclusive dialogue of an evening meeting of parents and teachers. The way organization functions at every level in the Reggio Emilia preschools and infant–toddler centers reminds me of the way Wheatley and Kellner-Rogers (1996) describe it in *A Simpler Way.* It is organic instead of rigid. It serves a larger purpose. It is not neat and tidy; rather it reflects the complexity and the order of the universe. In some ways, it is as if the organization already exists, waiting to be discovered. It evolves; it is flexible. It has flow and movement. It honors the integrity of all involved. It is not imposed from the top; rather it grows out of a dialogic group working closely together.

Many of the most respected educators, psychologists, and researchers from all over the world acknowledge that the Reggio Approach is the most exceptional example of the highest-quality early education that the world has ever seen (Bruner, 2000; Dahlberg, Moss, & Pence, 1999; Gardner, 2000; Katz, 1998; "The Ten Best Schools," 1991). At the same time, most of them are somewhat stumped when asked to pin it down, to say exactly how and why this is so. Even more daunting than describing it is venturing to transport this jewel, to export it out of Reggio Emilia to other countries and cultures.

Recognizing these challenges, Howard Gardner and a team of dedicated researchers from Harvard's Project Zero worked with Carlina Rinaldi and a team of esteemed educators from the Reggio Emilia preschools during a 3-year period of joint study and research. This research culminated in *Making Learning Visible: Children as Individual and Group Learners* (Giudici et al., 2001). This book includes the most clear and challenging writing of Carlina Rinaldi and other Reggio educators that I have ever read. The writing of the Project Zero team adds to the collection of thoughtful, provocative observations and reflections on this approach by researchers from all over the world. Additional references to this book will appear in my Epilogue.

In his final reflections in *Making Learning Visible,* Howard Gardner (2001) writes:

> I have found it challenging to make sense of the Reggio experience, one that I thought I understood moderately well when we began this collaboration but one where I now have as many doubts as certitudes. Like many other smoothly operative but deeply introspective entities . . . it has a "feel" to it that is self evident to residents but not easily caught by others. . . . Such communities are best captured by art and metaphor. (p. 339)

THE CONTEXT FOR OUR WORK AND THIS BOOK

In order to make sense of the stories in this book, it is important to understand some of the history behind our work in St. Louis and to meet some of the key characters who will appear in the narratives. As I mentioned earlier, from 1992 to 1995 a group of St. Louis schools from diverse settings received funding from the Danforth Foundation to support educators in a focused study of the Reggio Approach. Entsminger (1994) discusses and analyzes our work during these years from the teachers' perspectives. When the funding period ended, it was clear that three of the schools had made significant progress in understanding how the fundamental principles of the approach could take root in their programs (Cadwell, 1997) and that the teachers and administrators in these schools were committed without reservation to continued work and growth together. In 1995, the educators from these schools established themselves as the St. Louis–Reggio Collaborative. Brenda Fyfe, professor of education at Webster University who co-directed the 1992–1995 Danforth-funded effort with Jan Phillips, has been a member of the St. Louis–Reggio Collaborative since its inception.

Each of the three schools in the St. Louis–Reggio Collaborative has strong roots in innovation and integrated approaches to learning as well as administrators and teachers willing to grapple over time with challenging issues in a collaborative context (Entsminger, 1994). Although all three schools are located in middle-class neighborhoods, they share a commitment to serving diverse populations. A description of each school follows.

The College School was founded in 1963 as an innovative and experimental laboratory school for Webster College (now Webster University). Now a private, independent school of 270 students from preschool through eighth grade, it is a unique school in the St. Louis area, basing much of its curriculum on thematic and integrated approaches across many disciplines. In the chapters that follow you will meet my friends and longtime teammates Jennifer Strange, teacher of the 4- and 5-year-olds; Sally Miller Hovey, teacher of the 3- and 4-year-olds; Skyler Harman and Kathy Seibel, kindergarten teachers; and Jan Phillips, retired head of the College School. You will also meet two former colleagues, now gone from the area, who brought fresh perspectives and youthful energy to our work—Mark Wyndham, teammate of Jennifer, and Christi Meuth, teammate of Sally.

The St. Michael School, founded in 1969, is an Episcopal school for children of all faiths serving 115 children from preschool through sixth grade. In the following pages you will meet my colleagues from the St. Michael School: Chuck Schwall, studio teacher (English term for *atelierista*); Karen Schneider, Melissa Guerra, Frances Roland, and Sue Morrison (preschool teachers who move up with the children and then rotate back again); and the headmaster of the school (and also my husband), Ashley Cadwell.

Over the past 26 years Clayton Schools' Family Center, the school district of Clayton's early childhood and parent support program, has evolved into a multifaceted resource program serving more than 400 families. From the Family Center you will hear from other close colleagues with whom I have lived and worked for 10 years: Lori Geismar Ryan, the director; Catherine Katz, curriculum coordinator and teacher of 3- to 5-year-olds; and Cheryl Breig-Allen, teacher of 3- to 5-year-olds.

Although there are many other educators in our three schools, these are the colleagues who take the lead in the particular stories that I tell in this book. As a large group of educators in these three schools and one university, we work closely together in myriad ways. We meet regularly during the year as a whole and in smaller groups to share our progress and to cooperate on research projects. We observe in each other's classrooms and act as peer coaches for one another. We travel to attend and to present at conferences and workshops together.

The single most important factor in our history together is our work with Amelia Gambetti, now the co-ordinator of Reggio Children and consultant to schools worldwide. Amelia has worked with us, beside us, in the middle of us—talking, wondering, commenting, noticing, questioning, doing, showing us through example and with her own hands how we could push ourselves beyond where we are. She has worked with us for week-long to month-long periods several times a year off and on since 1993. With her support and the support of Reggio Children, we have hosted conferences and visiting days for educators from the United States and other countries since the fall of 1996. You will find Amelia's reflections on her work with us in Chapter 6.

In addition to the working relationship that all of us developed with Amelia in St. Louis, I had the privilege of working alongside Amelia at La Villetta School in Reggio Emilia the year that I was an intern there in 1991–1992, during the last of her 25 years as a teacher (Cadwell, 1997). It was at La Villetta that I also met and worked with Giovanni Piazza, the *atelierista* there, and Carlina Rinaldi, who served as the *pedagogista* of the Villetta School and as my appointed mentor during my internship in Reggio Emilia. Carlina was also a neighbor and friend to our family, as were Amelia and Giovanni. In the stories that follow, in addition to Amelia, Carlina, and Giovanni, you will hear from other friends and mentors from Reggio Emilia: Vea Vecchi, who is retired from her position as *atelierista* of 30 years at the Diana School and continues her research both independently and as a member of the Reggio Children team; Marina Mori and Paola Strozzi, teachers from the Diana School; Isabella Meninno, the present *atelierista* at the Diana School; and Paola Ricco of Reggio Children.

THE FALL OF 2001: A TURNING POINT

The last 4 months of 2001 deeply affected everyone everywhere. Many of us felt as if the world had turned upside down in the aftermath of September 11. We felt our world shrink, our sense of security vanish, and our priorities change. Here in St. Louis we lived this semester alongside Carlina Rinaldi, the worldwide leader and mentor of the Reggio Approach to early childhood education. She had been asked by our colleague, Brenda Fyfe, to be a visiting professor of education at Webster University during the fall of 2001. Carlina accepted what was to be her first professorship outside Italy. In addition to teaching at Webster, Carlina was able to spend significant hours with the educators of the St. Louis-Reggio Collaborative in our schools. We, the teachers and administrators of the schools, fully acknowledge our good fortune and will always be grateful to Brenda, Webster University, and Carlina for the way they organized the semester to include us all.

At the same time, during the entire year of 2001, we hosted the traveling exhibit entitled *The Hundred Languages of Children* for the second time. (It was first in St. Louis in the fall of 1991.) Carolyn Edwards, Lella Gandini, and George Forman (1998), the editors of the book *The Hundred Languages of Children,* whose title was taken directly from the exhibit, introduce the exhibit in this way:

> On tour in the United States since 1987, the exhibit is a beautiful and intriguing display that narrates an educational story and weaves together experiences, reflections, debates, theoretical premises, and the social and ethical ideals of many generations of teachers, children and parents. It describes and illustrates the philosophy and pedagogy of the Reggio Emilia Approach, through photographs depicting moments of teaching and learning; explanatory scripts and panels (many containing texts of children's words); and samples of children's paintings, drawings, collages and constructions. (p. 10)

They go on to explain that the exhibit was authored and composed by a group of teachers in dialogue with one another who designed the exhibit to immerse the visitor in a multisensory, spiraling journey of learning that is representative of the documentation these educators engage in on a daily basis in the preschools in Reggio Emilia.

These two presences from Reggio Emilia in our midst—Carlina and the exhibit—have pushed us beyond where we were, and I, for one, am not exactly sure where we have landed. I think of them both, Carlina and the exhibit, as forces to be reckoned with. In a way that is at once gracious and tenacious, these two refuse to be taken for granted. Together, they move in a dynamic duet.

During our last evening with Carlina in December, educators from the schools of the St. Louis-Reggio Collaborative and Brenda gathered together at the exhibit in downtown St. Louis. We had come together in a holiday spirit with hors d'oeuvres and wine, white roses and candles, small gifts and enormous thanks to exchange. We wanted to acknowledge and to celebrate one another and to say goodbye to both Carlina and to the exhibit. With the tall display panels of *The Hundred Languages of Children* enfolding us like wings, Carlina asked us what it had meant to us to have the exhibit in St. Louis.

We shared as in a chorus: "It has brought us together; inspired us to search for deeper and more complex meaning with the children in our schools; helped us to reach out to other educators; brought us closer to the parents of the children whom we teach; brought us out of the suburbs into the heart of our city. As you have, Carlina, the exhibit has become like a friend who has raised the bar for us. Raised the stakes. We want to reach for more, to understand more, to accomplish more in our individual schools, among our schools, with our colleagues in other cities, and around the world."

After we had shared, Carlina spoke: "What has the exhibit in St. Louis meant to me? To meet you all here has given the exhibit new meaning for me, too. You can have feelings about the exhibit, but you cannot hold the exhibit in your hand. It is like a butterfly. It is elusive. You think that you have it, and then it has flown away. It represents a permanent search for something. It is like creativity itself. Maybe there are things that we can express better; maybe there are things we can never express. It represents a process. We all are a process. There are moments in life when you are ready for meeting something and something is ready for meeting you. The right moment for us was this one. Through this we can understand that friendship is the most important value for life."

It is in this spirit that I offer you, the reader, this book. In many ways, I will share a process with you. Better yet, a collection of processes. I will share a period in time— 6 consecutive months of our work. Incorporated into this slice of time will be reflections

FIGURE **P.1.** Sharing Our Work: St. Louis–Reggio Collaborative Meeting at the *Hundred Languages of Children* Exhibit with Carlina Rinaldi, Fall 2001

on and gleanings from all we have learned during the 10-year period that we have journeyed with the inspiration of the Reggio Approach before us. I also include stories from my life-memoir, which fits inside the puzzle of trying to make sense of these ideas in a personal context, not only a professional one. I plan to do this, as I did in my first book, *Bringing Reggio Emilia Home,* through telling stories. I will use my journals and our many collected notes, tapes, video clips, and photographs to recall the concrete, small details of real-life dramas in school and string them together through narratives. I will tell stories about what develops with children, with the parents, and among ourselves as teachers at the College School and also among the teachers who belong to the St. Louis–Reggio Collaborative. I will tell about our travels to seminars and to Italy and about those who travel to see us in our schools. This is the most powerful way to share our experience that I know of.

Six chapters follow, one for each month of the first half of the new millennium, January through June of the year 2000. Chapter 1 describes each phase of a day that is composed from a series of rich experiences as seen and lived from my perspective as *atelierista.* It follows the flow of a day and the many layers of ideas and practices that are a part of our lives in action and in concrete scenes of daily life. It frames what is to follow, shows where we are in our practice, and gives a sense of the whole in the microcosm of a day. Chapter 2 reveals the journey that we are on with parents, the partnership that we have forged, the trust and openness that exists, and the many ways in which we support one another. Chapter 3 examines what it means for us to work in collaboration as teachers. It includes stories of the challenges we face and discoveries that we have made living together, thinking together, researching together, and building organizational structures for our work.

Chapter 4 focuses on the transformation of the space in the *atelier,* which is the room that I call home and in which I most often work with children. I will tell practical and detailed stories of change in space. Chapter 5 illuminates the innate intelligence and creativity of young children through vignettes from projects in which children invent ideas, stories, and theories through working with materials and having conversations about the world. It explores the possibility that the Reggio Approach offers us a new vision and a new worldview in education, in our lives, and for the future of humanity and the planet. Chapter 6 recounts the significant highlights of a week-long study tour in Reggio Emilia. It illustrates both connections with our work and the pull to dream of constructing even more refined and strong systems that draw upon all our ways of knowing and that are based on the core values described in the previous chapters.

Through all of this, I am compelled to write in order to uncover what I don't know, to travel with ideas until they take me beyond what I know to reveal new and deeper sense. In writing I am on a quest. There is more to discover. One way to search is to tell stories to each other and to listen carefully with our inner ears for the particular soundings these ideas create in our lives and in our practice.

I write with the humility of one of a group of educators who lives within a process of, as Carlina says, "a permanent search for something." We continue as if we are part of an ever-flowing river, always learning, always growing alongside the children, the parents, and one another. The approach is so rooted in a way of being that it becomes, for sure, more of a practice than a technique, more about living values than mastering a set of skills, more about a shift in our worldview than a different way to teach. I offer you our stories as a friend with the hope that for you and for us in the St. Louis–Reggio Collaborative it will be the right moment to meet.

CHAPTER 1

January

The Arc of a Day

1/2000

I remember writing about a day at the Diana School in the first chapter of *Bringing Reggio Emilia Home.* In some ways, now, I am nostalgic for that time when I lived my days at that school of schools—like Oz for those of us who aspire to learn and grow through continuing to study the Reggio Approach.

Along with my nostalgia, I also begin a description of a day at our school with a sense of pride and real joy in our own journey. We have come a distance together. We share a distinct sense that we are traveling, learning new skills and techniques from one another as we go, gathering collective experience and wisdom, and looking toward the future and our next adventures.

A great many of our days this year seem related to the days when I lived in Reggio Emilia at the Diana and La Villetta schools. I say "related" because the way that we live our days in school now seems remarkably familiar to me, as if I dreamed it in a vivid dream. This year at the College School both children and adults feel a sense of purpose and teamwork in research and discovery. All of us feel the expectation of great pleasure in one anothers' company and in our work together. We move through both our physical space and the mental and imaginative space of ideas, pos-sibilities, and dreams with familiarity and anticipation as well as challenge and delight.

The values, ideas, and ideals of the Reggio Approach seem woven together for us now. We have slogged through countless difficulties to get a grip on each idea through continuous cycles of experimentation, adjustment, failure, breakdown, excite-ment, renewal, and reexamination. Now, in this year of the new millennium, it feels to me as if they are, in some way, a part of us. We have digested them and practiced them, learned with them and through them, until they have finally come together as a way of being and living in school that feels right. What we have come to value as fundamental includes our appreciation of the bright, original, competent children we meet every day; our strong collaboration as a team of teachers, as partners with chil-dren and with parents; the ever evolving, transforming, layered place in which we live called school; the many materials that entice children as well as teachers and par-ents to engage minds, hands, whole selves with the world in order to make sense of it; our disposition as researchers who wonder, imagine, speculate, and think together about the nature of the work we do with children; and our commitment as teachers to render the children's, the parents' and our own thoughts and ideas readable in clear, appealing, and accessible ways in the school.

These ways of working as we have understood them and learned to practice them will appear over and over again in different forms as the stories in this chapter and in the following chapters unfold. One amazing attribute of a complex, dynamic system is that even a small part of it reflects the whole contained within it, reflecting out like light from a prism.

THE START OF THE DAY

On the west side of Big Bend Boulevard, hidden behind the storefronts and fast-food restaurants of Webster Groves, is the large, three-story, red-brick building that houses the College School. At 7:30 A.M. I pull into the mostly empty lot and park in my usual spot next to my colleague Sally's diminutive gray pickup truck. Sally, the teacher of the 3- and 4-year olds, and I have agreed to meet early this morning to catch up and organize ourselves for a class project.

As I walk up the hill of the parking lot carrying notebooks and camera bags in one hand and balancing two caffe lattes in the other, I remind myself to appre-ciate this time of quiet before the day begins. Over the roof of the school I can see rolling white clouds in the intensely blue winter sky and, closer at hand, misty puffs of air that float before me as I breathe. Often, during moments like these, I feel a pro-found sense of gratitude to work with the group of people who has come together in this particular place and time, all of whom share a deep commitment to our com-mon goals.

The Corridor

Once inside the door, I walk up the half-flight of stairs to the first floor and turn to the right toward the preschool entrance. Almost every day, when I walk toward the preschool, I think of our evolution and feel amazed at how much we have accom-plished together (see Plate 1).

There are layers of history all around me, pieces of a puzzle that have been added little by little, day after day, in our search to uncover and communicate who the children are, who we are, who the parents are, and all that we have to offer to one another.

To the left, along the wall, a long, buff-colored bulletin board holds a large collection of 8-by-10 color photographs that convey the life of our school. The heading, in bold, black, child-written letters, declares The College School and the Reggio Approach. Here, there are photographs of boys and girls with open faces among green branches, exploring; teacher and child together at the piano trying to find the right notes to compose a song; close-ups of small fingers in clay, shaping and discovering ideas; parents and children, faces lit up in the glow of candlelight, looking over a table overflowing with favorite family delicacies.

Next to this striking display is a synthesis of the history of our work: the inspiration we take from the municipally funded preschools and infant–toddler centers of Reggio Emilia; our beginnings with the support of a Danforth Foundation grant; the decision to form the St. Louis–Reggio Collaborative with the early childhood teachers and administrators from the St. Michael School and the Clayton Schools' Family Center; our continuing study and research together as a collaborative of schools as we host educators from around the United States and other countries who wish to see schools where the founding principles of the Reggio Approach have inspired educators to continually strive to create optimal settings for young children and their families.

From here, the entrance to the preschool seems to beckon all who enter. The doorway itself has become almost irresistible. Windows on either side of a glass-topped door allow one to view the rainbows of color and treasures that lie inside. Let me walk you down the hall.

On the wooden panels underneath the windows, the children's faces in black-and-white portraits greet you, smiling and pleased. In between the photographs inside the lower panel of the door, you will notice a composite of leaf portraits, also in black-and-white, drawn carefully by the group of 4- and 5-year-old children last year as part of a year-long project about the outdoors.

In between the window and the lower panels, a thin, horizontal, child-height band of mirror stretches across the length of the entryway. Every now and then, I like to bend down and imagine how it must feel every morning to see oneself twice reflected—once in a photograph among all your friends; once fresh, new, and in motion as you grow through the seasons of the year.

Running the length of a wooden panel above the door, robust clay dinosaurs and trees sculpted out of thick slabs of clay, fired and glazed in a range of blues, earth tones, and greens, dance across their narrow landscape. The now-sixth-grade children who invented these forms during a kindergarten study of prehistoric creatures glance up at them as they pass by and remember being 5 and fanciful.

Child-made mobiles hang in each window. To the left, clay leaf forms in yellows, ochers, and deep greens suspended from small bent branches turn with the movement of the air currents. In the right window, beads strung by 3-year-olds glisten down in dropping rows from a substantial, rough piece of bark.

The Plexiglas covering the portraits and drawings, the glass of the windows, the skinny strip of mirror, and all the shiny, colored glazes of the dinosaurs and leaves and beads catch and reflect the light and sparkle down the hallway, pulling you toward them.

Once down the hall, closer to the door, black-and-white photographs of the teachers catch your eye. In a vertical format on the fabric board, their faces line up, welcoming children, families, and visitors. Accompanying each photograph is a child's portrait of the teacher as well as a child's description.

This morning I notice my colleague Sally's face and the few black lines that her portraitist, Ben, used to portray her. Ben described Sally as follows:

> This is Sally. She is my teacher. She is nice to me and she plays the guitar and she knows songs that we sing like, "Old Dan Tucker." Sally loves clay and so do I. I made a turtle. Ben, 3.6 years.

The photographs and the text that appear outside the preschool on the corridor all hang on fabric-covered display board. It provides an elegant, clean backing to the subjects and, coincidentally, Velcro sticks to it. We back these pieces with foam core and then attach small pieces of hooked Velcro to them for hanging. In this way, we can make adjustments in the overall composition and also update and add new information as necessary.

Before entering the preschool, I turn to my right and admire the Parent Board, which is a daily reminder of the presence of the parents in our school (see Figure 1.1). Large, bright photographs show the many ways in which they contribute to our lives. You can see fathers baking pies with the help of many small hands; mothers painting a puppet stage given as a gift to the children at holiday time a few years ago; mothers and fathers at parks and on adventures with their children; mothers and

FIGURE **1.1.**   Parents at the Parent Board at the College School

fathers pictured around tables alongside teachers, discussing, thinking, taking notes, making decisions.

A calendar made by parents indicates important gatherings and meetings that will take place this month as well as special events with children. There are often copies of recent letters and flyers sent to parents and opportunities to sign up to help with and participate in upcoming events. Minutes of parent–teacher meetings also hang on this board.

This board not only communicates to the parents; it also represents them. It is created by the parents in collaboration with the teachers. It always includes children's work—small, seasonal collages and drawings created for the calendar and enticing examples of work-in-progress in the classrooms.

As I write today, I think of Amelia Gambetti's presence here in this hallway and her intense work in the three schools of our collaborative for short periods between 1993 and 1998. This morning I can easily imagine her standing beside me. It is thanks to her that we have understood the importance of all these small details within the layers of our history that we have represented here. When she began to work with us, she insisted that we ask ourselves, How could we show our history, our context, our intentions, our connections and deep respect for the parents and the children? How could we imbue this place with the feeling that it belonged to a community of particular people, all of whom had contributions to make? How could we make this entrance enticing, irresistible, layered, updated, ever evolving?

Time after time, she confronted us with our own values as she asked us what choices we wanted to make. Amelia made us look at the reality of what we had, as she inspired us to imagine something better. All this, of course, had to do not only with how we might change the corridor but also how we might transform what we did with the children and the parents and one another. She would often discuss possibilities with us. But then it would be time for her to leave. We were left with a strong desire to transform a lot of work before us on many levels.

I have heard that the surroundings you create are a direct reflection of who you are. It makes sense that this would be true. Because of many years of reflection, work, reconsideration, dedication, and tenacity on the part of many people, what surrounds us now reflects all of us—a community of children, teachers, and parents living exciting, multidimensional experiences in which everyone's voice is important. We live in a school where discovery, wondering, working together, and clear communication serve as guideposts for all of us. The complexity and depth of what we do here is palpable. The respect that we hold for one anothers' lives is present on the walls. The truth and joy of childhood is honored to the best of our ability. All these qualities and values fill the atmosphere even when the building is quiet and no one is here.

In 1992 this entry to the preschool was made of heavy, dark-stained wood fitted with one-way viewing glass. This bleak beginning led into a dimly lit cave of a room. There was nothing in the hallway or on the doorway that indicated what part of the school this was. In retrospect, it seems that no one saw the possibilities hidden in the space. Perhaps teachers underestimated the importance of creating rich and readable environments.

Imagining Amelia: Revisiting the Entryway

Sally had turned on the lights in the central entryway that we call the living room (see Plate 2). Now that I have invoked her presence, Amelia follows me in. I remember our work in this room together, examining each corner together. I relived this day with Amelia when I wrote about it in *Bringing Reggio Emilia Home.*

She and I ended up that workday back in 1994 sitting on the bench that is still tucked in the same place under the windows that look into the *atelier,* across from the entrance to the preschool. In 1993 the bench was a wooden one made out of plywood and painted, outfitted with cushions. The old one has been replaced with a park bench that is better suited for the outdoor room we have worked to create in this space.

This morning I imagine sitting here with Amelia for a few minutes to survey the room and how it has evolved since our workday together in 1994.

"So, what do you think of it?" I imagine Amelia saying.

"That's just what I was going to ask you," I smile at her. "*Dai, dimmi.*" (Come on, you tell me.)

I can hear her inside my head, "Well, I love that piece on the table near the door of the full-body portraits of the children moving through the woods. I remember we discussed making it much more evident that nature and the out-of-doors was a very important aspect of life at this school. This effort really does that."

I explain that it was a culminating experience for the 4- and 5-year-old children who were involved in a year-long exploration of the out-of-doors with their teachers, Jennifer and Jamie, last year. They had studied photographs of themselves in motion outside and played with movable mannequins before drawing themselves. They had worked on portraits of trees with similar care. Then they all worked, teachers and children, on standing themselves and the trees up on a base and surrounding the portraits with an outdoor context using bark, seeds, moss, grasses, stones, and dried flowers (see Figure 1.2).

In my mind, Amelia continues, "I like it. It is delightful. So are the mobiles in the windows. I think the explanation and context that you composed about the outdoor experience is good. Simple but good. But I don't like it covering the tree mural on the wall like that. It seems disrespectful to the tree. And it also appears confusing, with too much going on behind the panel. Can you find another solution?

"The terrarium in this other corner is very nice. I like the lights shining on it. But don't you have other ongoing experiences with these animals with the children? Where does this living part of your room figure into the children's daily life at school? Do the children play here? What kind of support do you give them? What do they do here? Have you observed them closely?" (see Figure 1.3).

Looking up, directly in front of us toward the end of the short wall that separates the entryway door from a cubby area, I scan the series of five Lucite boxes that hang vertically down this column and feel Amelia's eyes do the same. Each holds an $8^{1}/_{2}$-by-11 piece of paper for every day of the week and every week of the schoolyear. These pages are composed by teachers and children together to highlight important events of each day. The pages are posted here so that parents can read them. We call this sequence of pages the daily journal (see Figure 1.4).

I hear Amelia observe, "I think the daily journal looks very appealing. You must have really worked on this. There are many details, photographs, and examples of children's work. I can tell that you have explored many new possibilities and invented new ideas that might work well for you here in this school. What about the other collaborative schools? How is each school's approach to this idea unique? And, by the way, do the parents really read this? How do you know? Have you ever talked to

FIGURE 1.2. Close-Up on Portraits of Children in the Woods at the College School

FIGURE 1.3. Children at the Terrarium at the College School

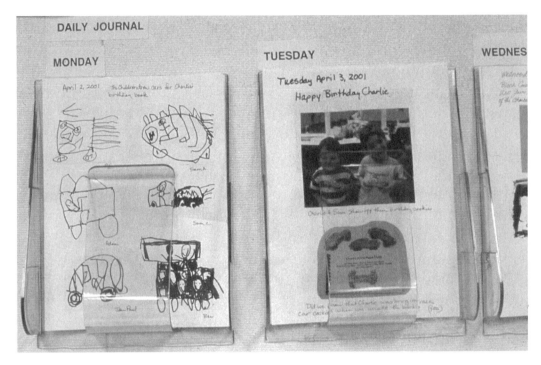

FIGURE **1.4.**   Example of Daily Journal Pages at the St. Michael School

them in depth about this as a group? What can they tell you about it? Do the children understand it, too? Do you talk about it often with them in meetings? Have you thought of actually initiating an ongoing dialogue with the parents around the daily journal? This looks very rich, yet I do not see evidence of the parents' understanding and response."

My reverie with Amelia continues. I see her get up to walk around the corner to look at the children's work above the cubbies. I imagine comments that she might offer on the three-dimensional, rainbow-colored collages made by each of the 4- and 5-year-old children this past autumn. "These are fine, beautiful really, and, again very simple. Be careful that you do not become focused on being too decorative. What are these related to? What did the children discover? Do they have a chance to work with these special kinds of papers again? Can they invent more ideas about what to do with them themselves?"

In my mind's eye, I see Amelia turn to look at the opposite wall above another set of cubbies at two large documentation panels that I worked hard to compose about children's work with clay in the beginning of the year. "And these panels?" she asks, "Where did these experiences begin? Where is the larger context? What happened next? You need to pay attention to these things so that the experiences that you represent do not appear to be fragmented, because I assume that they are not."

I realize that what I am doing is giving myself a critique using Amelia's eyes. I can literally hear her voice in my head—her tone, the specific words that she chooses, the way she moves around the space and considers the whole as well as every detail at the same time. As a group of teachers who have worked with her closely, those of us in the St. Louis–Reggio Collaborative often exchange smiles and admit to one another that we can almost hear Amelia talking. In certain situations, especially when we begin to ask each other questions, somehow we can feel her presence, almost feel her on our shoulders speaking to us.

Projecting with Sally

"What are you doing out here?" Sally queries when she finds me sitting on the living room bench. "I want my coffee!"

I tell Sally about my morning reverie and some of the ideas and provocations that I have dreamed of with my imaginary companion. She responds with interest and tact and adds that we had better stick to business or we won't get done what we had come to school early to do. This directness laced with kindness is one of Sally's traits that I admire and appreciate in her as a colleague. Linked to this is her ability to focus, not letting herself become distracted by the myriad things that we all juggle. We all must cultivate this kind of concentration if we are to do each piece of our work thoroughly and to the best of our ability.

We had decided to meet early, as we like to do periodically, to review the work that has occurred recently at the message center with the 3- and 4-year-old children and to consider what could happen next. We have been following the progression of the work here as a group of three, *atelierista* and two teachers. Christi, the other teacher, who lives an hour away, will join us when she can.

Sally and I begin by studying our notes in the collaborative spiral notebook that we began to keep this year in the 3- and 4-year-old classroom. In September, we decided to keep an observation notebook that would include notes from all three of us in one place. We each keep our own notebooks and records as well, but this would be an experiment in keeping a shared observation notebook. We came up with this idea for a number of reasons. During a trip together to Reggio Emilia in the fall of 1997, we learned how teachers there were creating more and more ways to both follow and demonstrate the chapters of learning that occur in the everyday life of the classroom, not only in projects. We have found that both before and since that trip, whenever we engage in observations of "normal life" we are always amazed at what we notice through paying close attention.

This fall, we discovered through reflection and conversation that Sally, Christi, and I were all curious about what was really happening in the areas of the room. We also realized that we wanted a way to keep collective notes so that they would be public, accessible, and, also, give us a chance not only to build on one anothers' observations but also to learn from one anothers' styles of note taking. We envisioned using this notebook in an informal way. We wanted be able to jot down notes, phrases, and words or to make quick sketches without worrying about presentation. We hoped that this notebook would permit each of us to read the others' notes and begin both written (by including comments on one anothers' notes) and spoken conversations about what we observed.

We decided to begin using this notebook for one area of the classroom so as not to become too fragmented and confused ourselves. We choose the communication area, or message center. We agreed to take turns observing there for several mornings and then to share what we had noticed. In order to do this, we had to cover one anothers' responsibilities with the children.

In the 3- and 4-year-old room, which we call the Big Bend Room (named after the street it faces), the message center is located near the front of the room against a wall near a window. A table large enough for three children provides a surface to work in fairly close contact with classmates. This area is defined on one side by the back of a section of cubbies. This 4-foot-tall open area offers an ideal space to hang the transparent mailboxes (shoe organizers), one for each child, identified with his or her name and photograph (tiny reductions of the larger black-and-white photographic portraits on the entry-door panels of the preschool).

On the other side of the message center table, a bank of three shelves holds materials to make messages, including various sizes, colors, and types of paper; different-sized envelopes; high-quality stamps and stamp pads; copies of each child's photograph and name in postage stamp size; soft, sharp colored pencils of many hues, black lead pencils, and black fine-lined markers; and small glue bottles and glue sticks (see Figure 1.5). There is also a divided bead box with enticing collage materials such as small, colorful buttons, bits of ribbon, dried flowers, sequins, tissue paper bows, and transparent stars. You can find similar materials in mini-*ateliers* and in the *ateliers* of all the schools in the St. Louis–Reggio Collaborative (see Plate 3).

These materials are collected, maintained, and enriched by small groups of children with a teacher or parent almost daily. Sharpening pencils, cutting paper, sorting and replenishing collage materials are part of caring for a place like this. In this way, we work alongside the children to create a culture of respect and care for the space and the things in it. Often, when I work with children here, we begin by taking a trip to the *atelier* shelves next door to collect and organize materials in the message center collage box. This feels like a treasure hunt for them, and they love

Figure 1.5.   The Message Center in the Kindergarten at the St. Michael School

it. Standing on tiptoe, they search with big eyes through transparent jars for new possibilities, for colors, for textures, for shapes that catch their attention, that they could fall in love with, that they want to touch and feel and play with and attach or wrap or tuck away in an envelope as a surprise for someone or even to keep in their own mailbox.

Over time, we have developed the message center as well as our way of maintaining, enriching, and using it with children through our study of the Reggio Approach. It is meant to foster the innate inclination that most children have at this age to notice small treasures such as acorns, ribbons, and bits of paper, to pick them up, to pocket them, and, further, to offer these things that they have found to others as a way of connecting, sharing, and exchanging. If I have understood correctly, the idea to support the exchange of messages in Reggio Emilia was originally based on Italian educators' observations of these gestures by children as well as their desire to provide a place where connections and relationships could grow through communication and exchange.

Last fall, before Sally, Christi, and I agreed on what questions would frame our observations, we realized that if we were going to keep collective notes, we needed a collective framework. If we were curious, what exactly were we curious about? What questions were we looking to answer? To begin with, we would include the time and date and names of the children who were in the group and how long each of them stayed in this area.

Had they chosen to come, or was it suggested to them at morning meeting?
What did the children do here?
What materials did they choose to work with?
If collage, did they seem comfortable and successful using glue?
If colored pencils and drawing materials, did they seem at ease holding and
    using them?
Did they show respect for the materials?
Did they return pencils to the Lucite boxes that held them? Did they open
    and close glue bottles?
What about their compositions? What did they actually make?
Did they make any attempt at pretend writing (made up letters and signs) or
    letters or numbers?
Did they write their names?
What was the interaction among children?
Did they talk? What did they say?
Did they influence one another in any aspect of their message making?
Did they seem to know about the mailboxes?
Were they making a message for someone else?
Did they deliver their message to another mailbox? Were they curious to see
    whether their friend found it?
What surprised us as we observed? What did we notice outside our frame
    that we had not anticipated?

We also agreed that, initially, we would not become directly involved with the children unless we were needed to clarify how to use a material or to mediate in some way. We would be present as an enthusiastic support for the children; however, our role would be primarily to observe their independent use of this area. Through sharing and discussing our observations periodically, we hoped to accumulate knowledge of the children and their understanding of this place. Eventually, after the children and we had settled into the year, we planned to put our heads together, so to speak, to project about the future of the life of the message center:

> What provocations might support the children, with their individual responses to this area, in moving deeper into the possibilities offered by making messages and communicating with others?
> What might we change to further enrich the space or the materials?
> What collaborations could we imagine with the parents?
> What other forms of documentation and communication did we want to consider?

This morning, drinking our lattes in the quiet of Sally's sunny, east-facing room, we look over the fall semester's notes. We read an entry written a few days ago by Sally:

> Noticed Brett in the message center making drawings, putting them in envelopes, taping the envelope shut, and delivering them to friends. He made several: for Libby, Catie, Annalise, Claire, and Logan. I asked what his message said and he said, "Nothing, just some stuff." I noticed him quietly hand-deliver each envelope. Annalise received hers with a shy smile. Catie put hers in a special pocket in her backpack. Libby said, "Brett made this for me, and oh! it is lovely!"

Looking back to earlier months, we review the observational snippets and vignettes that each of us has been able to capture here. An entry that I wrote while stationed at the message center for the morning as an observer in early November reads:

> Claire, Catie, and Samantha choose to work at the message center this morning during meeting time. They are turning out to be the "regulars." I notice that they all love gluing and are quite competent at it. With the girls, I suggested that we walk into the *atelier* to choose some new collage materials for messages. They picked out feathers, sequins in the shape of flowers with petals, several different types of ribbon cut in half-inch pieces, and rolled tissue paper balls in multi colors. We added these things to the divided box for collage materials.
>
> Catie wanted to make a message for her Aunt Patty and her mom. She said, "Because she is my Aunt Patty and I love her." Catie used all the new collage materials lovingly. Samantha wanted to make a message for her mother, her sister, and her grandpa, but when she noticed the photographs of her classmates, she changed her mind. She made a message for Lucy by gluing two photos on the new graph paper and then carefully composed a purple collage around it including feathers, sequins, and origami paper, balanced and beautiful. She said, "Lucy will like this because it is pretty."

These entries reveal the excitement and pleasure that the children find in making something and delivering it to someone, and also in receiving a message from someone whom they care about—a friend, classmate, or family member. In reviewing other observational entries in the notebook, we realize that at this point in the year most of the children are successfully using this space independently. They are caring for the materials, and they all are making messages for friends and parents and teachers. Some seem to prefer collage; others, drawing. Some children always seem to engage in both pretend writing and writing letters that they know, especially their names. Sally has noted that many write in pretend cursive from left to right.

Sally continues, "Christi's observation notes lately in the message center and the mini-*atelier* often refer to a group of children who draw themselves on their messages all the time—Noah, Sarah, Brewster, Logan. Maybe we are ready to ask all the children to draw self-portraits. We have been waiting for the time to be right."

I build on that idea: "We could each follow a third of the class and share our notes as we have been with this notebook. You know, what if we do it by each taking a group of six, but just two at a time, into the *atelier*? We could begin by staying in the observing role as much as possible as we have with the message center. We could focus on paying attention to the sequence of the marks they make and what they say and their interaction with the other child if there is any. What do you think?"

Sally adds more strands to this verbal weaving of ideas: "This could be an extension of our collaboration with this observation notebook with a very specific, focused provocation. Maybe we could even have two sessions with each group, changing the setting and the questions the second time around after we share our first notes."

At this point, it is 8:05 and Christi arrives. For the next 15 minutes we continue to brainstorm together about these new possibilities.

This morning, Sally, Christi, and I have engaged in a practice that is at the center of our work as teachers. Out of the energy and context of our previous work together, we have come up with a collective vehicle that allows us to better "listen" to the particular individuals in this class of 3- and 4-year-old children and to do so in a dialogic way. We have used a collective and evolving document—the observation notebook—to learn about the children, to learn about the area, and to learn with and from each other. When we come together, all three of us feel the power in this seemingly simple gesture. Keeping this notebook together means that we become part of a larger community in a very concrete way: We are committed to recording and to reading what we each contribute; we are connected to a process over time; we are following the multilayered processes of children not with one set of eyes from one point of view, but as team. In keeping this notebook, we become a team of researchers looking for the particular ways in this specific place in which these children make connections with one another, with pencils and pens and the beautiful stuff of collage, and with the idea of communication.

This morning we have used the notebook as a writer might use a journal, as, in the words of my friend and writing mentor, John Elder, "a seedbed of ideas." We have chosen several ideas from what we have observed as well as from the way we have been working together as teacher-researchers—from out of our collective seedbed, so to speak—and planted them. If the conditions are right, the seeds of the ideas may grow, among other things, into a collaborative way to both observe and support children as they draw self-portraits.

BEGINNING WITH THE KINDERGARTEN

In the *atelier,* I begin to prepare for the group of eight kindergarten children who will come to me from their classroom at 8:30. This morning I need a tape recorder, new batteries, and tapes. I also take out a folder of the children's drawings of birds, including owls and penguins, that they have been working on lately when in the *atelier* with me. This is the second year that I have had the privilege of working with the kindergarten children and teachers as their studio specialist. My role with both the kindergarten teachers and the children differs somewhat from my role in the preschool.

In the preschool I am part of a five-person team. We collaborate closely on every aspect of our work, which includes designing and redesigning the environment, maintaining plentiful and varied materials in every area of all the classrooms, meeting with parents for many different purposes, reflecting and projecting together on all the ongoing projects that are in development, and planning for and coordinating the documentation of these projects.

My role with the kindergarten has evolved differently. During my first years at the College School, I very much wanted to work with the 5- and 6-year-old children whom I had followed for 2 years and come to know well. I wanted to see the work that we had done together come to fruition as I had witnessed with the oldest children in Reggio Emilia in layered, complex, long-term projects like "The Tree Project" at Diana School (Cadwell, 1997) and "The Amusement Park for the Birds" (Forman & Gandini, 1994).

Kindergarten in the United States, however, is different from in Italy. In Italy, there is no expectation that the children will learn reading, writing, or math skills before they arrive in first grade. In the municipally funded preschools of Reggio Emilia, about 60% of the *grandi,* or 5- and 6-year-old children, leave the schools having learned to read, write, and count. This is not because they are taught in any standard way. It is because reading, writing, and mathematics are important languages that are part of the children's environment and their investigations from their earliest times in school. In addition, unlike in English, a consistent and predictable relationship exists between spoken and written Italian. Once children are interested in writing, this aspect of their mother tongue must be a help to them. Nevertheless, because of the absence of pressure to teach and learn academic skills in kindergarten, the teachers, and therefore the children, have more flexibility.

When groups of American teachers see the video of the "The Amusement Park for the Birds" (Forman & Gandini, 1994), many are completely overwhelmed with the complexity and sophistication of the work of the children and the teachers and *pedagogisti.* This project is truly a masterpiece that showcases all the fundamental principles of the Reggio Approach. The work is both awe-inspiring and humbling.

For very valid reasons, the kindergarten teachers at the College School were cautious. They decided that they wanted the Reggio Approach on their own terms. They liked many aspects of the curriculum they had developed, and they did not want to change them. On the other hand, they appreciated many aspects of the Reggio Approach, and they were curious.

In retrospect, this made a lot of sense. Some of the schools that we worked with under the Danforth Foundation funding tried too much too fast and, in the end, went back to previous practices. In the kindergarten at the College School, ideas have simmered, and we have had a long time to adjust ourselves to new possibilities and find avenues for growth and change that suited our particular situation.

We recognize that the philosophy of the College School is not that distant from the Reggio Approach. The school was founded on the strong belief that an integrated, thematic, experiential approach is the most effective and powerful way to educate children. Outdoor and adventure education augments and provides structure for many parts of the curriculum throughout the school. Documentation and the lively display of students' work are impressive. This becomes especially true in the upper grades when the students themselves produce and coordinate the presentation of their work, including creative writing, scientific charts and graphs, high-quality photographs and videos, drawings, prints, and sculpture.

It is with all the above history and knowledge in mind that the kindergarten teachers, Kathy and Skyler, and I agreed to begin to work together to create a new way to collaborate that would provide continuity for the children and a stronger bridge between preschool and kindergarten.

Teacher as Listener

In the kindergarten room the children and teachers have been studying birds since the fall. The interest began when several children brought in birds' nests and stories of baby birds being born in their yards and on their porches. Their investigations continued when the class went on field trips in November looking for owls. In December, after a trip to the St. Louis Zoo, the focus moved to penguins. This occurred because many of the children and the teachers seemed to fall in love with these playful creatures. They became fascinated with their body shapes and behavior as well as their habitat. This way of following the emerging interest and fascination of a group of curious children and adults is one example of a change in the kindergarten. Both teachers are now open and excited about experimenting with a more emergent curriculum than they used to be.

In a meeting last week, Kathy, Skyler, and I agreed that it might be a good time to organize conversations with the children in which they could have the chance to reflect about their experiences, knowledge, intuitions, questions, feelings, and thoughts about birds in general and penguins in particular. We agreed that I would lead the groups in these conversations and that I would start with the first group of eight on Monday morning.

The children have been talking about their ideas about birds all along—at their group meeting in the morning, on field trips, and during related experiences in class with me and with their classroom teachers. However, the act of having an organized conversation under the best conditions that we can provide is a different experience for the children and for us as teachers. We intend to make listening our top priority.

We are not listening for "right" answers. We want to know what the children think, feel, and wonder. We believe that the children will have things to tell each other and us that we have never heard before. We are always listening for a surprise and the birth of a new idea. This practice supports a mutual quest for understanding. It is a practice of searching together for new meaning. Together, we become a community of seekers.

The teacher has no idea what will happen. Our job is to listen, to stay on our toes and try not to get in the way. We strive to promote an atmosphere of excitement and adventure and journeying. We want to set a tone that pulses with the pursuit of knowledge. This is the opposite of traditional teaching, of transmitting knowledge; rather, for the teacher, this is the ultimate act of letting go, of listening and wanting to know, of participating in the act of wondering alongside the children. This is a practice that we have developed because of our study of the Reggio Approach (Cadwell, 1997).

This is also a practice developed by Karen Gallas (1994, 1995) while she was a teacher of first and second grade. She has written about her experience in structuring dialogue and about classroom discourse as a cornerstone of her approach to teaching and to learning as a researcher. In reading her work, I recognize many of the scenarios and themes that she describes and analyzes as ones that I have encountered. I also recognize how much I have to learn about and from this practice.

The following conversation is an example of what Gallas would most likely call "science talk." In sharing it with you, I will reflect on my part in it and on the thinking and dialogue of the children involved. My reflective comments appear in italics. As you will see, the conversation is fast-paced, and I am doing the best I can to facilitate without dominating, to guide while at the same time giving the process to the children. This is not an easy thing to do, and, in reading the transcript of the conversation, I found many places where I wonder why I said what I said. This practice is a humbling one, but it is forever fascinating and revealing of children's thinking and creativity in using all their experience, no matter where it comes from, to try to make sense of things. The practice of listening to children's talk in contexts like these drives home with absolute clarity children's passion to uncover meaning; to make relationships between what they experience, notice, hear about, see, and feel in the middle of living in the world; to create a collective discourse; and to keep going. This means that they are constantly building and rebuilding theories. For them, there is no end; there is no one "right," isolated answer.

A Conversation About Birds

We sit around a hexagonal table in the middle of the *atelier.* I want to begin with an entry point into the dialogue that will both give the children a number of possible choices as to the content and form of our conversation and turn the lead over to them.

"You know so much about penguins—where they live, what they do, what they eat, and how they are alike and how they are different from the other birds that you have learned about. Kathy and Skyler and I thought that we could have a conversation about all the things you know, or think, or wonder about penguins and maybe other birds. What do you think? Where do you want to start?"

"Where they live, yeah. Penguins live in Antarctica," Alex begins definitively.

Archie adds, "But some live where the biggest turtles live."

Molly chimes in, "My dad told me that some live on smooth islands where there is sand."

In these first comments three children have given the conversation a direction as well as shared three habitats and revealed one information source. In reflection, I think that I thought I would help them articulate qualifications about penguins' habitats when I asked, "So, they don't live in St. Louis?"

All of the children look at me as if I am a little slow and say, "Nooo!"

Molly gives us a reason: "They don't live in St. Louis because there are tons and tons of people, and they are scared of people."

Archie disagrees and attempts to clarify the issue himself: "Penguins aren't scared of people, but every penguin needs water. They get it from the ocean."

I think that I wanted a rationale for the ocean choice, which was a further clarification of Archie's comment after he says, "Every penguin needs water." "Could you tell us more about that? Could they live near a lake, in your opinion?"

Archie says, "No way, José."

Luke adds with a curious kind of voice, "They can't live near a lake. They need an ocean. I am not sure why. They need fish to eat."

Archie feels that we are all not getting to the heart of the matter: "It would break the food chain if they didn't have water. They wouldn't have fish."

Now, with the last two comments, the children are not only taking the question of habitat further but also introducing another idea and term. In thinking about this now, it seems that the subject of penguins is too limiting. Gallas (1995) points out that children sometimes use terms without knowing what they mean. Further, some children may understand the term and others may not. For these reasons I ask curiously, not for them to answer to me, but to explain to themselves, "What is the food chain?"

Luke steps in again: "It's like this. A fish eats a little fish, the penguin eats the fish, and then the killer whale eats the penguin!"

Archie continues, "And then, the whale shark eats the killer whale! And I know the biggest thing in the ocean eats the smallest! Do you know what the killer whale eats? Plankton. We can't even see plankton."

Alex muses, almost to himself, "That is so small for a killer whale to eat plankton. Whales would die, too, if they didn't have water."

Sienna cringes: "If they didn't have water, their skin would dry out."

Now the parameters of the conversation have vastly widened. This is one of several places where I wish I had either kept quiet or asked more about either of these powerful ideas—the largest animal eating plankton or these ocean creatures' need for water. Instead, I steered the conversation back to penguins. I am sorry about that.

"Well, what do penguins do?" I ask.

Molly smiles: "They play around. They play with each other."

Sienna says shyly, "They slide on their tummies."

Molly adds, "They toboggan on the ice."

Ga-Young comes in for the first time: "The penguins talk in penguin language, and they learn the games that way."

Archie frowns and says in a practical kind of voice, "Well, I don't think that they play games. And they don't talk. They do different things. They catch fish. They take care of their children."

I once took a seminar entitled Human and Animal Play. I remember seeing a film clip of penguins having a great old time. I wondered why Archie was being so serious. Perhaps he did not want to go along with his classmates' theories that penguins talk and invent games. I posed the question to him.

"But don't they have fun?" I ask.

Alex says sadly, "Penguins can't even fly."

Archie quips, "But their ancestors could."

I ask, "Who were their ancestors?"

Luke says immediately, "Their grandmas and grandpas."

With this mention of families, Sienna returns to the care of the penguin progeny: "This is about the babies. The moms and dads keep the babies under them because it would be a little too cold for the babies. They keep the babies warm by keeping them under their skin."

Archie corrects her: "It's the dads."

Molly continues, "The dads keep the babies under their warm feet to protect the babies. And the mother goes out to get food for the babies and the dad."

This last exchange is an example of what seems like a confusing sequence, but when studied it reveals itself as logical and sequential. Alex laments that penguins can't fly. Archie, who is playing the expert, affirms that their ancestors could. I ask what he means and Luke connects with his family to explain the term. This gives Sienna and Mollie, who love to relate to the family dynamics of the penguins, opening to take off on particulars and Archie a chance to be the expert again.

The sequence also brings to light the stances or worldviews that children are adopting in this conversation. These stances seem related to but not the same as what Gallas (1995) cites as "overarching beliefs about the world" (p. 27). In thinking about these children's stances based on beliefs about and dispositions toward the world, in this conversation I would characterize Archie as one who believes that everything is connected, that science is his domain, and that he has expert knowledge. Luke identifies personally with the penguins and personifies them, as does Alex. Sienna and Molly are intrigued with animal behavior and family systems. Ga-Young and Allison (who has not spoken yet) are not accustomed to science talk and do not take an active part in the conversation. They are, however, intent listeners. Given more of a chance to practice in conversations like this one, I am sure that they will each develop confidence in "thinking out loud" (Gallas, 1995, p. 44).

I say truthfully, "You know a lot about penguins!"

I am not sure why I decided to make this comment. I suppose I really was impressed with their knowledge. In any case, I could have asked more questions that would have been more systemic in nature and followed the lines of their thinking. In making the comment that I did I seemed to encourage the children to impress me more with statistics.

Molly says, "The emperor is the biggest. He's 12 feet tall. Well, maybe 3 feet."

Luke says, "Look at my foot. This is about a foot." (We stop to get a ruler to measure the children's feet, which, we discover, are about 6 to 8 inches long.)

Molly picks up with her list of penguin types: "There is also the king and the emperor and the fairy. The king is up to here on me." (She puts her hand up to her chest.)

Allison, who is new to the kindergarten this year, contributes for the first time: "The rock hopper has feathers coming out of his head."

"And the fairy is the smallest," Sienna croons.

"We like penguins," Archie announces. "We study penguins!"

Luke opens the conversation up to flying again: "They are the only birds that can't fly."

"Ostriches can't fly," Molly disagrees.

Archie interjects, almost thinking out loud, "They can't fly because they don't have hollow bones. It is more important for them to swim and catch fish. A kingfisher dives into the water. Maybe ducks also dive into the water."

I say, "It sounds like you are saying that penguins have a body designed to swim." *I was trying to be what I understand to be "an active listener," interpreting what I hear using the politically correct language—"it sounds like you are saying. . . ." But Archie doesn't take it that way. He all but yells at me to emphasize his point.*

Archie is emphatic: "They can't fly for one reason! They don't have hollow bones!"

Allison is quizzical: "But we have hollow bones."

Luke shakes his head and smiles: "But we are a little too heavy to fly."

Archie is building his case for the attributes necessary for flight: "And we don't have wings or feathers." But, then, he veers off into a new dimension: "I know how the blood gets to the bones. It is made of molecules and atoms and we can't see them."

Allison is making the connection to human bones and raising a very good question. If flight is all about hollow bones, and we seem to have hollow bones, then why can't we fly? Luke adds that, in his opinion, humans are too heavy to fly. Archie concedes that something about feathers and wings, not only hollow bones, contributes to birds' ability to fly. But then he goes off on a new tangent—blood, molecules, and atoms. He is being the expert again. And I really am feeling overwhelmed with this diversion. I somehow feel a pull to return to the top of the conversation again. Maybe I need some form of adult order and logic, and I am imposing it on the children.

"Could we return to the beginning of the conversation when Alex started with where penguins live? He said they lived in Antarctica, or I think I've heard it called the North Pole or the South Pole. Where are those places, anyway?"

Luke says, "Antarctica is on the bottom of the world."

"There is no bottom of the world. On the globe there is but not on the real world. Because, if you were on the bottom, the sky wouldn't be up, it would be under your feet," Alex says, cocking his head to one side.

Luke tries to reassure him: "There is no up and down in space."

Alex says with an amazed voice, "Space is everywhere. It doesn't even stop, space."

Archie can't stand it: "Can I tell you something, Alex? There is sides and bottom."

Alex is sure about his position: "Not on the real world."

Archie: "You are thinking things on the bottom would fall off. But they can't."

There is a moment of silence, and everyone looks at Archie and Alex. Then, very softly and with grave seriousness, Alex says one word in a knowing tone: "Gravity."

Archie gains speed: "OK, gravity. It's still OK."

Alex continues to challenge Archie: "On the real world, on the bottom the sky is up. How come it is not down, then?"

Archie departs from the essential query and gives a bigger answer: "There is no sky in space! All there is are black stars, meteorites, planets!"

Ga-Young adds, "And aliens."

Alex is not giving up: "There is no bottom of the world!"

Luke interjects in an instructive tone, getting weary of this argument, "On the globe, we would say on the bottom of the globe and the top of the globe."

I am amazed with this spin-off. I never expected it. I am trying to both follow the train of thought and keep up. I think maybe a clarifying question would help them. I interject, thinking that it might help them to make distinctions, "What is the difference between the globe and the real world?"

Allison seeks a concrete answer: "I know. The globe has writing on it and the earth doesn't."

Out of nowhere Archie says, "And it's called the North Pole because St. Nick lives there."

"There is a little pole that is red and white like a candy cane. That is why it's called the Pole," Molly offers.

If I wanted logic, I got it. Not what I expected, I thought.

Archie has been pondering: "I know the difference between the globe and the real earth. The earth spins!"

Alex stands up to demonstrate: "We are going around and around, but not this fast or we'd fall off."

Luke offers a more detailed explanation: "Our bodies are not turning right now because the earth moves pretty fast. We say that it moves fast and it does. See, a day for us is a second for outer space."

Molly adds, "One side of the earth is day and the other is night!"

Luke says, "The other side of the world is the future for us. They are like 17 hours in front of us."

Archie is still thinking about spinning: "I know why we're not going around and spinning. Because we are not supposed to."

Sienna, who has been very patient says, "When can we get back to talking about penguins?"

I find myself spinning with their quick comments. We are about out of time, but I wonder what would happen if I asked them a question that might bring together fact and imagination, as they have been doing all along, as well as provoke them to take their identification with the penguin families ever further. "Well, we are about out of time for now, but one last thought. Would any of you like to live in Antarctica or be a penguin, even for a little while?"

Alex laments, "I would not like to be a penguin. Do you know how old they are when they are grown-ups? Two and a half! Their life is so short. They have a baby when they are two and a half."

Luke says softly, "Well. The sooner I'd go to heaven and see my grandpa."

Molly has the last word: "I would like to live in the North Pole because I'd like to see what Santa was giving me for Christmas."

I turn off the tape recorder, feeling a little stunned as the children hop up and skip down the hall to their classroom. I had never expected a conversation about birds to turn into a heated debate about space, gravity, time, infinity, and the spinning earth. What we would do next, I had no idea. I did feel as if I had been in the midst of a rapid-fire conversation among a group of children who were accustomed to the practice of dialogue.

I thought about our mentors in Reggio Emilia—about *atelierista* Vea Vecchi, who has often said that given the chance and the support, children will connect everything, making a web of relationships as they go. I also thought of Loris Malaguzzi, the principal founder of the Reggio Approach, and his insistence that children be free to mix fact and fancy, logic and the imagination in any way that their journey leads them to make sense of the world.

I thought of Karen Gallas (1995), who writes:

> In the process of teaching young children, I have rediscovered, through them, the joy and wonder that the natural world provokes. It is a response that celebrates the attitude of not knowing and wanting to find out; that requires that all questions be asked unself-consciously. And it is contagious. (p. 9)

These children were as animated as I have ever seen them in conversation. I feel exhilarated. I duck down the hall to tell Kathy and Skyler that something exciting happened and that I hope to transcribe the conversation by the end of the day.

MOVING TO THE NEWPORT ROOM

Attending the morning meeting in the Newport Room gives me a chance to sit on the risers next to children, to catch up on what is going on from their perspective, to feel a part of the big group of children and teachers. At this gathering I can sense the pulse of the whole community of this 4- and 5-year old class (see Figure 1.6).

I make my way to the second tier of the two stepped blue risers that wrap around the corner under the window in the end of the room. The overall sense is one of closeness, coziness, and sharing. I come in toward the end of the meeting, which Jennifer orchestrates masterfully. That is one of the reasons this meeting is a pleasure to attend. Mark, her teammate, keeps records of children's comments and of the organization of the group for the day and who is doing what.

Now, John stands beside Jennifer in front of everyone. He has just returned from a ski trip. Both children and teachers are laughing. Apparently, John is showing his report card from ski school. Practically everyone is curious about the trip and the plane ride and what it must be like to ski down a hill.

"Would you like to take some questions, John?" Jennifer asks, looking directly at him. "Maybe two or three for now."

John takes over the management of the meeting. Children raise their hands. "Was it really cold?" "How do the skis stay on your boots?"

After this exchange, Jennifer widens the conversation, including everyone. "What other special trips did you take and what other interesting things did you do

FIGURE 1.6.   Morning Meeting in the Newport Room at the College School

over the holiday? Last week was so busy at meeting times that we haven't really had a chance to talk about the holidays. Did anyone's grandparents visit? I went to see my mother with my family, and we drove 3 hours all the way to Indiana."

"I went to St. Joe to visit my grandparents, and we made cookies together." Emmy bubbles over with pride.

"And we drove to Illinois, and I went sledding with my cousins on a big hill." Daisy bounces up and down with pleasure, eager to share her adventure.

"What about drawing some of these adventures today at the small table in the mini-*atelier*? I can see some of these pictures in my mind of skiing and sledding and making cookies with grandmothers. Maybe some of you would like to do that."

Daisy and John say they would like to.

"Then what else do we have going on today? Luke, you are having a special guest, aren't you?" Jennifer says, smiling at Luke.

"My mother is coming to make waffles with us for snack, and kids can help!"

"Who would like to help make waffles?"

Many hands go up. "Let's see, last month Jake's father came to make pies. Who was a pie baker that day? What do you think? Should other children have a chance today to work with Luke's mother? Luke, would you like to choose three friends who didn't cook last time to work with your mom today?"

Luke considers his enthusiastic classmates and selects three children slowly and thoughtfully. Luke, who can be less vocal than some other children, has had a chance to be in charge and to make important decisions.

"OK, what else is happening today?" Jennifer continues.

"We want to keep working on our store in the blocks," Sarah announces. "We'd like it to be open today, but we need to make more prices and signs first. We decided to sell more things, and we need time to organize it." This entrepreneurial venture emerged after a November trip to the city's biggest and oldest outdoor market. Because it was the off-season, several vendors took time to make friends with small groups of children, even inviting them behind their stands to weigh vegetables and add up the bills on brown paper bags. Now an interest in produce and products, lists and inventories, pricing and presentation has drawn a group of dedicated girls into the big block area almost daily for a month. On some mornings, Mark stations himself here as a documenter, recording children's actions and conversation in words and digital images.

"So, you and Allie and Emmy will be in the store today? Is that right?" Jennifer clarifies the arrangement. "And we have books in progress, don't we? There are several authors who are in the middle of books. Mark, aren't you planning to work with a book group?"

"Yes, I'm looking forward to that today. Who is in that group?"

Gabriel and Hannah jump up to stand next to Mark.

"And Nicholas and Greg, I think you have books in progress, too, don't you? Are you four ready? Your books are in the book basket. Let's get going," Mark says, leading the way. He is the pied piper of the books today, making them out of textured papers and binding them with spirals and mat board covers with the children. Many members of this class are developing skills in telling stories both in careful drawing sequences and in accompanying words. This turn of events grew out of Jennifer and Mark's close observation of children's pleasure in writing in pretend cursive, random lettering, and inventive spelling in the Newport Room message center. They have also witnessed many children's spontaneous desire to "take notes" at meetings using these same writing techniques. These observations and subsequent team meetings about them are based on choices that originate in a document that we call the declaration of intent, which includes projections and questions prepared early in the year. More about this document and how we use it will be explained in Chapter 3.

When several children brought in handmade books that they had written at home to show at meeting, making books at school seemed a natural next step to both enrich and follow children's developing literacy. Jennifer and Mark kindled this desire further by providing time, materials, and group support as well as offering their encouragement and excitement to the children. The practice of authoring and illustrating books is fast becoming almost a craze in this classroom.

"And I know that several of you are working in the *atelier* with Louise on paper sculpture." Jennifer adds to the multiplying list of enticing ongoing events.

Maggie, Erin, and Rebecca have come over to stand by me during the last few minutes. They are eager to return to the story and the place that they are building with paper in the *atelier*. The groups are peeling off now, each with its own mission, its own focus, to begin the morning's work.

I suggest to Jennifer and the small group remaining: "There would be room in the *atelier* for several children to work with the transparent paper sculptures at the light table—the ones for the composite we are making for your classroom window. Who would like to do that?"

Claire and Natalie wave their arms: "Me! Me!"

I head to the *atelier* with five girls, holding two hands, through the already busy classroom, filling with the pulse of excitement, the whir of ideas, the pleasure of friendship, the aroma of warming oil heating and maple syrup.

I think to myself that this respectful and expectant atmosphere, this dynamic and paced rhythm, this pervasive sense of well-being, this moving flow among people, places, ideas, and events, this "rich normality," as Ceppi and Zini (1998) call it, has evolved over time. It is difficult to dissect it, to pull it apart, or to say exactly how it came to be or even precisely what it is. Perhaps this is what frustrates educators who want to pin this all down and see it in measurable, quantifiable chunks. Perhaps this is what seemed daunting to us to begin with. How can we emulate what we do not fully understand? How can we adapt or embrace or translate into our own practice what seems elusive?

For us, working with the Reggio Approach as an inspiration has become something like learning to be gardeners. We have chosen to devote years to learning, practice, and patience. In the end, though, as with a garden, the ecology of the whole takes over. Rather than making things happen, we become participants within an ecosystem that begins to bloom around us.

Paper Sculpture

We have loads of paper in the *atelier*—all types and colors, patterns and textures, sizes and shapes: bright colors of shiny foil, rich golds, royal reds, deep blues; corrugated cardboard in earthy tones with washboard textures in fat rolls; intricate Asian floral patterns in origami squares; crinkly, iridescent, transparent cellophane; wispy sheets of tissue paper in all the colors of the rainbow.

We have all been collecting paper for a long time. By all of us I mean teachers, parents, children, and members of the school community. Whenever I unwrap a chocolate candy covered with silver foil, I peel the paper carefully, smooth out the folds, and save it for the transparent envelope on the *atelier* shelf that has colored foil in it, or I add it to the small Lucite box over the light table that holds candy papers of all kinds—the ice-clear, twisted papers from peppermints, the fiery pieces of cellophane that hold cinnamon hard candies, the amber foil around caramels.

A collection of children have also become paper scavengers. They arrive in the morning at the *atelier* door with an armful of Mylar from a birthday balloon or a clean doily saved from a meal out over the weekend, eager to make a contribution. And parents leave surprise bags and folders full of stationery, wrapping paper, wallpaper, or card stock samples marked "For Louise" or "Can you use this?"

All this paper, along with the other kinds of materials that are collected in similar ways—threads, yarn, buttons, pine cones, shells, wire, ribbons, trinkets—is sorted, organized carefully, and kept on visible shelves in transparent boxes or envelopes. Children and teachers sort it, or a parent volunteer and a group of children spend the morning categorizing it. This practice is an ongoing organizational part of our shared life. The practice of developing extensive collections and of sorting and organizing them originated in our work with Amelia in our classrooms and in our intrigue and amazement at the wealth and variety of materials that we have seen on our visits to the schools of Reggio Emilia. We know now that order, abundance, and variety of materials create fertile ground for making meaning out of the pieces and parts of our collective lives (see Figure 1.7).

FIGURE 1.7.   Kathleen and Libby Sorting and Organizing Materials at the College School

Up until last spring, most children used paper for flat, essentially two-dimensional work. Collage plays a daily role in both the children's and teacher's experience in the classroom mini-*ateliers* and the message centers, as well as in the *atelier.* All the paper collections are available for collage, along with countless other materials such as beads, buttons, feathers, dried flowers, and sequins.

Last spring, the teachers in the Newport Room and I decided to focus on exploring paper research and paper sculpture with the children. This decision was based on several factors. A number of children in the class had shown both curiosity and intuitive ability to build and construct with paper. Two boys, in particular, loved to play with paper—curling it, looping it, and standing it up using glue, tape, and staplers. In observing this, the teachers all realized that we had not, to date, actively supported children in exploring paper sculpture as a language.

This would be a new learning opportunity for me. I had not had much experience with paper sculpture. I felt a growing sense of anticipation and excitement about playing with paper and learning new skills myself as the children and I made our way together. I wondered what would develop. I called my *atelieista* friends, Jennifer Azzariti and Chuck Schwall, to ask what they had done with paper sculpture and where I could go to learn more—books to read, artists' work to research. I knew that sculpting paper would take us all somewhere new; it would give children a chance to create the basis for a rich and complex lifelong relationship with a material that they will always use. It would offer children and adults new worlds for invention and discovery, narrative and intrigue, physical and metaphorical knowledge and understanding that would not reveal themselves in any other medium in quite the way that they would with paper sculpture.

At about this same time, Chuck Schwall and I made the decision to stay in much closer communication about materials exploration in our schools. In a meeting it occurred to us that we could follow the development of paper sculpture as a language at both schools together, sharing our framework for observation and our notes at regular intervals.

Together we composed a series of questions to frame our research, which we shared with the teachers in both our schools, asking for their input. These questions included the following:

> Where is paper stocked in both our schools?
> How easily can children find paper that they might use for sculpture in addition to collage?
> What do children seem to do instinctively with paper?
> How do they use paper three-dimensionally before we focus on any specific explorations and provocations?
> Will we begin by collecting and preparing papers for sculpture with the children?
> Should we initiate a paper collection with families?
> What kinds of provocations might we start with? Perhaps simply, "Can you build up with paper? Can you make paper stand up?"
> Paper sculpture can be built on a base or constructed hanging from above, can be small or large, can be made by an individual child or a group. How would we choose to frame these explorations so that children would have a range of experiences?

Once we had started, would the children tell paper stories?
What tales might they tell while they shaped worlds with paper?
What techniques would they invent?
What techniques might we support?

These kinds of questions—like the questions Sally, Christi, and I generated to frame our observations at the message center in the 3- and 4-year-old classroom—serve as a backdrop for our work and support us in staying in the mode of inquiry and investigation as teachers.

Sometimes visiting teachers ask us, "How do you observe? What do you write down? What are you looking for?" The practice of thinking together about what we might do, might look for, and might discover gives us a beginning structure to hold our wondering and our curiosity, as well as our provocations and speculations. It gives us a collective, organized place to begin, heightening our anticipation.

Although the questions may seem basic and even perfunctory, they are more developed and far-reaching than the questions we asked ourselves as individuals several years ago. We had not developed the practice of thinking and preparing a framework together. Still, the practice of generating beginning questions together requires organization and time; it also presumes a mutual commitment to follow through in discussing and sharing, interpreting and critiquing the work of the children and our work as teachers. We are not always so organized. We are successful some of the time.

Chuck's and my collaboration spurred on our research with colleagues and with children. Now, 8 months later and into another year, the language of paper sculpture has begun to take hold in both of our schools. At the College School there are visible examples of children's work from last year on the *atelier* shelves, with short stories about them and who made them. Paper for building is found in our environment not only in the *atelier* but also in the classroom mini-*ateliers,* in the block areas, and even—on a small scale—in the message centers. We teachers have begun to think of paper sculpture as one of the many languages in which we and the children can play, invent, construct, and make meaning.

In the *Atelier*

Natalie and Claire head for the light table—a table covered with semitransparent Plexiglas that is illuminated underneath. On the table, I have organized the materials that they will need today: pieces of square, leftover laminated plastic that have been trimmed and saved to serve as bases for their sculptures; strips, arches, "stairs," spirals, and other three-dimensional shapes of transparent colored gel, cellophane, and clear wrapping papers made by children during the past few weeks; and clear craft glue. Each child in the Newport Room has agreed to construct a small, transparent paper sculpture that will be attached to those of his or her classmates to make a quilt to hang in a window in the classroom. Both the children and the teachers would like to make the room more beautiful and to create the possibility for casting colored shadows on the floor.

Today, I point a few things out to the two girls. Do they remember that they will need to hold the ends of the arches or spirals or other forms they create down on the base for a few moments until the glue catches? Do they think that they can work here on their own and make a wonderful square to contribute to the classroom project? They say eagerly and earnestly that they can.

I return to the other trio. "Where is 'Girl Land'?" Maggie asks, casting her eyes up and around the shelves and tables.

"I had to put it up here to keep it safe," I say, standing on a chair to reach a high shelf. Down comes a mat board, 2 foot by 3 foot, revealing the beginnings of an intricate puzzle of low-relief standing papers of all kinds, colors, and forms.

"Remember these steps?" Rebecca says, pointing to an accordion-folded rectangle of bumpy, textured, handmade paper. "This is the way to get to our playground, the one just for girls."

"And this is our swimming pool," Erin adds, rustling the transparent blue-striped paper that came from a party favor bag.

"Do we have more of this, Louise? We want a bigger swimming pool, right, Maggie?"

Rebecca and I are assembling the baskets of different papers that the girls have been using to construct their collaborative paper sculpture, "Girl Land" (see Plate 4).

The baskets make me think of fantastic hors d'oeuvre trays offering countless delicious possibilities. These paper baskets have become richer over time, with the children and the parents all contributing.

One parent in particular, who has become almost like an *atelier* teammate to me, has made the most significant contribution to the creation of these baskets. One day several months ago, Kathleen Sprong asked me what she could do to help. She had started to come in for several hours a day 2 or even 3 days a week to help with materials organization, the organization of the *atelier* environment, and the display of children's work.

I suggested that we had so much paper that I was beginning to become overwhelmed. The individual family collections that had come in at the end of the summer had been sorted by the children into categories invented and labeled by them, such as "pink patterned paper," and "leaf paper," and "clear colored paper." The paper groupings were put in legal size, clear, plastic envelopes and stored between bookends on an *atelier* shelf.

I saw the primary difficulty to be organizing this paper in an appealing, accessible way so the children could see it, choose what they wanted, and keep a sense of organization for the paper at the same time.

Kathleen reached down to pick up a stack of baskets that I had rescued from my mother's attic 2 years earlier. "Why don't we try these flat, wide baskets for containers? Maybe we could make spirals and accordion folds and other wrapped surprises that could be part of these baskets so that the children could get more ideas. Let's mix all kinds of papers but maybe organize them by colors, like a blue/green basket and a red/yellow basket and an earth-tone one and one with whites. What do you think?"

"I love it," I said.

These baskets appeared at the end of that morning, and they have remained our paper-organizing system ever since. The baskets need to be reorganized and replenished almost every day, but that is part of the fun. Once the children became part of the organizational system, they loved to sort by color, arrange by type of configuration, find and add to and embellish the assortment from the clear envelopes with the support of a teacher or parent.

Today, Erin begins to pick up and consider papers in the blue/green basket. "Let's see," she almost sings, "what should we make the boy trap out of?"

"Boy trap?" I ask. "What is the boy trap?"

"We want to be able to play without the boys because they chase us, so we want to make a trap for them. Maybe it will just be part of our playground. Maybe we'll invite the boys when we want them to play, right, Rebecca?"

"Maybe we will. We don't know," Rebecca says, tilting her head to one side in a moment of consideration.

I put some Celtic music on, and the girls begin to work on their playground, hovering around the baskets, testing the glue bottles, helping each other, negotiating decisions, imagining the place that they are inventing and inhabiting in their minds.

I slip out to borrow the digital camera from Mark in the Newport Room so that I can capture some of the sequences of the story the girls are building together. When I am looking for this camera, more often than not it can be found around Mark's neck.

The digital camera literally stops action before your eyes. I move away from the table to get a distant perspective of all three girls, the range of materials, and the whole context of the scene. I want to capture a sense of their give-and-take, their way of interacting and choosing materials together, the excitement of this experience for them. I look through the 2-by-2-inch screen that replaces the lens on a normal camera and wait for a moment to best show what I am witnessing.

Then I move in closer. I'd like to illustrate the intensity on particular faces, the depth of consideration that these children are demonstrating in this work. Again, I focus in on their expressions and wait for a composition that will shine. Push the button, wait, the image freezes on the screen, and the girls continue. I get the feeling that the last one wasn't quite what I wanted, so I check it out on the review mode of the digital camera. My suspicion confirmed, I wait and try again.

Lastly, this morning, I'd like to show a close-up of their hands, the intelligence in the moving of their fingers, the fine detail of their work, the searching their hands do in the midst of the emerging structures of paper.

As the practice of composing questions together helps us to construct a shared framework from which to observe, we have all developed an eye for what to look for behind the camera. This also takes time, patience, and practice, as well as a strong desire to learn.

At about 11:00 we begin to clean up. The girls know to close the glue bottles and return them to their shelf. They place unused and still-possible-to-use-paper forms in the baskets or containers where they belong. They throw small scraps into the wastebasket, and Rebecca volunteers to wipe the table and the light table with a sponge. I join in these clean-up procedures, helping the girls to stay on task and to make decisions about papers.

There is a feeling among us that we are all part of taking care of this place together. This is a feeling and a responsibility that has developed over time, along with the development of the layers of the environment. There is an order now and an underlying structure we have all created together that make it possible to maintain the level of complexity that I have described.

Taking care of the place and developing all the skills and habits needed to do so (for example, judging how much water to squeeze out of the sponge and then doing it rather than splashing a watery sponge around to create pools and waterfalls on and off tables) require consistent and cheerful support from all of us every day. Children, teachers, and parents work together to support this culture of complexity and richness in the environment.

MIDDAY

Today, Sally and Mark are working over their lunch hour at our new G3 Macintosh computer to continue to edit a short movie that Sally filmed of the family events that occurred in December. Now, after we had viewed all the footage as a team, Sally and Mark were learning to use the video editing program, Avid Cinema, that we acquired as part of our new computer system this year. Actually, this is the first year that we have had a computer that works well, a digital camera, and a color printer for our team. All of this equipment is located on a built-in desk at the far end of the *atelier*. Our five-person preschool team and the team of kindergarten teachers use this system.

We coordinate the time before and after school, during our lunch hour, and sometimes during a meeting when one or more of us will be using this equipment to view, catalog, and/or print digital photographs; or to type observations, conversations with children, or organizational lists from our meetings; or, as Sally and Mark are doing now, to edit a video.

This new system gives our team a new way to function together. We all have access to our shared documents, both written and photographic. We can work on these things during school hours. We do not have to leave the building to access and review photographs together. We are able to use photographs in the daily journal because we are able to print them immediately.

Because I have lunch duty, I head downstairs to supervise all three classes of children who will eat their lunches brought from home in a ground-level multipurpose room. Then Kathy, my colleague from kindergarten, and I, who are a lunch-duty team this year, will be joined by another colleague to accompany these 64 children outside into the crisp January air for half an hour of running and romping, which they need after a busy morning.

I miss the long and delicious teachers' lunches at the Diana School and the meandering, intriguing conversations that evolved around the table. And I have always wished that the children here could enjoy a nutritious hot lunch prepared at the school for them, seated at tables in small groups, as the children do in Reggio Emilia. This remains a dream. Maybe someday, somehow, we'll be able to move in that direction. Until then, we have many other things to work on.

After I return from the playground, I take a break and eat my own lunch of last night's leftovers in the empty teachers' room. It is 12:45 now, and most of the other teachers are back in the classrooms. In the preschool, the teachers are reading the children stories and helping them settle in for their rest time, which will last until after 2:00 for the 3- and 4-year-olds, most of whom sleep, and until 1:30 or so for the 4- and 5-year-olds.

Often I attend a team meeting with either Jennifer and Mark or Sally and Christi on Mondays from 1:30 to 2:15, but today we have rearranged things as a team so that Sally and Mark can continue to work on the video. It is taking them longer than they thought to learn the way the system works at the same time that they edit the footage and add background music and titles.

In the *atelier*, Sally and Mark are concentrating on the monitor, deciding where to enter the music and where to fade it out, so I don't disturb them. I take this half hour or so to go to an upstairs computer lab in the middle school with my tape recorder and headphones to begin to transcribe the kindergarten conversation from the morning. I can't wait to do it. I am anxious to share it with Kathy and Skyler, and

I want to leave it with Jan Phillips, the director of our school and former science teacher, who understands and appreciates "science talk." I hope that she will join our team to consider this conversation and the possibilities for next steps.

THE AFTERNOON

At 2:00 the lights in both rooms are on again. I suggest to Sally that several children who are awake in her room might like to continue working on transparent boxes of treasures at the light table, a project they had started last week. Noah and Sarah come in. Both 4 years old, they are competent at using glue and working independently.

Now that the computer is free, I have a chance to look at the digital photos that I took this morning of the Newport Room girls working on "Girl Land." I ask Jennifer whether they could come in to work on the daily journal with me. Gathered around the computer monitor, we pop in the disk from the morning. The images appear full of color and life, huge on the monitor. Every time, I am amazed that this can happen. The children ooh and aah.

"I like that one of me. Let's print that one," says Erin right away.

"But I want to be in the daily journal, too! That's not fair, Erin," Maggie whines.

"Let's use all of them," says Rebecca. "We do that with Mark. We tell the story with pictures in the daily journal. Lots of us get to be in it."

"Well, I guess we could," I say. Up until this point, I have usually used only one photograph in the daily journal because I haven't learned how to reduce them to print miniature multiples. Luckily, Mark comes into the *atelier* for a few moments to hand me his notebook with the morning groupings of children in it to include in today's daily journal page. With these groupings at the top of the page, parents can read about who made waffles, who worked on books, and who was where during the morning. While he is here, I ask Mark how to adjust the photos to practically a postage stamp size. He shows me—leaning over my shoulder, quickly clicking the mouse—how to create a canvass page and print multiples. Now, I have learned something new.

The three girls are delighted. The pair of Big Bend children have come over now, too, admiring the little photos. We all go over to sit at the table with the paper sculpture of "Girl Land," and the girls give me captions to write under the photos, which we have glued across the bottom of today's daily journal page, Monday, January 10.

"Where's the boy trap?" Noah queries fascinated, but a little concerned.

"Right here!" says Erin gleefully. "But don't worry, Noah. It's not for you. It's only for the boys in our class."

When the journal page is complete, Rebecca stands on a chair in the living room to reach the top Lucite box, which holds the Monday daily journals, and proudly drops it in.

"I wonder if the moms and dads will worry about the boy trap?" she asks Erin as she steps down from the chair.

"But it's only paper!" Erin says as they disappear around the corner to the Newport Room. It is 2:45 and time for the children to go to the risers for a last goodbye before the parents come and the hustle-and-bustle of departure begins.

I am eager to return to transcribing the kindergartners' conversation, which I plan to finish before leaving school today. As I wander down the hall to get a cup of tea, I begin to muse. I think to myself that today is like a web—a web of experiences that are all related to one another. Beyond this, each part of the web of today is inter-connected with many other experiences that have led up to today and that stretch on into the future. I remember the acts of folding paper to invent a landscape, stretching as a group of minds to the ends of the earth and beyond within the context of a "science talk"; stirring delicious ingredients together with the companionship of a visiting mother; stitching together moving moments of video for a community of families. I trust that these, as well as today's many other acts of insight and discovery, questioning and searching, pleasure and perplexity will remain memorable moments—moments that will nourish us, join themselves generously with others to create patterns of meaning for all of us, and, in this way, last a lifetime.

CHAPTER 2

February

The Power of Partnership with Parents

The air is full of mist and moisture, and the snow is melting. This morning I filled the bird feeders, hoping the neighborhood cardinals and white throats would return to find a satisfying meal after our recent cold spell. I've noticed that the cycles of days are beginning to turn toward the light, to point toward spring. Even in the midst of the winter months, the light is returning.

Among the flowers in the corners of the supermarkets at this time of year, I look for spring bulbs in small pots—crocuses, hyacinths, tulips, daffodils. Yesterday, I bought one of each for our kitchen table. I love to watch the blooms open. They emerge from under their green shoots, displaying the colors of Easter eggs, and begin to release their spring perfumes into the alcove of our kitchen, which looks out over the back garden.

My birthday falls in early February, and I have always felt happy at this time of year. Perhaps it is natural to feel a fondness for the point in time during the earth's turning when we were born. After all, it was our first experience in the world. Our very first sensations were of this weather, this light, this sky. I, for one, feel rooted in both the time and the place where I was born.

My mother died on February 2, 1998. Her obituary was printed in the *St. Louis Post-Dispatch* on my birthday, February 5. I remember the surreal feeling in the newsroom on February 4 when I suddenly saw her face enlarged on the monitor, three men hovering over it. "She is a handsome woman, but this photo will never work. One side of her face is shadowed. Do you have a different one?"

At home, I found another photo—one of the two of us together taken about 12 years earlier. We are sitting side by side on a love seat, both looking at the camera and happy, really happy. Proud of each other, fresh, soft, at our best. We have the look of soulmates. I took this photograph back down to the *Post*. They cut me out and used half of the picture. People loved that photograph. Her friends said they were glad they could remember her that way.

Like the end of a long and treasured story, her obituary is with me always. When I imagine her face in that photograph and remember the well-written and impressive list of her accomplishments and those of her family, secretly I know that I am the other half of that picture in life and in death. Much of what I am is due to her and to the love and education that she gave me.

Another part of my birthday heritage brings the memory of my father, who died on February 8, 1996, just 3 days after my birthday. At this time of year, I remember caring for both of my parents in the last days of their lives in the house where they lived for 60 years, in the house that I grew up in, just a few blocks away from where we live now.

I suspect that house will always be home for me in my heart of hearts, for my memories of it are wedded to the relationship I shared with my mother as a child. When I was still small, my mother taught me that the house was designed in a Tudor style, framed in dark beams with cornerstones of granite and a steep slate roof. A studded, arched front door adds mystery to the house, as do the wisteria-draped trestles and ivy-covered walls. In the front yard, a stately American elm towers its gracious umbrella crown over the roof.

After we returned to live in St. Louis in 1992, my family of four used to spend every Sunday evening with my parents in that house, cooking them a good meal, sitting around the dining room table together, laughing at my father's collection of jokes, warming ourselves in front of the flickering flames in the generous hearth of the living room. My parents had reached a certain period of old age when everything seemed to be held in timelessness.

Then, all of a sudden, one night, my father fell and broke his hip and suffered a stroke. We brought him home from the hospital to his own room, where he lived for 3 weeks, unable to speak or smile or laugh. I used to sit with him and hold his hand, breathe with him and sing to him. He died quietly one afternoon, the low winter sun flooding the room and haloing his white head in golden light. The anniversary of my birth is now book-ended on either side by the anniversaries of my parents' deaths.

Now, as the seasons turn, as the millennium lives its first bright year, as the light returns once again, I have arrived at my 51st year. In this first February of the 21st century, I have found myself reflecting on many of my previous birthdays and the gifts from the past that I treasure, many of which are intangible.

My mother kindled in me many of the essential values and practices that the educators in Reggio Emilia had stood by, insisted upon, and invented in their schools long before either my mother or I had heard of the Reggio Approach.

I remember the feeling I had that we were friends even when I was still a little girl. We explored the world together side by side as parent and child. She had time for me, time to explore, time to wonder, time to play, and time to invent possibilities and ideas along with me. She looked for a kindred spirit in me and she found one.

The days we most looked forward to were during the long, lazy months of summer. We left the stultifying heat of the Midwest and the city and traveled to the Maine coast. There, we walked together on the soft, pungent needles of the deep woods on treasure hunts for ferns growing out of rocks, red bunch berries, and shafts of light shining down in filtered rays through tall stands of hemlock and spruce. Together we marveled at the varied sea-green lichens on huge rocks along the path, felt the carpets of so many different kinds of moss beneath us, and listened to the pure, sweet sound of the white-throated sparrow.

We played with round, smooth pebbles shaped by the waves and collected from the beach. We built homes for imaginary creatures out of moss and sticks, shells and stones. We painted with watercolors out on the porch watching the clouds float in majestic towers above the dark-blue sea.

The love of the world and rooted sense of place that my mother nurtured in me remind me of Scott Russell Sanders's (1991) words:

> I learned a thousand natural facts from my parents but above all, I learned how to stand on the earth, how to address the creation, and how to listen. . . . My mother was alive to design everywhere—in the whorls of her palm and the spirals of the chambered nautilus, in the crystals of milky quartz, the carapace of a snapping turtle, the flukes of a mushroom, the whiskers of a mouse. (pp. 230, 241)

My mother gave me these same gifts of seeing and listening, of wondering and imagining. With my mother as guide and companion, I learned to be present in the world, to seek meaning, and to recognize beauty. What greater gift could there be for a child? As my birthdays come and go in these years without her, I remember her and thank her for giving me the gift of who I am.

These early experiences gave me my career. My love of materials and children are woven together and part of the fabric of who I am. My impressions of how essential a teacher is in the life of a child, how an adult presence can kindle and awaken a lifelong love of the world, deeply cherished values, and even life work were already seeds planted in my childhood. I am indebted to my mother, who was my first teacher in all of these ways.

BUILDING RELATIONSHIPS: THE PARENTS AND THE SCHOOL

When I first saw images of Reggio Emilia and longed to go there, when I was blessed with the privilege of living and studying in Italy for a year, I did not have the parents and their participation in the schools in the forefront of my mind. I was impressed that parent participation played such an important role in the approach, but I did not spend much time trying to understand why or how this is the case.

At the time, I was seduced by an endless fascination with the materials, such as the different grays of moist clay in enormous blocks, the collections of pointed clay tools, the pools of tempera colors in jars, the bits of twisted foil, the tiny mirrors, small seashells, and rounded pieces of aqua glass. I was intrigued by the way children worked with these things, played with them, explored their properties in boundless ways. I was amazed to see the way the teachers organized and prepared these materials and the way they followed the children's hands and faces, the children's amazement, and the children's ideas born out of relationship with all that surrounds them.

It was as though, for a time, I was under a spell. I could focus my full attention only on the world of materials and the depth of meaning these materials could evoke for the children and for the teachers. While I was living in Reggio Emilia, I missed the importance and the significance of the parents' role. I think that I assumed that I understood it and that it was straightforward. I was wrong.

When I began at the College School, parent involvement took the following forms. In each classroom, two parents, usually mothers, served as room parents. They helped to post sign-up sheets, to organize field trips and parties on Halloween and Valentines Day, and to encourage participation in schoolwide events. Usually, parents helped to organize birthday parties for their children at school. Parents came to parent–teacher conferences, and we hoped that they read the letter written by the preschool teachers in the school's weekly newsletter. There were no events organized especially for families or for the parents in the preschool.

Over the course of my first year at the College School, in an attempt to initiate a more meaningful context for building relationships with the parents, the teachers hosted several informal discussion groups for parents on subjects of interest to them. We also organized a family party just before the holidays.

However, we were several years into our work in St. Louis before we realized that we did not really understand how to involve the parents in deeply meaningful ways. It was around that time that Amelia Gambetti, during her third visit to St. Louis in 1994, suggested very strongly that we organize a Parent–Teacher Committee that would meet regularly once a month. She told us that, in her opinion, unless we had a structure and an organization to serve as a vehicle for the growth of understanding of the potential of parent participation for both teachers and parents, we would not make much progress. Soon after Amelia's recommendation, we asked the parents to help us take this step.

At the same time, she asked us to consider designating a place for parents to literally see themselves as important protagonists in their children's education. We chose a floor-to-ceiling bulletin board just outside the preschool as the designated spot for the new Parent Board. Over the years, the Parent Board has become one spot where parents go for information—where photographs of parents participating in many ways, parents' quotes, minutes of meetings, current fliers, and a calendar of events made by and for the parents give the parents a voice (see Figure 1.1). This diversified and well-organized board, now maintained by a committee of parents and teachers, highlights the enormous and indispensable value of the parents' presence. Without something like this, we all now realize, the parents' place in the life of the school would be invisible.

We are now on a journey with the parents. As teachers, we are discovering, alongside the parents, just how meaningful their participation can become for them, for us, and for all the children. We are not headed for a particular destination, when our work will be done. Rather, we are moving along together, and we are in it for the long haul. The way has been endlessly fascinating, challenging, rewarding, frustrating, and joyous, just as are all the other aspects of our work.

One of the most precious gifts that we share with each other through living in partnership is a mutual awe and wonder at the power of childhood, the freshness of the children's viewpoints, and the strength of their minds and imaginations. As adults, we know that we have much to learn from listening to the children in our lives. We know also, as my mother understood, that we have much to offer to them. This offering becomes immeasurably rich when teachers and parents work together.

FORMS AND STRUCTURES FOR PARENT PARTICIPATION

Looking back over the last 8 years, I feel as though the teachers and parents of the preschool have been weaving a tapestry together. As I recall the way our practices have evolved, it is clear that each piece has been woven into the already existing framework, making the tapestry richer and stronger as a whole. We did not understand or envision the whole before we began. With the support of Amelia, we gradually came to see the role of each form and structure for parent participation. This is the story of one school's growth toward rich and meaningful parent involvement.

The forms and structures that we have developed fall into two categories. The first are events, times, and places for specific types of participation and exchange with parents. The forms and structures vary from school to school among the three in the St. Louis–Reggio Collaborative, but the following themes are constant:

> A parent committee that meets with teachers on a regular basis
> Evenings or afternoons of sharing and dialogue with parents about children's work
> Jointly planned and orchestrated celebrations for parents and children
> Introduction and orientation to the school and the program at the beginning of the year for parents and families
> Parent-child collaboration on collecting the child's impressions of significant experiences over the summer in some kind of book, notebook, folder, or box that can return with the child to school in the fall
> Opportunities for parents to explore and collect materials
> Parent volunteers who help enrich and maintain the classroom environments or share hobbies and skills with children, such as cooking, storytelling, and guitar playing

In addition to these forms of parent involvement, there are other ways in which we communicate with families to inform them about the ongoing life of the school and invite their participation. Forms of written communication at the College School include the following:

> The daily journal—a minidocument posted Monday through Friday that often features children's words and work with materials as well as a teacher's or a group of teachers' observations, interpretations, and/or questions to parents (see Chapter 1)
> Flyers and letters that go home announcing important information or inviting parents to attend events (often dictated and illustrated by the children)
> Minutes of the Parent-Teacher Committee meetings
> The weekly letter in the school newsletter, *Collage*
> Longer stories of developing work that we compose on panels or in books

The Holiday Party and Gift Exchange

When we tell the story of the evolution of parent involvement at the College School, we all seem to begin with the tradition of the holiday party, which we initiated the second year that I was at the school, in the winter of 1993. That fall, I shared with my colleagues my memories of the events surrounding the holidays at both La Villetta and the Diana School in Reggio Emilia.

My internship at the Diana School took place primarily during the fall semester, culminating with the celebration around the holidays. The children and teachers had prepared gifts of the children's paintings of leaves that were connected to an ongoing project on plants and trees, which I had followed with the 5- and 6-year-old children and their teachers (Cadwell, 1997).

The paintings, done on delicate tissue papers of blue or yellow hues, were placed in festive folders with protective sheets of white tissue paper inside. I will never forget the night when the children presented these carefully made and beautifully wrapped gifts to their families. The central piazza space of the school was darkened, and a large screen filled one end of the large, open room. Parents sat in chairs waiting with great anticipation as the surprise unfolded for all of them. One by one, huge images of each child's painting were projected onto the screen as each child voiced a thought, a specific idea about leaves or plants that he or she had spoken as part of a conversation during the fall.

After the image of the painting was projected and the words spoken, each child emerged from behind the screen and walked to his or her own family to present the original painting (see Figure 2.1).

Later that evening the parents presented the children with a wondrous collection of new games for the school. Earlier that fall, the parents had decided, with the help of the teachers, what gift might be fitting for the children and the school. Then we all filed into the dining room that is attached to the kitchen as the lights came on to reveal traditional holiday cakes and other delicacies made by the beloved cooks of

FIGURE 2.1.   Painting Leaves at the Diana School: A Surprise for Parents, 1991

the school, Nadia and Ida, laid out in abundance on embroidered tablecloths. That night, parents, children, and teachers together enjoyed the intense pleasure of festivity, delicious food, and shared company as well as the satisfaction and appreciation of having witnessed the culmination of a significant experience in their children's lives. It was a celebration of the power of childhood, of the imagination, of the intellect, and of the strong relationships forged from respect and love and hard work among all present.

Sharing these memories with my teammates at the College School created a desire in all of us to invite parents to participate with us in planning a shared holiday event. Our beginnings were modest. We met with a small group of parents who volunteered to help. We all decided that it would be lovely to share favorite family recipes. We hoped that we could also share music and singing. These were the elements that we started with the first year.

By the second year, we wanted to share the idea of the parent-made gift with the parents. That year, we were fortunate to have a parent who is a sculptor and paper artist volunteer to assist parents in making books for their children. This idea had arisen at an earlier parent–teacher gathering at which we asked for parents' ideas. One parent said, "The children make so many beautiful things here at school. I would like the chance to make something beautiful for my child." This prompted the proposal by another parent to make books.

The tradition has grown and evolved now for 8 years. Parents and children anticipate the events that lead up to the party with great pleasure. Now many parents are involved. We become more organized every year. We are all open to new ideas. This is partially due, I am sure, to the fact that every year we need to invent ideas for handmade gifts, to be made both by parents and by children supported by the teachers.

What the gifts of parent and child will be is always a matter of much anticipation and delight. We think together—teachers and children, and teachers and parents, respectively—about what could fit, what would work out for this particular year, and then the clandestine work begins. The teachers are the only ones who know both ends of the mystery. Everyone else works in secret—or tries to.

This year, we had a new idea for the party. One day in a team meeting in October, when we were reviewing the comments about the previous year's inside party, which had not been as huge a success as other years, my colleague Jennifer mused, "I wish we could have this year's holiday party outside. It would really fit with this school's mission of outdoor education, it would fit with our continuing study of the out-of-doors, and I just think it would be fun. We need a change."

We all looked at each other and almost simultaneously said, "Why not? That is a great idea. Let's take it to the Parent–Teacher Committee."

Indeed, by mutual agreement, the holiday party happened outside on a misty, damp, Sunday afternoon, in front of the school. There were lights hung in the trees, tables of evergreens, and sparkling silver wire with stars and tiny pine cones to make crowns. There were pots of peanut butter and large pine cones and twine for stringing Cheerios as treats for the birds.

There was flute music and guitar music, along with singing and a surprise entrance of a small troupe of parent and teacher musicians, singers, and jugglers. Gifts of delicate child-made ceramic bells and shimmering parent-made wind chimes were exchanged under the wide and soft eyes of both parent and child. There were marshmallows to roast and hot chocolate to drink and later there were candles lit as quiet descended and the last songs were sung. This had been a simple and perfect afternoon, created, orchestrated, and appreciated by all of us (see Figure 2.2).

FIGURE **2.2.** Outdoor Family Holiday Party at the College School, 1999

The educators and parents at each of the three schools in the St. Louis–Reggio Collaborative have developed their own traditions that involve planning and organizing committees with parents, festivities with parents and children, and special gifts made by parents and children at different times of the year. The values of participation; creative and inventive use of many materials by both parents and children; meaningful exchange among parents, teachers, and children; and ritual and celebration are present in all our schools. These values grow stronger each year as we grow with them.

The Parent–Teacher Committee

Amelia's provocations of 1994 propelled us forward. At that time we did our best to reach out to parents to explain that we wanted to establish a committee of parents and teachers that would meet regularly to discuss and support various forms of parent participation in our preschool. We did not fully understand the purpose of this committee, how it would evolve, what we would discuss together, how lines of communication would open, how we would structure meetings, who would be in charge, or what would come of it. In fact, we were somewhat fearful about the idea. Would the parents want to take over? How would we establish a balance? We wanted this committee to be productive, but we did not initially understand the benefits that establishing it would yield. We knew only that we trusted Amelia and that we wanted to give this idea a try. The stated purpose of the committee was and still is to work to support each family in finding a sense of belonging and well-being in the school, to work together as parents and teachers to reflect on the components of family participation, and to constantly enrich and support family involvement.

In order to take this step, we became willing to take the risk of shared ownership of our work. We became willing to open ourselves to parent opinion and parent voice. Over time, we decided that we wanted to know how the parents really felt about every aspect of life in school. We wanted our forms of communication to serve the families well. We wanted to listen even if it was hard to listen. We became available for the concerns, joys, and questions of parents. Even in the early years, we realized that we needed the parents' knowledge and their understanding of their own children. We realized that we, parents and teachers, were responsible together for the optimal growth of the children.

During the first years we faced challenges and disappointments and still kept going. At various times, we had too many parents on the committee, too few parents, lack of clarity about our collaborative roles and about the tasks and purposes of the committee, disgruntled parents, disgruntled teachers, trial and error of all sorts. By 1998, however, the Parent-Teacher Committee had become one of my very favorite meetings to attend. We all began to feel a growing trust in one another. We laughed a great deal and genuinely enjoyed one another. We all had a shared sense of purpose and knew what we were working on together. We all became comfortable thinking together and creating together. I think we began to feel a shared joy in having knocked down a barrier, equalized each other as human beings, and eliminated the distance that sometimes exists between parents and teachers. We accepted and respected one anothers' expertise and wisdom. We began to feel the satisfaction and pleasure of collaborating.

Although the Parent-Teacher Committee is still evolving, this is the way it functions now: Participation on this committee is open to all parents. The committee meets from 3:30 to 5:00 the first Monday of every month. I attend as many meetings as I can, and the teachers from the two classrooms rotate, usually by semester. The parent members volunteer to serve for 1 year at a time. There are usually three parents from each room and at least two parents who are serving for a second year. This provides continuity and a sense of history for all of us. The parents know and agree that six parents and three teachers make up a workable size for a committee. One parent volunteers to be the facilitator of the group and one to be the secretary. Minutes are kept in a committee notebook, posted on the Parent Board, and sent home to every parent.

As a group of parents and teachers, we always generate the agenda for the next month's meeting while we are together. As the time for the meeting approaches, we teachers always check in with one another to review this agenda and to think together about anything we might want to add. The parents do the same thing at the beginning of each month's meeting.

This February 7, the first Monday in February, the main topics on the agenda are

- Reflect on the January Parent-Teacher Exchange evening
- Review organization of the upcoming Delegation Day visits by educators from around the United States
- Consider content and format for the St. Louis-Reggio Collaborative Parent-Teacher Exchange planned for April
- Review forms of parent-teacher communication.

Since 1994, the Parent-Teacher Committee has grown and changed. In retrospect, I have much admiration for those first brave parents who were willing to work with us to form a vision and a practice that would evolve into the Parent-Teacher Committee that we have today. I am also grateful for our willingness to take the risks that we took as teachers in jumping into this invitation and practice, because it was only in this way that we learned. Now, after 8 years, we have learned a great deal together, and we continue to learn every day.

Parent–Teacher Exchanges

A year after we had launched the Parent–Teacher Committee, Amelia asked us, "Do you have evenings with the parents when you discuss what the children are doing? Do you show parents slides of experiences you have had with the children? Do you read conversations that you have had with the children with the parents? Do you talk and discuss together what the children are really doing, what you are doing? What do the parents understand about what is going on here?"

"Well, we don't really do that yet," we responded.

"Then it is time to begin," Amelia said, urging us once more to go farther and deeper with the parents.

"You should be able to assess your program by how the parents respond, you know. How much do they understand about what you do? How happy are they with the program? Do they feel comfortable communicating with you, with asking you anything? How willing are you to consider their challenging questions? It is critical to get the parents. By this I mean to reach them, to bring them into your work, to enter into a real exchange with them. To work with them so that they, too, are changed in the way that they live their lives with their children and with you and the school. Once you get them in this way, they will never leave you."

Amelia roused us again to try new forms of exchange with the parents. Looking back, it is hard to believe that we did not have some way to share with parents the nature of the work that we and their children were doing. Up until this point, the twice-a-year parent–teacher conferences, the end-of-the-year report card, and informal conversations were the only vehicles to communicate with parents about a child's life and growth in school.

There were no group dialogues about what and how children were learning. And there was no forum in which to consider the larger picture together. This larger picture includes, for example, the community of all children and adults as learners; the important links between home and school; the parents' hopes and dreams for their children; and the parents' desire to uncover and appreciate the joy their children experience by learning in the context of a group. We realized that an evening of sharing would give us the time and the space to consider this important larger picture.

We decided to call this kind of an evening a Parent–Teacher Exchange. The first one occurred in the winter of 1996. We decided as a staff to show a series of slides accompanied by children's comments about their experiences in a community garden that fall. We discussed our plans with our newly formed Parent–Teacher Committee, and they agreed on the content and format of the evening. As I recall, it was a cold and snowy night and about half the families were represented. We gathered in what we call the Commons of the College School, where chairs and a slide screen had been set up. I remember our nervousness in anticipation of this presentation of our documentation and interpretation of these parents' children's work. I recall our uneasiness and curiosity about what they might say when we invited their comments, questions, and critique. However, afterwards we felt exhilarated. However difficult or awkward the beginning, we had launched a new forum for communication and dialogue with parents, and we could already feel the positive effects.

Amelia is fond of saying, "If you invite the parents and they don't come, it is not their fault." This is a turn of phrase that keeps one on one's toes as a teacher. The idea behind this statement is that it is our job to keep pursuing the parents because their participation is vital to us, to their children, and to the whole community. Parents are busy like everyone else. They are not used to coming to school for these kinds of events. There could be any number of things keeping them away. Maybe they are tired from working all day. Maybe they don't have child care. Maybe they are shy. Maybe they don't know what to expect. Maybe they feel that they are already participating enough or that they already know enough.

At any rate, being upset and/or disappointed that they don't come does not increase the attendance rate; it decreases it. By understanding that all these changes in ways of learning and living together in school require reaching out over and over in diverse ways, we can draw all of the parents in eventually.

We use many forms of reminders and invitations now. We list the important dates and events in the school roster. There are three scheduled Parent–Teacher Exchanges—one in September, one in January or February, and one in April. In addition to these, others occur as the impetus grows and the need arises.

We remind parents of these evenings with special letters and flyers written and illustrated by their children as well as personal phone calls. Announcements are posted on the Parent Board and in the school newsletter. All these forms of communication are enticing, and each one draws parents into the community as they become curious about the evening. By this time, in the year 2000, we have developed a culture of parent–teacher community in which parents are genuinely eager to attend evenings like these. We all know that they will be fun, thought provoking, and community building. We, teachers and parents, go into these evenings expecting to learn from one another and to make our community life richer and deeper because of our thinking together and our mutual participation.

I am always touched to remember how deeply parents are connected with their own young children, how high their hopes and dreams are for them, how much they want them to be happy and free from pain and difficulty. I remember that being the parent of a young child is often a trial by fire. Most of us have no idea what hit us when we have children. We can't imagine that we could ever be so in love with a baby. As our children grow, we cannot believe how much time they take, how much patience they require of us, how much nurturing and care they need. Young parents also need nurturing and support, and they need to feel their own power as creative, strong, immensely capable parents whose children need their stability, their complete presence, their intelligence, and their wonder and joy in life. All the forms of partnership that we share with parents give rise to these qualities of life.

Now, in the year 2000, our Parent–Teacher Exchanges take many forms. Teachers and parents are used to thinking out loud together, sending out questionnaires to solicit all parents' responses and wishes, listening to one another, chatting and networking. We have had evenings when parents viewed examples of their children's words and work with clay, followed by an invitation to work with clay themselves in small groups. We have shared video clips and discussed the social dynamics of different groups of children. We have read and interpreted conversations of children together. We have projected and brainstormed future directions of a project together (see Figure 2.3).

This January, the Parent–Teacher Committee had heard from a number of sources that the parents wanted a social component to the evening, a chance to talk informally and to enjoy one another's company. At the same time, one of the parents on the committee wanted very much to give the preschool parents a chance to experience the new climbing wall in the gym. Adventure education and risk taking in a safe setting are all part of the College School experience, and Steve Walters, the committee's facilitator, felt that many parents would love the chance to climb the wall! The teachers were eager to share the edited video of the winter holiday party that had been the first to be held outside, as well as slides and voices of both children and parents during the experience of making gifts for each other in secret.

We all thought that these ideas could blend. It made sense to revisit the experiences of making secret gifts of ceramic bells and metal wind chimes, to see the events of the party that we had created together, and then to listen to parents' responses. And it made sense to follow this with a social time of sharing refreshments in a setting that offered parents a new experience, one of climbing.

From all of these ideas at the Parent–Teacher Committee meeting on January 3, an evening was born. Parents were invited in the school newsletter that Friday, January 7. Parents organized the preparations for the evening, including sign-up sheets for delicious refreshments (bringing especially good food has become a tradition during the last 4 years of Parent–Teacher Exchanges), gathered the necessary equipment for the event (helmets, ropes, and harnesses), and found spotters for the climbers. Teachers organized the equipment to project the video in the central Commons area of the school.

FIGURE 2.3.   Parent–Teacher Exchange Evening at the College School: Parents and Teachers Reflect Together on Stories Children Composed in Small Books

On Monday, January 17, a letter of invitation, composed by Jennifer along with several Newport children, went out to all the preschool parents. This is what it said:

Dear Parents,

We would like to invite you to a special meeting on Thursday, January 27, from 7–9 P.M. You will see a movie of you working on wind chimes, and you will see a movie of the Outdoor Winter Celebration.

You and the teachers can ask each other important questions about things like going outside and being in the sun. The kids at the College School know that it is nice to be outside. A long time ago, Mrs. P [Jan Phillips, the director] invented the idea of going outside, hiking with backpacks, and climbing up rocks at school. Would you like to try the climbing wall? We know how to climb. You have to wear climbing shoes, and don't wear dresses. Wear pants for climbing. If you want, you can try it, and the teachers will help. Thanks and we hope you can come!

Sincerely, Tessa, Sarah, and Chase and everybody in the preschool

When the evening came, most parents arrived dressed appropriately and curious about the proposed activities. The challenge of the climbing wall offered a group of parents a new perspective—a chance to see each other and to know each other freshly. Some parents were experienced climbers; some were brave beginners. Some were timid and finally ventured forth to give a climb a try, trusting that their belayer would hold them if they lost hold of the wall. Some parents simply watched and enjoyed the spectacle.

The following comments appeared in the minutes of the February meeting of the Parent–Teacher Committee. They communicate the success of the evening.

Reflections on the "Climbing Wall Parent–Teacher Exchange"

Most feedback gathered both in informal conversations with parents and on the reflection forms available that night indicated that parents and teachers found the most recent exchange more relaxed and comfortable than others. Possible reasons: Time was made available for several different types of learning experiences: Presentations by teachers, Question and Answer and Dialogue, Hands-On (and Legs-On!), Exploration, and Socializing.

All agreed the video format of the documentation of the holiday party edited by Sally and Mark made a strong complement to other presentation formats. Based on the success of the January Parent–Teacher Exchange and the awareness of the many different types of meetings and gatherings we participate in together, we propose to dedicate most of a Parent–Teacher Committee meeting in March to exploring and evaluating all the meetings that occur during the year.

Connections Between Home and School

In the fall of 1996 Amelia spent 1 month with us, dividing her time among all three of our schools. After she had observed and toured the environment in each school, she had a number of things to say to us, but the most pressing questions for the teachers in every school were the following:

Where is the connection between home and school? I don't see it. I am sorry if I have not communicated the importance that we give to this in Reggio clearly enough. I don't see any evidence of families in the school or of families' and children's interests at home being visible at school. Do you have a time for families to visit the school before they begin? Do you have a way to introduce them to the work that you do, to the way that you organize yourselves with their children, to the flow and organization of the day, to the environment? Do you give the families a book or something to do together over the summer, parents and children, to inform you of their styles of learning, their interests and their family? It seems as if there is no connection to the families, and this is the beginning of the school year. Do you think that these kinds of connections are important for you and the children and the parents in this school?

Orientation for New Families

Amelia's questions to us in the fall of 1996 about how families are introduced and brought into the life of the school prompted us in the spring of 1997 to organize an occasion that we hoped would serve those purposes. Every year since then we have planned an orientation meeting with new parents that welcomes them into the school community.

In the early summer, after children have been accepted and are enrolled in the school, parents are invited to attend an orientation in which several seasoned parents and all the teachers speak about the school in ways that invite the new parents to directly experience the flow of the day, the variety and quality of experiences we engage in, and the richness that grows from a disposition to learn together as children, teachers, and parents. In order to do this, we often show slides or video segments of recent work and share examples of documents, such as conversations with children, daily journal pages, and letters home to parents written by children. The Parent-Teacher Committee prepares a packet for new families that orients them to the school and to our ways of communicating and working. We invite them to complete a questionnaire in which we ask what skills, hobbies, or interests they might be willing or eager to offer all of us. We give them their summer book, and an experienced parent shares a summer book that he or she has made with his or her child. There are other examples of past summer books to leaf through and admire.

This gathering gives the new families a sense of the strong community that they are entering. The teachers and parents welcome them together and communicate to the new families how rich a network school is and how vital their presence is. At the same time, this gathering is meant to be a beginning—not to overwhelm them. Above all, we want to welcome and orient new families, as well as to communicate our pleasure in their arrival; we aspire to reassure and excite as well as entice these new members of our community.

Summer Books

Amelia's questions about home–school connections motivated us to consider other ideas: Once families are a part of the school, what forms or structures would facilitate more connection between home and school life? What might make children and families feel more at home in school and, at the same time, lead them to think of their connections to school life when they are at home, especially over the long summer months?

Our present custom of designing and passing out books for families to work on over the summer originated with Amelia's urging us to find ways to sustain families' connection with school over the summer and to keep their connection to the school alive.

I had seen and read a number of summer books when I lived in Reggio Emilia. We had all heard of this idea. Again, it was a question of believing that this practice could work for us, being willing to give it a try, and inventing our own way to go forward with it.

With the help of the parents on a committee, we conceived of a small, blank book with many possibilities and invitations for children and their parents. They could make collections, select and paste in favorite photographs and postcards of experiences from the summer. Children could create drawings and collages. Parents could act as scribes, listening and recording children's comments, questions, and ideas. We included open questions and ideas that we hoped all children and families would enjoy thinking about together. The following are examples of ideas that were in the first book, the summer of 1997: "Tell about a favorite summer experience or memory." "Can you find a photograph of your family on vacation this summer to glue on this page?" "Here is a little envelope for a collection from this summer. Maybe shells, dried flowers, or stickers—whatever you like to collect."

In the fall of 1997, many of the books came back to school, and some did not. Some families had enjoyed them; others had lost them. Most of the children loved having their books at school, leafing through them themselves and sharing them with friends. In the spring of 1998, we asked for feedback from the Parent–Teacher Committee and made changes accordingly.

The book format evolved from a laminated, spiral-bound book made at school to a purchased, sturdy, yet inexpensive 6-by-8-inch white, blank book to which we add children's drawings to fashion a different cover every year. In the years since then, the books have further evolved to include many questions and ideas formulated by the teachers that pertain to possible projects for the coming year. All the books come back to school now, though some sooner than others. Most of the families look forward to getting them and anticipate the pleasure of a shared summer focus. In the fall, the teachers in each classroom take time at meetings to feature each book, with the child as author sharing his or her book and facilitating the discussion.

The summer books have now taken on a life of their own. Some families use the book as a fabulous scrapbook, gluing in ticket stubs and postcards and other memorabilia. Others use it as a photo album, creating collages on various themes. Some parents pay particular attention to their children's words and fill the book with quotes accompanying drawings or photos. It is remarkable to look back on the evolution of yet another practice that could have been dropped early on because of lack of full participation or enthusiasm. Now, these books are alive; each one tells stories of particular people who each make up an integral part of our learning community (see Figure 2.4).

The Development of Parent Participation

Tracing the growth and evolution of parent participation in all our schools reveals patterns that I have not noticed so clearly before. I can see the layers of our evolution

FIGURE **2.4.** Pages from Summer Books from the College School

with the parents and the waves of effort on our part to reach out to families, to organize different ways of connecting with them, and, at the same time, to create multiple ways for them to connect with us, with the school, and with one another.

I don't think that Amelia had a list of organizational structures or various types
of meetings with parents to present to us one by one in order of priority. We were
familiar with every structure that she mentioned before she pushed us to incorporate
it into our practice. We had read about and discussed the possibilities of parent–teacher
committees, evenings when teachers shared children's work with parents, summer
books for families, and orientations for the families to the school. Anyone who visits
Reggio Emilia, attends seminars around the United States or other countries, or reads
The Hundred Languages of Children (Edwards, Gandini, & Forman, 1998) and other
literature will most probably hear and learn about parent participation in the many
forms in which it exists in Reggio Emilia. However, reading and thinking about these
ideas in theory is very different from putting them into practice in the life cycle of a
school.

As anyone who has tried knows, it takes faith to leap into new practices and
new ways of working with parents. Each new idea takes a great deal of energy to think
through, organize, discuss, troubleshoot, launch, debrief, evaluate, tweak, wonder about,
transform. Each new practice requires our energy, time, goodwill, and belief that it is
vital to our collective growth. Eventually, these new practices, like children who are
so challenging to raise, take off and begin to grow richer and richer each year, giving
back to us all in ways we never imagined possible.

In retrospect, I think Amelia pushed us because she knew these particular avenues had worked for the educators in Reggio Emilia over decades in constructing a strong and unshakable community of parents who share common values through the lives of their children. Amelia wanted this for us, for our children, and for our parents. She and Carlina Rinaldi, and Loris Malaguzzi before them—and, indeed, all the educators in Reggio Emilia who travel the world and receive visitors from every corner of the globe—want this for all children, all families, and all teachers. This is their drive and their passion.

At the same time, Amelia has come to understand, particularly in the last several years, how critical it is for these ideas to take root in different cultures in ways that can sustain themselves in a particular place. Parent participation in St. Louis, Missouri, looks different than it does in Reggio Emilia, Italy.

I remember the night that Amelia spoke with a group of parents who had gathered from our three schools to listen to her speak about her town of Reggio Emilia and the municipally funded preschools where she had worked as a teacher for 25 years. That was the week that CNN was here, the spring of 1997. We gathered at the St. Michael School in a big hall. The room was full of parents and teachers from all our schools and flooded with bright, white light. Cameramen and sound technicians crowded into the corners. We were all a bit flustered. Amelia began:

> I am really honored to be with you tonight and a little nervous. I am not so nervous about the cameras. It is because I feel moved to be with you, the parents of the St. Louis schools, for the first time. In my home of Reggio Emilia I have grown up in a place with a school culture where we have great respect for the parents and their importance in our work with their children. I want to communicate this to you, and I want to do a good job speaking to you tonight, because I have this same great respect for you.

I think that all of us there that night were changed. Witnessing someone with Amelia's charisma humbled by the presence of parents of preschool children in St. Louis touched us. In a way, it woke us up. This is work in which we are all humbled in the presence of one another. This is true for parents, children, and teachers. We can learn through this work to wake up and to see one another and listen to one another in a way that is truly present.

In all the three schools in the St. Louis–Reggio Collaborative, we have invented our own forms of parent participation, and we continue to invent more alongside the parents. Parent participation at Clayton Schools' Family Center and the St. Michael School has developed out of a different history and tradition than ours at the College School. Each school's forms and structures and traditions are unique. At all our schools, however, you will find parents who feel a strong sense of well-being for themselves and for their children. You will see parents who trust each other and the teachers, who are accustomed to being included, and who feel that their unique gifts and voices are not only sought out but also vital and necessary to the whole. This is not to say that we do not encounter problems and that we do not have conflicts and misunderstandings. We do. We have not reached a point in time when we live "happily ever after." This is life as it is in school, and every day we meet challenges of all kinds. What we have done is to establish forms of communication and partnership with the parents that we use to face and to find solutions to our problems. What we have created are strong communities of families and teachers working toward common goals.

PARENTS SPEAK TO VISITING EDUCATORS

It is Friday, February 25. Fifty educators from all over the United States have come to visit the spaces, teachers, children, and parents and to see and discuss our work in the three schools of the St. Louis–Reggio Collaborative.

Today, we have organized a panel of parents and teachers to speak about parent involvement in the preschool at the College School. During the last few delegation visits, parents have become more and more comfortable speaking to educators. The parents who do this say that they learn about the Reggio Approach from a different perspective through listening to the questions of visiting educators and to our responses in the ensuing discussions. They also share with us that they come to appreciate the educational community that we have created together over the last 8 years.

This time, during this first delegation of the millennium, we felt that the parents' voices should be featured in a panel of their own that would focus on their multiple perspectives of participation as parents in the life of the preschool at the College School. Invitations and sign-up sheets asking for volunteers went home to all families in minutes of the early February Parent–Teacher meeting and hung on the Parent Board. In the end, about five parents volunteered to give this new experience a try.

In a meeting to prepare for this day, we decided together that the parents would begin by sharing a bit of background information about themselves, giving several examples of their participation and what it had meant to them personally. The parents felt that it would be a good idea to be prepared with examples of documentation to illustrate different forms of parent participation. We brought the video of the 1999 holiday party and a video clip of a Parent–Teacher Exchange in 1998 in which parents worked with clay after hearing about and seeing examples of their own children's experiences with clay. We also brought several summer books, examples of the school newsletter, samples of daily journal pages, and the new parent journal. We hoped to offer our experience and to emphasize the values that are growing strong through our partnership.

Now, the room is beginning to fill up as the visiting educators enter, find a chair, and settle in. Prepared with tapes and a tape recorder as well as the digital camera and notebooks, the three teachers involved—Mark, Christi, and myself—will document this day. I will serve as facilitator. The teachers and I will offer comments and insights when we feel they would enhance the participants' understanding. Primarily, however, this discussion will be led by the five parents: Leanne Ridenour, Steve Walters, Kathleen Sprong, Terri Shearer, and Jennifer Hillman. The following is an edited transcript of the dialogue featuring the voices of the parents.

Leanne: I'll begin. I'd like to offer a microlook at our family and my children and my husband's and my experience here. If it "takes a village to raise a child," these teachers have been the village for our family, the experts, the neighbors over the back fence. My son's life is not compartmentalized. It is very connected. He feels that school is like another home to him. The *Collage* newsletter is my favorite form of communication that comes home, and I love checking in with the daily journal to learn about the specific things that the children are doing.

I was here with my husband last week as part of another schoolwide function, and we toured the preschool for a little while at the end of the evening. I wanted to show him the new clay panels that featured some of our son's work along with his friends'. He said to me, "It is amazing how the teachers find so many ways to honor these children. It must be empowering for them to see themselves and their words and ideas every day that someone cared enough to write down and put up here."

My sister-in-law was just here and she said to me, "I was completely afraid of adults as a child, but your children talk to us. They expect to be listened to, to share their ideas." I have to say that I think that is true. Because they are in this environment, that is what this school does for my child and my family. They reinforce things that we believe at home and put them into action.

Steve: This is my second year on the Parent–Teacher Committee. Last year was just to get my feet wet, but this year I feel like it all came together for me in the very beginning of the year. I volunteered to be a parent driver on a field trip with the Newport Room children and Jennifer and Mark. We went out to a lake near a school family's property. I am a very typical dad. I never spent time with kids until I had a child, and it was all new to me. I went into this day thinking it was going to be chaotic, went from being worried that we should have ropes on these kids so that they wouldn't leave us, to watching the teachers. I was learning all these things about how Jennifer and Mark were keeping the kids focused, and once the kids had that respect and focus, they began to lead us around. We must have spent 20 minutes around this one group of trees that had been chopped down by beavers. We talked about it forever. And I found myself in total amazement.

I thought I was going to have to be a ringleader in order to keep these kids excited about walking around a lake. After spending that whole day together, I learned what the school does. I also realized that the more I get involved, the better dad I'll be. The kids amazed us all day long with the things that they could be interested in if you focus with them. It is one of my big beliefs now—I make time. It was a turning point as a parent for me because now I can do a lot more things with Nicholas that I don't think that I grasped before. I say to other parents, "Go on a field trip. I think you'll understand what you can and cannot do as a parent." That has been my personal experience.

Kathleen: I want to say a few things about constructing the role that you play at school. This is my second year. I have two children, and I am very split between the two rooms and the *atelier*. It took me a long time to find my niche and what I wanted to bring and how I fit in. For me, the idea of "the environment as the third teacher" is very important, and that is where I contribute the most. I work a lot in the *atelier*. I work with materials. I work with Louise. But also, the environment in the whole preschool and the dynamics in each of the rooms are very different, so my role changes. I have a daughter in one room, a son in the other, and a friend, Louise, in the third room. I feel like I bring different things to the different areas. This idea of constructing your role—for me it has been a slow process, but it is developing, and it is getting deeper, and each of the rooms provides a different opportunity to give.

I am really stimulated by the materials and the display of materials and the quality of the materials and the things that the teachers are doing with the kids. I love the work that is being created by the kids. I have a creative background, but I haven't done anything for a while, so it is stimulating to me in my personal life to do more. It is something I can share more deeply with my children and all the children because I have an appreciation for it. But it has been put to the side at home with cooking and cleaning and taking care of kids.

My husband does not spend that much time at school, but I feel that his participation is occurring at home. In Newport they are working on books. At home this week the kids have written books. They have illustrated them, and he has done the writing for them, and so we are doing books at home, and that is the kind of participation that extends from what goes on in the school even though he is not physically here.

Terri: I might be a little unusual. I am a single parent who had to change jobs, and now I have started my own company. Tiffany and I have found a real sense of family here even to the point that when I had pneumonia, the parents all stepped in to help bring Tiff to school and bring her back. Parents and children were sending me messages.

I am fortunate that I can afford to send her here. I am able to draw stability from two-parent families. Many fathers step in to be a role model for Tiffany. There is so much extension of school at home. We had the first sleepover, and now we have had them pretty regularly. Through these interactions I am getting to know the children's families better.

Jennifer: My mother-in-law, who lives in New York and is an early childhood educator, lecturer, and writer, went on a study tour to visit the schools in Reggio Emilia. When she got back, she called us and said, "There is a school in St. Louis, and there is this woman who lived in Reggio for a year teaching there, and in all my years of teaching I have never see anything like the schools in Reggio Emilia. They stopped me in my tracks. If I were you, I'd call and look into getting Max into that school."

I think it was June or maybe even July, and we called and found out that the school was TCS [the College School] and that the woman was Louise, and Max was accepted. Now Max is in fifth grade, Ben in third, and Natalie in the Newport room. We have been here for 7 years.

I was a career mom until about 3 years ago. I don't know that I am that much more involved in the preschool than I was before because I am trying to balance all three kids.

I will tell you about an experience that relates to third grade, but it could relate to any grade. Last week the third-grade teacher stopped me in the hall and said, "Jennifer, if you are not busy this afternoon, we are going to the library. We are going to walk down, have a tour, do some research, and then walk home. If you'd like to join us, that's what we are doing."

I was going to go home to work on the computer, but instead I decided to stay. This teacher grabbed me and gave me an opportunity—a 2½-hour opportunity. I spent more time with another mom, getting to know her. I am here all the time, but you find as parents and as families, even as children, you don't really know the other people across the room, in the other car, in the other household.

I can remember that when Max was here and I was working, I used to complain all the time that I didn't even know the kids' names, I didn't know the parents' names. I think there is great strength in what is happening with the parent–teacher relationships. It brings together community and how important community is.

I think of Mary Pipher and what she writes about in her new book, *The Shelter of Each Other* (1996). The community of this school didn't just happen by chance. There has been a lot of effort put in by the parents and the teachers. These kids will literally grow up together, and it is not just the kids, it's the parents. These are relationships that we will have as long as we are in this school community.

And I don't think that it's happening everywhere. There is a lot going on, and everybody is just too busy, and they forget to stop and talk. There is great strength in human contact between people. I was out of town for the event a few weeks ago when they did the climbing wall in the gym with the preschool parents. I am sorry that I missed it. I wish I'd been there.

When you get parents together on a casual basis, something different happens. When the kids are not with you, you get to see a different point of view. You get to know each other in a different way. As teachers it is really important to look for opportunities and all the different ways where you can strengthen relationships—the parent to teacher, the parent to parent, the parent to child. It happens in so many different ways during school hours and after school.

Kathleen: I just want to add one thing. I think that the communication lines in this school are wonderful. I really appreciate the fact that I can go up to Louise, and can tell her, "OK. I don't think that this area is working very well." There is no defensiveness. I can say, "Louise, don't take any more fabric!" She is not offended. She could be really offended at some of the things that I say, but she isn't.

I feel that this is so true with the Big Bend teachers and also the Newport teachers. I can talk to them, and they are really receptive. We can have a real exciting exchange about lots of things. I am not looking for them to tell me what Emmy is doing and what she needs or if she ate lunch. It is really about how Emmy is growing. It is a whole-child approach that you take with you from the school, to your home, to the friend's house. The teachers are so open, and it is not just about assessment; it is rather about the whole child and their relationships. The emphasis is on relationships.

The parents' introductory remarks turn out to be much more complex and rich than we had anticipated. Mark, Christi, and I are just as intrigued by what they say as the visiting educators. We are hearing their perspectives in this context for the first time. This is also true for the parents, who are listening intently to one another. We ask the visiting educators whether they would like to see the videos we have brought or use the remaining time to ask the parents questions. They choose to ask questions.

Visiting Educator: Can you tell us more about the Parent–Teacher Committee and other parent meetings?

Steve: When I got involved with the Parent–Teacher Committee, I thought, "Why would I be on that committee? I don't want to determine what they teach." But that's not what we do. We make it clear that we are not setting curriculum. We are an organized voice between the teachers and the parents. We facilitate parent involvement more than anything else. At the first Parent–Teacher Exchange of the year in September, teachers and a parent from the committee explain the committee. From there, one or two or three people take the lead. This year I talked to parents to see if they would be interested. I said, "Parents, call me. I'll explain what I got out of the Parent–Teacher Committee."

At the beginning of each committee meeting the teachers summarize what has been going on in the classrooms and where they are headed. Then we always have events that are coming up for which we need to start organizing a couple of months ahead. With the holiday party we start at the beginning of the year. This year we had a very successful party because the teachers were very open to spurring the parents on to design it.

Visiting Educator: Could you tell us more about other ways that parents are involved, like volunteering in the classroom?

Jennifer: I thought I would give an example of a field trip that I went on this fall to Soulard, one of the oldest outdoor produce markets in the city. I thought, "OK. I'll drive. I'll make sure they're safe, and I'll get to know them better." All of a sudden I started listening to what Louise and Jennifer were saying about what the children had been doing. They were really into color. I thought, "I am not just here to drive or watch my child and the other kids. I can really make a difference in their experience in this hands-on experience."

It was a fascinating morning because I took my kids, and we walked in, and I encouraged them to smell the smells, see the colors, the shapes, the flowers, and the people. We went into the meat market and the spice shop.

And then everyone else went to one area, and we ended up going to the other side of the market, where there was only one stall open. And there was this grumpy old man standing with all of his vegetables and fruits. We had the most amazing experience. I decided to say, "Who wants to shop?" And I'd say, "I need three zucchinis." And then the kids got involved and excited. As this was going on, the man behind the counter sits up and starts coming alive.

And then he begins adding all the prices up, and he lets the kids come back and count and sort and bag, and then they start pretending like they are selling. Then the next evolution is they came back to school and they started to do a little market in the block area of the classroom.

I see how important it is to think out of the box, and as a parent sometimes you don't know how to do that. It is really important to listen to the teachers and hope that they are thinking out of the box. Not, "This is how it has always been done and this is how we are going to do it." But that they help give you ideas for the kids.

Or, another example: The teachers know that this dad loves to cook, and it is the fall, and we have brought apples back from Soulard Market, and they get Jim Wood to come in. Here is a dad. He's a banker. They don't have a great kitchen in that room. You have to bring in all the equipment. It didn't matter. They had a great time. It was such an amazing experience. If it doesn't work the first time, don't give up on the parents. Ask them again. It is so valuable for these kids.

I was walking across the parking lot the other day, and I heard someone call my name. It was one of the kids. I know that I have connected with a lot of kids in this school, and they don't know me as Mrs. Hillman. To hear them yell across the parking lot, "Jennifer!" They are my friends. They are comfortable with me, and I am comfortable with them. So as a parent, I encourage you as teachers to reach out to parents. It is not all what is going on with the kids in the class. It is also what is going on with the parents.

Kathleen: I knew that I wanted to be on the Parent–Teacher Committee last year. For me, it was the continuity of hearing from the teachers about what projects were emerging, what the kids were doing, and what they were excited about. I began to realize what I might be able to offer. I think I went to Sally and asked if

I could plant the flower boxes in the windows with the kids—something really small, but it was fun.

I kept thinking of other things I could do, and then I thought of the skills that I possess and how I would bring them into the classroom. Somehow, I started to work in the *atelier* with the light table. We reorganized it, and one of our ideas was to keep the light table reflecting the different seasons. It was really good for me personally. It brought me back in touch with the creative part of myself. So, I took away a really good feeling from it. My point is that I did not just jump in and know what to do. It is something that has developed. At the end of the year I talked to Louise about becoming the *atelier* mom this year, and it has been a role that has just grown, really developed into a collaboration with a lot of trust. Working on the light table literally forced me to sit down on a child's level as opposed to approaching it on an adult level, which is looking down on it. I really felt that I was getting this peep hole into what my child was doing, and that was really exciting for me. And somehow, symbolically this reconnected me with the uniqueness of my children, and I could take that to my husband, who doesn't get into school.

Visiting Educator: I am really interested in the summer books that we saw in the classroom and that you have examples of here. When do the children work on them?

Jennifer: They are given to us in June. They are sent home. They are really blank books with questions in them, like "What are your favorite foods?" and "What are special things that you do with your family?" Steve and I put these books together last year. You work on them with your child as the summer goes on. It's a way for them to introduce themselves and their families and some of their experiences to the rest of the class. And I think these are just great.

Kathleen: The summer books got us in the habit of writing things down, so when I got to school I was excited to read everyone else's book, to meet the other families, and to see what their books were like.

Visiting Educator: Before, you mentioned that parents came to school to work with clay. What was that like? Did the parents like the experience? We have trouble getting our parents to attend events like that.

Steve: We got a fantastic response. In fact, that night was the impetus for trying other things, like the climbing wall.

Kathleen: That night, at the clay Parent–Teacher Exchange, we were challenged to do something not familiar. We were encouraged to try something different. There was a basket of natural materials in the center of each table—rocks, seashells—and we were to use those if we wanted to, to rediscover the processes as a child would. It was fun. You know, what I remember most about that evening was sitting around the table, and all of us were busy, and there were these great dialogues between parents. We were at tables of six or eight, and I got to know Mindy Bhuyan and her husband, Raj. It was a great evening of community building among the parents without the children present [see Figure 2.5].

Jennifer: I know we are nearing the end of our time, and I just want to add one last thought. I think that it is really important to look at the big picture of what this is really doing. As a parent, you come to hear about the children's work with clay and then try to work with clay yourself, or you come to make a gift for your child. But what you are also giving your child is the gift of friendships with families that will continue for the entire time that your child is in school.

FIGURE **2.5.** Parent–Teacher Exchange Evening at the College School: Parents Work with Clay

If you don't have that chance as a parent in the early years, it makes it more difficult as your children get older. It is so important for the teachers to draw the parents in, because when you are a parent it's hard. You are working, you have other kids, you don't know what to do, you are timid about it, you are in a rush, you think, "I can't help. I'm not a teacher."

I see now how important it is to engage the parents when their children are very young. As Steve said, he has the advantage of having learned very early in his child's life what it is like to be involved with a child, the child's friends and classmates, the child's friends' parents, the teachers, and the school community. In our society today it seems more important than ever to have a really healthy school community.

As the visiting educators filed out to board the bus back to their hotel, they thanked us all. With appreciation and admiration in their eyes, they especially thanked the parents. As they left, the evening when Amelia spoke to the parents in the St. Louis–Reggio Collaborative schools came to my mind. That night, we had all felt her universal commitment to and respect for parents and their place in schools all over the globe.

The atmosphere in the small room inside our circle of chairs was electric on this day in much the same way. As educators, we were all stunned by the power and insight of the parents' voices. An underlying desire was kindled to continue to <u>forge</u> partnerships, to reach out to one another across barriers, to create authentic relationships, and, together, to invent new possibilities for our children.

REFLECTIONS ON OUR LIVES WITH PARENTS

In order to arrive at the point where we were moved and inspired by the voices of parents, we had needed to envision the larger purpose and value behind each structure for participation, one by one, and then to make a commitment to change. For us it has required time and a steady determination to introduce and develop the new practices that have deepened and enriched connections with parents and nurtured our mutual growth as contributing partners in the education of children.

None of these ideas took off right away. None of them were wildly successful right from the start. In fact, the beginnings of each of our efforts—from the Parent-Teacher Committee to the summer books—now seem fragmented and lackluster. To realize how each practice has grown and taken off, as if with a life of its own, is gratifying and also, at times, astounding. Each system, each structure, each ritual contributes to the life of the school that we all share.

"The life of the school" seems an abundant phrase. We learned it from Amelia. Before working with her, I would not have used it. Now, I love it. It says everything. Does the school have a life? Is it full, rich, exciting, on the edge, brimming over with possibilities and ideas and inventions? Is it growing? Does it pulse with the minds and imaginations of all who live there—the children, the teachers, and the parents?

In retrospect, it feels as if a culture of partnership has developed over time, with the evolving history of our shared experiences and a growing awareness of the aspects of life together that are most important to everyone. Looking out over my desk as I write this evening, out the window to the snow-covered lawns and the pink evening sky and the new February moon, I find that my gratefulness for parenthood is renewed. This gratitude is at least threefold: for my experience as a child with my own parents, for my years with my own two sons as they have grown into men who are my friends, and for my daily life of meaning and joy with the parents of the children with whom I live at school.

March

Teachers Living in Collaboration

We fly in over a sea of twinkling lights that float over the undulating landscape of northern California surrounding San Francisco. It is March 8, 2000, 2 days before the Conference on Documentation and Research will begin at Mills College. We have arrived early to be with our mentor, Amelia Gambetti. We come both to study together as a collaborative of teachers and to renew our relationship with Amelia before she returns later this month to St. Louis for the first time in 3 years.

This trip is a dream come true for us: professional development as a group of teachers from the three schools of the St. Louis–Reggio Collaborative with a bonus of traveling to a conference in California. We have worked hard to earn this trip by saving the funds from hosting delegation days and conferences in our schools for several years.

LEARNING TOGETHER AWAY FROM HOME

The next morning dawns cool and fresh in Oakland on the campus of Mills College, where most of us are housed in a dormitory for visitors. The bay air rolls around the

Spanish colonial buildings and over the green lawns of the campus, bathing us all in sunlight and warmth. Magnolias bloom in fuchsia and white. Their velvet petals fall open luxuriously on bare, black branches. After breakfast we stroll slowly in the soft air as if in a heavenly dream.

We have arranged to meet Amelia in the room at Mills College where the *Hundred Languages of Children* exhibit is installed for a year. The exhibit is hung in a renovated library that feels as if it could be the spacious study of a stately home. The panels of the work of the children and teachers line the walls of stall-like areas. This arrangement creates the friendly possibility of intimacy with the work and with one another as colleagues. (See description of the exhibit in the Prologue.)

The version of the exhibit that we see here today includes some of the documentary panels that most of us from St. Louis have studied before and some new ones that have been produced with digital technology. These newly documented experiences offer us and other visitors not only current examples of children and teachers' work in classrooms but also the Reggio educators' most recent strategies in examining, analyzing, and presenting that work publicly.

Many of us have spent hours with this exhibit in other cities in the United States. It was in St. Louis in the fall of 1991 and it will return to us next winter. One of the reasons we wanted to be with Amelia here at Mills is to think ahead to the time when we will host the exhibit in the Midwest.

The Project Zero Protocol: A Framework of Questions

We hear Amelia's voice speaking to Susan Lyon, director of the Innovative Teacher Project at Mills and longtime colleague of ours in the study of the Reggio Approach, as they approach the entrance to the exhibit. Amelia exudes pleasure and delight in finding us all here, this group of teachers from St. Louis with whom she has worked intensely.

We are a giddy group of teachers—thrilled to be together, honored to have been offered this private time with Amelia, and filled with the anticipation of learning and exploring new territory. Our St. Louis–Reggio Collaborative group is joined by two friends and colleagues from Oregon, Judy Graves and Lynette Engstrom. (We are indebted to Judy for tape-recording and transcribing our discussion that morning.)

"Why don't we sit in a big circle so we can see each other and I can meet some of you that I don't know yet," Amelia suggests. "What shall we do this morning? Do you have ideas?"

My colleague, Lori Geismar-Ryan, director of the Clayton Schools' Family Center, looks around the circle for tacit agreement and then begins.

"In thinking about these days, we mentioned to you that we wanted to share a framework for discussion that we have used in many contexts with ourselves and with other groups of teachers. In the fall of 1998, I came across a series of questions for examining children's work in the professional journal of the National Staff Development Council [Lewis, 1998]. The framework was developed by Project Zero at Harvard University. We have found it useful, and we'd like to see what you think."

"Well, let's try it. Why not?" Amelia smiles, a little skeptically.

"We have talked about it a little, and we would like to start with the exhibit's Metaphors and Scripts panels about the work in wire with toddlers," Lori continues.

"OK, let's go," Amelia says. We all stand and move our chairs to the other end of the room to be near the panels about work with the youngest children. We sit on the floor or in chairs facing the almost-life-size photographs of excited 2-year-old children sitting at tables with long strands or bunches of wire.

"Here's how it works, Amelia," explains Lori. "We start with a 'presenting teacher' who shares the work with us but does not interpret it. Then, the process of thinking together about the work begins. First, a member of the group who volunteers to facilitate asks the participants to share what they notice about the work without interpreting or forming opinions about it. The group chooses a recorder to write down what the participants say.

"The second task of the facilitator is to ask the group what they are wondering about and what questions they have about the work presented. After collecting the questions, the facilitator suggests that the group speculate about and imagine the nature of the learning that is occurring. After this, the presenting teacher can finally speak and address questions and respond to the ideas that the group has generated. The process ends with the whole group sharing the implications for teaching and learning that could be drawn from this work."

"It sounds very American," Amelia says with eyes twinkling. "I will try to play the game."

We laugh. We think it is worth trying. For us, this Project Zero "protocol," as it is referred to, has offered us one way to organize ourselves as researchers within a straightforward group process. We began to use it in the monthly meetings of the St. Louis–Reggio Collaborative several years ago. We find that using the protocol provides a strong motivation for the presenting teacher or teachers to prepare themselves well to introduce us to whatever they have to share about a particular piece of ongoing work. This might include conversations they have had with children or with parents, children's drawings or work in other media, photographs, slides, or video clips.

In this way, we take turns bringing to the table what is in progress; through sharing it with our colleagues from three schools, we involve more voices, more perspectives and invite wider possibility and greater scope into our particular experiences. We become a think tank. I like this concept. We stop, gather artifacts and collections of "data," put forth ideas, ask questions, wonder, imagine, dream. We all come away having learned from each other and as a group.

In 1999, some of us began to use this process with other educators at workshops and conferences. We have discovered that this way of thinking together never fails to create a group dialogue in which presenters and participants become learners and researchers with equal footing. This means that we, as presenters, do not claim expertise and knowledge about all that we offer to an audience. We come to a group with the idea in mind that we will examine work together and that we all bring fresh insight to this process. My colleague Brenda Fyfe believes that using this protocol in this context gives us the chance to simulate a teachers' meeting in which we look at work together, raise questions, speculate on what is unfolding and what might happen next.

Through studying the panels today, with Amelia, we want to learn more about the animated toddlers whom we see in these photographs and the processes that are followed. We also want to introduce Amelia to a practice that we have found to be an invaluable stepping stone in our research and in our collaboration as colleagues.

Lori orients us to the context for this morning: "Since we do not have the Italian teachers who worked with these children or any of the team who worked on the documentation, Chuck said that he would be willing to read the introduction and the text out loud as well as serve as the facilitator. Frances has offered to record. And Amelia, would you be the one who addresses the questions and the 'wonderings' that are raised?"

"Of course," Amelia nods.

Chuck smiles, stands up near the panels, and begins to lead us in the first step of the protocol. He is a clear and articulate reader. Hearing him speak the words out loud grounds us and brings us into the present together. We all follow Chuck as he moves across the piece, pointing out references and orienting us. He begins by reading the title and the introduction.

Step 1: Presenting the Work

"*Metaphors and Scripts.* Using metaphors and analogies to transform reality and create other realities through processes of allusion, substitution, and imaginative metamorphosis, are some of the basic elements of the creative process but also some of the strategies that young children use naturally in the exploration of the world."

Chuck continues, "The subtitle reads, *The Intimacy of Wire,* which refers to the three sequences that you see here. The first of three series is titled *Alice and the Whale.*"

We all look at the first photograph of a girl named Alice, aged 2 years and 3 months, holding a single piece of shiny copper wire bent in an arch over her head between her two outstretched hands. She is smiling. She has curly brown hair and deep brown eyes (see Figure 3.1; in order to fit on the page, the arrangement of the photographs in Figures 3.1–3.3 differs from that on the exhibit panels).

Chuck reads the related text: "Alice is playing with some copper wires. She says, 'I make a fish. Now, I make another fish.' "

In the second photo we see a boy near Alice looking down as he plays with a collection of cut pieces of wire. Alice looks up in the air at the wire she holds.

Chuck continues to read from the panel, imagining and imitating Alice's excited voice: "Alice exclaims, 'This wire is really big!' "

In the third photograph Alice has stretched her arms over her head. Her brown eyes are as wide as saucers.

"What a big fish!" Chuck says in a delighted voice with wide eyes himself.

"It's a whale!" Chuck continues to read Alice's words: "What a big mouth you have! The better to eat you—Chomp!"

Now we move to the fourth photograph. Chuck points down to the last part of this first story, where Alice sits smiling with an open mouth. "And the text reads, 'And the whale swallows the little fish.' "

Lori and I exchange smiles. We are thinking of a very similar story that we followed several years ago with our colleague Catherine Katz. Catherine had observed and recorded in photographs a 4-year-old girl in Clayton who made a family of whales out of wire.

Chuck moves our attention to the second section of the large free-standing structure that these panels are mounted on.

"The second series is titled *The Wind of the Fair.* We see a girl named Elisa, aged 2 years and 5 months, stretching a large coil of silver wire in front of her face [see Figure 3.2].

"The text here reads, 'Elisa is playing happily with a friend with a coil of wire, often following its movement, extending and rewinding when she probably assimi-

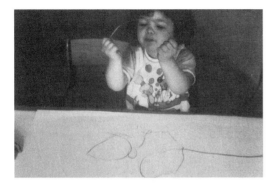

FIGURE **3.1.** Alice and the Whale

lates the structure of motion.' Then in the next photograph, she is holding the coil in front of her face with the opening next to her mouth. The text states, 'At a certain point she blows into the coil.' " Chuck leads our eyes down to the last photograph, where Elisa has let go of the wire. It flops in circles and spirals, some standing straight, some flat on the table in front of her.

"Here it says, 'Then she drops it, letting it unwind, and gives a name to the performance: 'It's the Wind of the Fair.' "

Whether we have seen these panels before or not, paying such close attention to every detail together begins to stimulate a lot of anticipation in us as a group. We are each feeling that we have ideas in response to these ministories with toddlers. But over time we have learned to wait, to be patient, to simmer within this well-thought-out process.

"The last sequence is titled *The Horse Chair*," Chuck begins again (see Figure 3.3). "Under this first photograph of a few pieces of wire the text reads, 'Marco

FIGURE **3.2.**   The Wind of the Fair

is playing with some pieces of wire.' The next piece of text, under a tilted photograph of a wrist with a piece of wire wrapped around it, reads, 'He takes one piece, which becomes a bracelet on his teacher's wrist.' "

"Continuing down here"—Chuck bends down to the next in the series—"you see this photograph of Marco's hand attaching the wire to a chair. 'And then it becomes a horseback rider on the back of a chair.'

"And in the next photograph you see that he has moved the position of the wire on the chair and the text reads, 'And then it becomes—What? "Ear," says Marco, bending the wire and setting it on the top of the side of the chair. He makes the same gesture with another piece of wire, setting it on the other side of the chair. Then he moves away a bit and looks at it and says aloud, "horse".'"

Chuck points to another photograph that is tilted on its side to the right of the panel at the end of this sequence. There we see an image of a sculpture by Picasso.

Referring to the text under this image, Chuck reads the last pieces of text on the panel: " 'This process of reinvention is quite similar to that used by Picasso when he created a bull's head from the seat and handlebars of a bicycle.' "

At the very bottom of the panel, in a placement that echoes the first two stories, the age and name of the child are printed.

" 'Marco, 2.5 yrs.,' " Chuck states conclusively as he finishes this first section of the protocol procedure.

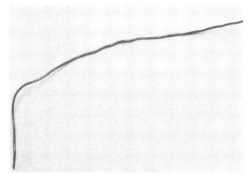
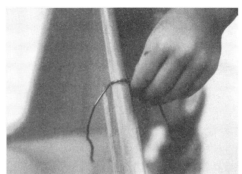
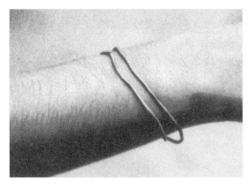
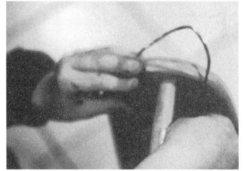
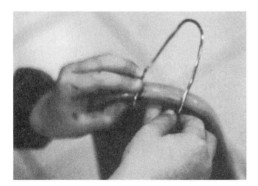
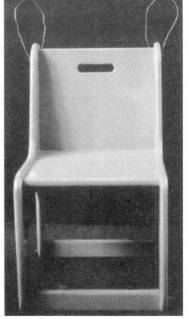
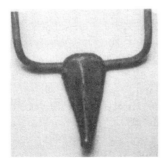

FIGURE 3.3. The Horse Chair

73

Step 2: Describing the Work

Chuck moves on without missing a beat in his role of facilitator in this adaptation of the Project Zero protocol that we are fashioning for this situation.

"What to do you see here? What do you notice?" Chuck asks.

We begin to toss out responses in different voices and varying styles.

"I see a little girl playing with a large amount of silver wire."

"I see a girl at a table with a boy. They are each using one continuous strand of wire."

"I see children of a very young age picking up a material and going with the movement of wire."

"I see that the wire is made available to the children in at least two different ways."

We speak slowly at first and then pick up the pace, as is usually the case when we use this framework. Often, even we who are accustomed to this framework are hesitant to start, thinking that we may sound foolish to voice what seems obvious. Then, in hearing ideas spoken, we listen to their significance. We begin to see more, to notice more, to enjoy this process of seeing and voicing together as we create a tapestry of meaning, a collective understanding of what we are witnessing.

"I see gesture and animation."

"And pleasure."

"And a comfort with the material."

"And body movement."

"I see a playfulness with the material."

"I see that they are really engaged with the material."

"I see pride. Alice is so proud of what she did."

"I don't see a teacher hovering. I see children with autonomy."

"I see that someone is listening because we see the photographs and we can read what happened and the children's words. I see an invisible teacher/observer."

"And the children seem to be surprised at what these materials will do."

"The children appear to approach the material without expectation or limitation."

"I notice that the children keep going with their ideas. They don't stop with one. They keep building on the first."

"I notice that they are making connections between the materials and their experiences in life."

"I notice that they are representing ideas with the wire."

Step 3: Raising Questions

"What if we move on to questioning now," Chuck suggests. Amelia begins to fidget. She looks impatient to speak but is also trying hard to go along with our format.

"I wonder how long it took Alice to make the story of the whale and the fish. How long was she at the table before she did this?"

"I wonder how experiences like this vary. Was a lot of patience given to this process in particular, or is this typical of work done with toddlers?"

"I wonder what kind of interaction is going on with the teacher or with other children. I wonder if a wide-angle lens would give us a view of the social context and a view into interactions with a teacher/observer or other children."

"I wonder how many children were present in the room and whether they were all working with wire."

"I wonder what the teacher did and did not do to allow these wire stories to unfold."

"What happened next? What happened before? How did the work with the wire coils get started?"

"I wonder how these ideas occur to the children. Where do they come from?"

"I wonder if the teachers have demonstrated any wire techniques to the children."

"I see a simple, straightforward format for presenting this work that is very powerful. I am wondering about the selection of these quotes and photographs and sequence. What thought process is behind it?"

Step 4: Speculations on the Nature of the Work

"Let's move on to speculating about what is behind this piece. What do you speculate that children are learning?" Chuck moves us along in the process.

"I speculate that children have had experiences with wire before and are comfortable with it and can tell stories."

"They are learning to use their hands and fingers in ways that are beyond what I think we might expect of toddlers."

"I think that this material provides them with a way to tell stories, that it is a reciprocal process."

"In working with materials like these, children learn about change. They can transform something into something else."

"I think they are learning about sequencing. First one thing happens, then it leads them to the next, and then the next idea."

"They are learning to take initiative, to start something, to make something that has meaning out of something that is neutral to begin with."

"I speculate that the children see that the connections they make are valued. They are seen as authors already at age 2."

"I speculate that experiences like these with wire would strengthen these toddlers' confidence in their own abilities and initiative. They are taking a risk in a way, both teachers and the children. Neither party knows what will happen or not happen."

"I speculate that these stories were surprises to the adults who were observing."

Step 5: Amelia Responds

Amelia cannot contain herself any longer. "May I speak now? I think that I may have something to offer you."

Having lived through these simple yet powerful sequences together, we are eager to hear how Amelia will respond. She begins like a horse out of the starting gate. She is passionate and strong in her words and in the connections that she makes with what we have noticed, wondered about, and speculated about.

> These panels are the first in the whole exhibit after the introduction. We think of them as a powerful introduction to our work. They are also meant to make a strong impact on the viewer with very few images and words.

This is to create a kind of open door to the complexity that you will find in this exhibit that all comes from this first attitude of the child and the teacher to research.

Materials—for example, many different types of wire—this is something that we have even for the very youngest children. We do this so that children will have many different possibilities to explore the world. It is the same with paper, and the shadow screen, and the light table—many different materials and ways of exploring them are available to the children.

Some of you mentioned time. The time the children work can be short, or it can be long. The strong statement is that children have time—time to stay there, to go back and forth, to return and see things from a different point of view. Something like this can happen in a very short time, but there have been many other times that have made it possible.

Someone mentioned the steps—the exploration and then the story and which comes first. The exploration, the connections, and the story can happen simultaneously. This depends on the children and the teachers and their way of thinking.

Now, let's think about the adults' expectations and the children's thinking. Even though we don't see the adult, we can imagine that there must be a teacher there who is capable of giving the children a lot of credit for what they can do. This is also a teacher who has high expectations of the children. The adult has also provided this context with the environment and the materials so that the children can become aware of the power of their thinking.

This is not so common for young children. Usually, there is an adult who is more directly intervening instead of believing very strongly in the context that is around the children. Every time I bring the conversation back to how much the educators believe that it is important to have a rich context in which the children can have many different kinds of experiences. Then there is the conversation about the quality of the experiences and the quality of the materials.

In Reggio we have the highest-quality kinds of materials that that we can find, not so the children can become geniuses, but so that they and we have many opportunities to discover their learning processes and their ability to think. I believe that when you give this to children when they are so young, when you empower them in their thinking, it stays with them forever—as Malaguzzi used to say, like an extra pocket. They understand the power of their intelligence.

How many actions take place in daily life, and we do not see them? This short documentary is also meant to show that maybe we have around us a whole world and we just see villages. This piece shows a great deal of respect and dignity for the daily life in school. In daily episodes you have the richness of possibilities for children to learn from their own potential.

Hearing Amelia's voice, and her passion, takes many of us back to memories of our work with her in our schools. Much of what she says is familiar to us, close to our hearts. Yet every time we address these issues in a new context we go deeper. Using the exhibit panels and this framework of questions gives us the chance to re-search for new, shared understanding and meaning.

Step 6: Implications for Teaching and Learning

Lori asks, "Should we move onto the sixth step and a dialogue about the implications for our work? Amelia, did you have more to add before we go on?"

"No, it's OK. Go ahead."

Chuck moves in as facilitator and participant in this last phase of the protocol: "Who has thoughts about what we've shared so far or how this relates to our work?" The group begins to think together again.

"It's amazing where the children go given time. There is not a teacher coming in trying to help the child move on from bracelet making. The child is supported to continue his or her own series of explorations."

"Maybe when the children begin to see that adults value what they are doing, they keep going and are continuously open."

"It reminds me of that quote of Carolyn Edwards about the delicate balance of the role of the teacher and the need to be a dispenser of occasions. Looking at these panels together, we are all saying that we want to listen more, to pay closer attention to children in our schools."

"And to show it better. These moments can be so elusive. We all have questions about how we are documenting. How can we capture these small episodes and make them visible?"

"It is something that you try every day. It does not have to be this huge piece."

"I want to raise a question about the use of Picasso's work at the end and whether it is helpful or not. Is it saying that the child's work is only important because a famous artist did something similar?"

Chuck jumps in now with a passion close to Amelia's.

"I find that it has exactly the opposite effect. It is very provocative. I don't know if all of you know the background of this piece. It is one of a whole series that was totally revolutionary. Picasso did not change the bicycle seat. He did not change the handlebars. He turned the objects. He put them together in a juxtaposition without actually changing the objects and created something entirely new. It was a conceptual idea that in the 1940s was completely revolutionary.

"So, as Amelia was saying, it is a revolution to see a 2½-year-old in this way—making wildly creative relationships between objects and his or her experience. Maybe in the same way Picasso caused a revolution and jolted the whole world when he put two things together like that. I think these sequences are meant to say to educators, parents, and even children that this work is as powerful and imaginative as one of the greatest artists in the world."

Lori responds, thinking out loud, "And how we end a series of panels is essential. I am thinking of a series that Cheryl and I worked on years ago with Louise. We had ended with questions that didn't so much provoke your thinking as they left you wondering, 'What were they thinking?'"

"Or, maybe, what *weren't* we thinking," suggests Cheryl, laughing at herself, at which point we all break down into belly laughs.

"I want to add something on a more serious note," Frances says as we settle down. "One thing about these panels, too, is that they evoke a kind of sadness in me at what is missed. We all recognize that we see these kinds of things all the time, but how often do we successfully take on the responsibility of conveying to adults what the children are doing?"

"Can I add something now?" queries Amelia.

"Of course," smiles Chuck.

"These stories are an invitation to an attitude. As I mentioned in the beginning, the origin of documentation is a continuous attitude. We try to understand, we follow a sequence of events, then we understand a little more and we visit it again with a co-teacher. Then we go to others. What matters is that parents see that teachers have this disposition, so that they, the parents, can also give more credit to their children and grow to have a stronger image of the child."

At this point we are all feeling astounded that we have pulled so much provocative thinking out of these panels as a collaborative of teachers and with Amelia.

"Maybe we should take a break," Lori suggests. Everyone agrees. It has been a productive morning, and we are ready to move.

I climb down the stairs and head for a walk under the pungent eucalyptus trees, where I love to collect eucalyptus buttons. The trees are tall, with shaggy, rust-colored bark. The deep blue-green leaves taper to a slender point. The buttons, which contain the seeds, are the size of acorns, but they are flat across the top. The rounded side that reminds one of an acorn is at the back. Slender openings form a small cross in the middle of the flat side of the seed case, with four tiny circles on the end of each small opening. There are hundreds of these buttons under the trees. Perhaps the locals don't know that they are treasures.

The buttons can be used to make fairly deep imprints in clay, or they can serve as game pieces or food for pretend play in the house areas of classrooms. The seeds bounce around free inside their small encasement, so that each button is its own diminutive rattle. Each one carries the strong fragrance of eucalyptus and of the Northwest. I will give a small bag of them to the teachers from each school before we leave.

The Conference

The conference begins on Friday evening. Our group of 20 from the three schools of the St. Louis–Reggio Collaborative are joined by the 200 educators who have come from all over the United States to hear about a hopeful way to educate young children and a fresh way to perceive ourselves as teachers.

Teachers of many ethnic backgrounds from a variety of school settings have come to hear Carlina Rinaldi, Amelia Gambetti, and the educators who have accompanied them—*pedagogista* Paola Cagliari, who will speak on research and parent participation, and teacher Antonia Monticelli, who will share research and documentation on infants' and toddlers' exploration of what they call "theatrical languages."

Carlina and Amelia have each worked for 3 decades in the municipal preschools of Reggio Emilia. During this conference Amelia orients us and frames the work in the context of our efforts in the United States and the world. Carlina speaks to us of history and philosophy. They work together well, entering seamlessly into each other's comments and those of the other presenters when they wish to add a thought. The last morning that we are together, Carlina speaks to us of the values underlying the Reggio Approach.

She speaks with passion. Her eyes look out at us with courage and with truth. The following comments are excerpts from her talk:

> Values define culture and are one of the fundamental elements of society. Every community shares and constructs values. When we educate, we transmit values. Values are not universal. Every culture and society defines its own

values. Values determine the culture and are determined by it. As people we choose our values.

This is one of the biggest responsibilities that schools have, that all of us have. For us, in Reggio Emilia, school is a place where we create values, prioritize them, and emphasize them. The school is a place to transmit and also to construct values. But what values are we talking about?

The value of *subjectivity:* We are each unique and we will be unique forever. We see this as precious. For this we value *differences.* We pledge to listen to differences and also to accept the way that we will change. Mutual change is generated by true interaction. We might each lose something in this change, but we also find something new. We find the value of *participation*. Through our participation we are creating a democratic experience— one where each and every voice is heard. The value of *democracy* is a founding principle of our experience.

In this context *learning* is a value because we are aware that learning is relational. We move from a school of teaching to a school of learning. Learning is the emergence of what was not there before. Life is the place in which we educate each other, where there is emotion, compassion, and change. There we value play, enjoyment, feelings, curiosity, and a sense of humor. The cognitive act becomes the creative act of bringing something new into being for both the child and the teacher.

This brings us to the value of *personal and professional development,* which should not be seen as separate but as a lifelong adventure from birth ongoing throughout life—development in which we continue to construct ourselves in relation to others based on the values that we share and continue to shape together.

I think the values that I speak of are very different from those that surround us. That is why, in my opinion, our shared work is so important and political; this is why we need to be courageous, persistent, and optimistic. [Rinaldi, 2000b]

We literally breathe in Carlina's commitment to a new worldview of the young child, of the teacher, of true community, and of the preciousness and intelligence of life. Her words fill us with energy and hope. As Carlina finishes, we spontaneously rise as a group, clapping.

As the applause subsides, Amelia asks for responses to Carlina's speech. A dark-haired teacher in a red dress raises her arm. With a lilting and gorgeous Spanish accent sculpting her words, she says, "We are hungry for this. We have heard these things before, but no one directs words like these to us. We are hungry for this because we are teachers. We are hungry for someone to see in us the depth of our humanity, our feelings, our intellect, our potential."

LOOKING AT OURSELVES THROUGH AMELIA'S EYES

Since 1994, when we began to work with Amelia in St. Louis, we have adopted a schedule for her time that seems to work well for all of us. We divide the days that she is to be with us by 3 so that she will spend approximately equivalent times in each of our three schools. This March we planned that Amelia would begin at the St. Michael School, move on to the College School, and end at the Family Center.

In each school, we focus on what seems to be most important for our growth at the time. Amelia usually begins by walking through the space, noting changes and evolution since her last visit. Sometimes we ask her to observe one or more of us working with a large or small group of children. Often we share photographs, conversations with children, children's work, and our reflections with her and ask her for her input and feedback about what we have done and what we might do next. Sometimes we share slide presentations, asking for her comments and suggestions (see Figure 3.4).

In each school our meetings with Amelia take place during the afternoon, during the school day and after school is over. Teachers from the other two schools are encouraged to attend the meetings at the school Amelia is visiting that day. One of us at each school takes detailed notes on Amelia's comments and suggestions and the ensuing dialogue that the teachers in each school engage in. These notes are shared among all the teachers of the three schools.

Each school has faced difficult critiques at one time or another. Always, however, the observations that Amelia makes at one school help us in all three schools both to return to foundational principles and to forge ahead in new directions. This particular year the teachers at the St. Michael School received Amelia's most challenging critique, though she repeated many of her suggestions and comments in slightly different contexts in each school. Through all of these experiences, Amelia has been our most difficult and demanding teacher and mentor. We always grow and stretch—but not without discomfort and challenge.

When we review the notes from Amelia's previous consulting periods from all three schools, we discover recurring themes. Above all, she has asked us to consider why we do what we do with children and to evaluate whether what we are doing is

FIGURE 3.4.   Teachers at the Family Center Revisit Documented Experiences with Amelia Gambetti

worthy of their intelligence and time. Once we have determined this, she has pushed us to make the whys behind our choices absolutely clear and visible, not to take the values that motivate our choices for granted, not to leave them out. Over and over, she has led us to consider the school environment as a whole that can both engage children in discovery and communicate these experiences in respectful, thoughtful ways to everyone in the community. Many times, she has queried us about our parents. How do we reach out to them, how are they integral to our community, and how is our partnership with them readable in the school?

At the St. Michael School

The following are excerpts from notes taken by Chuck Schwall and Karen Schneider at the St. Michael School this year. They are representative of the content and style of the notes that we have shared among our schools over the years of working with Amelia.

> After a morning touring the classrooms and the studio, Amelia met with the pre-primary teachers and offered many criticisms and suggestions. After discussing this feedback from Amelia among ourselves, we summarize our collective reflections in these notes.
>
> 1. An alive environment needs constant attention and consideration. When you live with something or inside it, as in the case of the environment, you do not always see it as others see it. Our environment needs to work well as a whole, but, in Amelia's opinion, it feels fragmented. She commented that especially because our school is in a basement we need to pay extra attention to the care and organization of the space. She pointed out windows, shelves, and materials that need our attention and care. Amelia commented on the artificial plants. We had more real ones before. We might think about replacing fake ones with real ones. Growing plants contribute to our well-being just by being alive!
>
> 2. The environment should reflect our thinking, and, at present, ours does not reflect the high level of the thinking that we are engaged in.
>
> 3. We need to show the context for the experiences that we are engaged in with children. [We heard about this issue in all three schools.] We need to show the beginnings of our work, where it originated, and tie the beginnings in with our declaration of intent. As an example, she pointed out a panel about painting process in which we did not show the beginning of our process or that of the children. The process and evolution of what we initiated and followed is unclear.
>
> 4. Amelia encouraged us to create Parent Boards that were more clear in their communication with families. We could include parents in the research and documentation.
>
> 5. Another big challenge that she offered was this: How can we communicate the complexity of what happens in our school in a clear and ongoing way? Could we provide a space in the classroom where we follow what happens in the daily life of the class? Or perhaps we could create a monthly journal of the current year. We could choose one of the most important experiences in the classroom and update it month by month. She offered these ideas as possibilities. What other vehicles could we use to communicate the rich normalcy of our classrooms?

6. How can parents educate teachers? We could have a PPTC [Pre-Primary Parent–Teacher Committee] meeting and ask the parents to read everything in the room and then discuss it. Could we use our Parent–Teacher Committee to help us understand whether we are communicating well with the parents and how we could be more clear and effective?

7. In St. Louis we have an important resource: The St. Louis–Reggio Collaborative. In all of the schools it is hard to understand that this collaborative exists and how it functions. Maybe we could post a schedule of our meetings and other work that we do together. The professional development aspect of our work needs to be visible. Do we present outside the school? Do visitors come here? Do we learn from these events? Right now this is all invisible. We can all gain strength through making our collective work visible; so can other people—parents, visitors, even children. In this process we are giving value to our community, our research, and our desire to keep growing professionally.

At the Clayton Schools' Family Center

Early in the afternoon on the last day of her visit, the staff of the Clayton Schools' Family Center gathers in Cheryl Breig-Allen's classroom with Amelia for a final meeting. A few of us from the other two schools are there, including Chuck and me.

Every time that we come here, Chuck and I are intrigued with Cheryl's classroom. There is not an *atelierista* or a separate studio room at the Family Center, but somehow this whole room feels like an *atelier*. Materials are abundant in each corner, on shelves of every size and description, and in organizing grids on the walls (see Plate 5). Colors and textures in photographs and in the work of the children in paper and cardboard, wire and beads, seeds and buttons, cork and wood in many configurations adorn the walls and the ceiling.

Over the years the teachers at the Family Center have learned to find, scavenge, purchase, collect, and organize materials as a staff and in collaboration with parents and children in layered and appealing ways that work well for the whole community. One way that they began this work was to hang a bank of shelves in the central hallway on which they organized many of their shared materials by color: yarns, papers, raffias, paint, wood scraps, ribbons. This arrangement piques the imagination of child and adult every time they pass. It is like a rainbow of invitations to play with colors and textures, to take things off the shelf and begin.

Now, Cheryl's classroom has become a bounteous array of possibilities for the children and adults in her classroom as well as a connecting link to the hallway collection. Cheryl has shared with us that she has always valued an abundance and wide variety of materials to spark children's ability to meet challenges of all kinds in expressing their unique points of view. The roots of her work with materials and children go back to her beginning years, when she was a special educator. She says that studying the Reggio Approach has helped her understand much more about the power of materials as well as the nature of her role as a teacher-researcher alongside children.

This year, collage self-portraits—accompanied by children's quotes, recorded by teachers as they worked—hang at one end of the room. Portraits of the children's homes made in the same fashion hang at the other end. Today, Cheryl explains that when they do this collage work, the 3- to 5-year-olds in this class have come to treat the whole room of materials as their palette. The decision to challenge the children to construct collage self-portraits grew out of the children and teachers' mutual love of the medium as well as several children's spontaneous drawings and collage representations of themselves. In a booklet that Cheryl, Mary Jo Dieckhaus (her co-teacher), and Mark Katzman (a father who is a photographer) composed about the collage self-portraits, the teachers write:

> We encouraged the children to closely observe and examine their faces, bodies, and clothing in the mirror. Then we supported them as they searched around the room—at the light table, in the mini-*atelier,* at the workbench, and in the construction area—to find materials that they could use to represent particular aspects of themselves. The children made all their own decisions as to choice of material and placement. As teachers, we primarily aided in cutting thick fabric pieces, asking clarifying questions about the process, and suggesting techniques and strategies. The children approached this experience in different ways.

Before our meeting begins, I have a few moments to walk around the class. I go immediately to the collage self-portraits. Standing in front of them, I find myself intrigued with all of them individually as well as struck by the impression that they make as a whole. They almost dance in lively and vibrant motion. Today, I choose two to study in detail. Isaac had drawn himself before he started with collage (see Figure 3.5). As he worked he said:

> I need dark-brown-almost-black buttons for eyes. I also need black beads for the middle of my eyes. I like these (round seashells) because they are kind of round like ears. I need two cords for the mouth because that way it looks like a real mouth. I will use these pointy shells for fingers, and they would make good eyebrows, too.

Ali began with collage materials right away and did not include drawing at any stage (see Plate 6). As she worked she said:

> I want to use rose face paper, but I don't want the roses on my face. [Cheryl showed her how to cut around the roses, and she was pleased as she smoothed the edges with glue.] I need the right eyes. [She searched for a long time for button eyes and wooden ear pieces.] I will use this piece for hair because I have short hair. It will probably be too hard to make my dress [plaid]. [Cheryl suggested that she look for the colors in her plaid dress, and she did, choosing cellophane.] I will add this for the lines [plastic netting]. These are my leggings [green sticks]. And these are my feet [green flat marbles]. Even though I do not have them [glass slippers], aren't they just too beautiful?

During our meeting this afternoon, Amelia comments on the exuberant array of materials and children's work. "You can feel it here, all the possibilities in the air and the respect for the space and the people who live here, don't you think? Congratulations."

"Thank you, Amelia," Cheryl says.

All of us present feel the hard labor over long periods of time behind all that we see, all that we witness. Even though we are in Cheryl's classroom, we feel this

FIGURE 3.5.   Isaac's Self-Portrait from Clayton Schools'
Family Center

collectively. We understand together the work that needs to be done at the same time that we recognize the accomplishments that we have achieved and the road we have traveled. We accept one anothers' strengths and weaknesses as individuals and as three schools. We are committed to learning together and from each other. For this we are grateful.

Amelia continues:

> I want to end with two provocations for you. The first is about your explorations of St. Louis and the place that you live, about finding your identity in this in the midwestern United States, in this city. I see many beginnings in all the schools, and that makes me so happy. These fantastic homes of the children from all the different Clayton neighborhoods in collage make me think of that. I would try to go further. You have the book *Reggio Tutta* [Davoli & Ferri, 2000]. Try to use it as another provocation. Think of the exhibit that is coming and how you could make connections in this area with the exhibit. Try to work together on this.
>
> The second provocation is about working together as three schools. Try to do this more. Try to help each other more. Have more meetings that you can count on. You are a precious resource for each other.

We look at Amelia. We look at each other as the afternoon light falls into the room around us, and we know that Amelia is right.

ORGANIZING OUR WORK AND MAKING IT VISIBLE

During the remainder of the month of March, at all three of the St. Louis–Reggio Collaborative schools, we are spurred on by our participation at the Mills College conference and our time with Amelia to pull together into documentary panels children's work that we have been following for the last few months (see Figure 3.6). At the College School we choose to focus on the self-portraits in graphics in the Big Bend Room and on emerging stories in the block area in the Newport Room.

Drawing Self-Portraits in the Big Bend Room

In January Sally, Christi, and I had decided together that we would each follow three pairs of children as they drew their self-portraits (see Chapter 1). We made this decision based on several considerations. For the past 5 years we have developed what we call identity boards above the cubby space in the corner opposite the entrance to the Big Bend Room. We begin the development of the these panels during the first weeks of school, and they are added to as the year progresses.

FIGURE **3.6.** Making Learning Visible: Teachers at the St. Michael School Work Together to Reflect on, Organize, and Compose an Experience

The identity boards are a series of panels that feature each child in the room with a photographic portrait accompanied by a written interview with the child about favorite things at home and at school—family, pets, and whatever else each child wants to include. Over the years we have also included a piece of work in some media or combination of media by each child. These small pieces in collage or fabric or wire become another kind of self-portrait representing the child's preferences and style of working at that point in the year.

It has also become a practice for us to add a graphic self- portrait to these boards when the time is right. When we observe that most of the children are spontaneously drawing first representations of themselves, we make a team decision to ask each child to draw a portrait of him- or herself. In the past we have given children white drawing paper—about 5 inches by 5 inches—and a collection of black, fine-line markers to work with. We do not want to rush the children into this. At the same time, we want to give them the opportunity to consciously put pen to paper with the intention of drawing who they are, in whatever form that takes.

We initiated the practice of developing the identity panels after Amelia's first consulting visit to our school in 1994. She encouraged us to make the children much more visible. She challenged us by saying that she had no idea who came to this room everyday.

I can remember her voice now: "We need to hear the children's voices and see their faces. They need to find their own identity as unique individuals and as a group. You need to hear their voices every day; so do the parents. Why don't you look at the catalog of the exhibit of *The Hundred Languages of Children*? Find the section on 'The Importance of Looking at Ourselves.' You will get ideas."

At the time we thought about why we hadn't done this before and why it could be so important. Maybe, in our culture, we think of schools and classrooms more as functional places in which groups of children gather to learn about things other than and separate from themselves. Perhaps we do not place value on the identity of each learner and the importance of making his or her unique presence visible. Maybe we think of schools as places to serve children rather than as places that are created, in large part, by their contributions. Perhaps we are not used to seeing young children as central figures in our mental picture of school.

We reflected on these ideas together in all three schools and challenged ourselves us to come up with different solutions. If you visit, you will find an introduction to the protagonists in the classrooms at the St. Michael School and the Clayton Schools' Family Center, as well as at the College School. Each year, at each school, we revisit the practice and decide how we would like to proceed and present the central characters for the coming year (see Figure 3.7).

Until this year at the College School, our former colleague Dorris Roberts had both interviewed each child and set the stage in which he or she drew a self-portrait. Dorris loved to do both of these things. She developed interview questions, but at the same time she was very open and natural with the children and put them at ease. The children told her lots of stories about their lives. Dorris also loved to set the context in which children would feel content to draw their self-portraits in whatever way they chose.

At the beginning of the year, in a team meeting the week before school began, Sally, Christi, and I reconfirmed that we wanted to continue what has become a yearly practice of creating these identity panels with and for the children and their families. We decided to make this aspect of our work with the children part of our declaration of intent, as we call it. The declaration of intent is a document that we prepare for our-

FIGURE **3.7.** Close-up of an Identity Board at the St. Michael School

selves and for the parents at the beginning of the year and that we update in the middle of the year. It includes a collection of possibilities and projections for the year, areas of children's development that we intend to follow, changes and evolutions that we hope to initiate in the environment, and possible questions that the teachers, parents, or community wish to explore.

This document is not meant to include everything or every domain we consider important. To gain an understanding of the full scope of daily life at school, parents consult the preschool handbook, tour the rooms, and participate in many exchanges both as a group and in informal conversations with us. The declaration of intent is meant to highlight particular areas of interest of ours and of the children's, to point toward the areas that we would like to develop and follow more closely than others this particular year. The concept, design, and title of this document came from Reggio Emilia, where we were introduced to it by Amelia and other educators. The use of this document is evolving in its own way within our context. I will discuss this further in the story about collaboration and documentation in the Newport Room.

I return now to the development of the identity panels and our September team meeting. Sally agreed to ask Joyce Devlin, another former colleague who is an excellent portrait photographer, whether she would be willing to continue to take the black-and-white portraits as she has since we began this tradition. Christi agreed to organize interviews when the time came after the first month of school. We would decide how to proceed with one self-portrait in materials and one in graphics a little later in the fall.

Joyce Devlin's stunning 7-by-8-inch portraits of each child have been up since September. Christi had typed the interviews in an 18-point font so that they could be read easily by parents and other family members visiting the school. These hung next to the portraits, along with small collages of fabric and threads, beads and buttons made by each child. And now that we have arrived in March, the graphic portraits made by each child are there as well.

In a series of team meetings in January and February, Sally, Christi, and I created a framework for the experience of portrait drawing (see Chapter 1). Dorris had interviewed and supported the drawing as a single teacher, but we were all curious about the process. We each wanted a chance to observe a group of children. We chose to divide the class into thirds so that we would each be responsible for six children.

Based on all this previous experience, we decided to alter the framework of how to proceed this year in several ways. We would each work with two children at a time, and as a team we would decide on which children to put together, pairing children we felt would support and encourage each other in this process. After several years of structuring this experience so that one child worked with one teacher, we wanted to retain the integrity and focus for both child and teacher, yet we were also curious about interactions that would occur between children.

Dorris had initiated the idea of creating a respectful place to work. We chose to build on her initiative. We would organize ourselves so that each of us could go to the *atelier,* away from distractions, with our pairs of children. This meant that some mornings I would be in the classroom while Christi or Sally went to the *atelier.*

We also decided not only to closely observe how children worked, what they did and what they said, but also to use a common format for our notes that could be shared with each other, the rest of our team, the parents, and teachers from other schools and visiting teachers. Together we choose our approach by asking each other questions:

> What kind of materials would we collect?
> Would we have one type of drawing pen or several?
> Should we stick with roughly the same size of paper?
> What would we say to the children to invite them to draw themselves?
> Would we have mirrors and copies of the black-and-white photographs of
>   the children?
> Would we just observe, or would we interact and encourage the children,
>   asking them questions and making comments?
> What would we look for, and how would we record what we saw and
>   heard?

In the end, we decided to designate time for each of us to have two sessions with each pair of children. The first time we would not have mirrors or the children's photographs with us, and we would be primarily observers. We were curious to see what and how the children would draw with only the question as a provocation. The second time we would bring hand mirrors and a full-length mirror as well as the black-and-white photographs of the children. We decided to bring the children's first self-portraits to the second session. We wanted them to be available if the children wanted to refer to them.

On reflection, I think we planned for two sequential sessions with the children with these parameters because, to begin with, we shared a genuine curiosity about what each child might do with minimal visual stimulation. We wanted to observe the children in a situation similar to the times when they spontaneously drew themselves at the message center or in the mini-*atelier,* though we knew that just being in a quiet place with one other child would change things. We wondered how much. We wondered whether and how the pairs might influence one another. In the second session, we hoped revisiting the experience might give the children added incentive to notice more about themselves and their partner and, in the process of drawing a self-portrait, to make more sense of themselves.

For both experiences, we would each use an observation sheet for each child with three columns: one to sketch the progression of the child's drawing, one for what the child said and how he or she interacted with the other child, and one for what we said. We decided how we would set up the room, which table we would work at, who would prepare the materials, when and whether we would try to photograph or video this experience.

As I write this long list of thoughts, preparations, and questions that the three of us asked ourselves, I am reminded of an article by our colleague Brenda Fyfe (1998) in which she proposes sets of questions that teaching colleagues can ask themselves in order to proceed as collaborators in organizing and documenting their work. When I first read it, I remember thinking, "Who would ever have the time or a sense of the order in all of this to do all that?" Yet, as I think through and explain all the steps that we followed just to prepare for this experience before we even started, I realize that we were doing just what Brenda wrote about.

As she explains, as teaching teams mature, some ways of thinking and preparing become second nature. We just do it. Maybe it is like becoming a good crew on a sailboat. We know what needs to be done, we recognize each other's strengths, and we have adopted a certain rhythm and style of working together. After a while, it is fun to do these things well together. And, as on a sailboat, we don't know what kind of conditions we will encounter or where precisely we will go, but we are good at preparing ourselves to travel and, most of the time, we enjoy it.

As our experiences with each pair of children evolved, we shared our observations with one another at our weekly meetings. We could look at each other's observation sheets and see the sketches of how each child had proceeded, what he or she had said, and how the interaction between children had ensued. These notes, along with our verbal and gestural sharing, gave each one of us a fairly accurate picture of the whole as well as an exhilarating sense of pride and shared ownership in the fruits of our collective labors.

When all the children had drawn their self-portraits, Christi volunteered to ask them which of their two portraits they would choose as their favorite. She then made copies of the favorites (because we would put reduced copies at the message center and perhaps on their mailboxes) and hung the originals on the identity boards alongside the children's photographs.

Now, the three of us want to make our observations of the various processes that we have followed visible. We want parents and children to see and understand the many different ways in which the children went about thinking through how to make a drawing of themselves, what it meant to them, what marks they had each chosen to make, and how these marks were significant.

In the documentation panel about this experience that we are designing together, we choose to feature three children's processes and portraits, one from each of our groups of six, in order to give examples of some of the ways in which the

18 children worked. Figure 3.8 illustrates the work of Logan, Brewster, and Claire. Figure 3.9 provides a close-up on Claire and the process she followed to create her self-portrait. We decide to make the rest of the observation sheets available for parents and children. We plan to send them home with the portraits in the children's portfolios at the end of the year. As I reflect on the experience of representing ourselves both as children and as adults, I am reminded of the words of Daniel Walsh (1999):

> The goal is not to express ourselves but instead to construct ourselves and our relations with each other with our own descriptions in our own language. We are to create ourselves by telling our own stories. And [children] need the time necessary to begin doing that. . . . Usually a lifetime." (p. 22)

Through our slowed-down, carefully organized time with children, and our shared observations, Sally, Christi, and I feel as though we have witnessed one part of the continual process through which these children are constructing an image of who they are with a pen on paper in the company of friends. We have heard some of their stories, and now these stories are part of our community to be shared and appreciated by all of us. Through this process we have come to know ourselves, one another, and the children in a deeper way.

Creating Soulard Market in the Block Area of the Newport Room

I want to begin this story as a detective might, searching for the beginning traces of the experience, for it was not something that we projected or anticipated. Citing excerpts from the declaration of intent for the Newport Room will give a sense of the scope and shape of things as we saw them in September.

Outdoor Study

  The study of the outdoors and children's sense of place in 1998–1999 stimulated children, parents, and teachers in many ways. (Please read and enjoy the process of our adventures and discoveries on the panels hanging on rings in the meeting area of the Newport Room.) We feel as if we are just beginning to understand the myriad ways in which children find their place in the out-of-doors and within our community. Therefore, we propose to continue this study into school year 1999–2000 with a new emphasis. We have several proposals and questions for 1999–2000.

  1. In 1998–1999, our outdoor experiences took place mostly in spaces away from buildings. Because we know that the city where we live is fundamental to the children's growing sense of place, this year we would like to add outdoor experiences in the city to our explorations. We question:

    Could we visit city parks, or Soulard Market, or the riverfront and the arch? How will children respond to these outdoor city experiences?

    What will they notice, remark upon, wonder about?

    What will they enjoy, and what might they find intimidating?

    Just as the trees and leaves intrigued the children last year, will the architecture of city buildings interest the children this year?

    How might the children represent what they experience?

    How can we best document these new experiences?

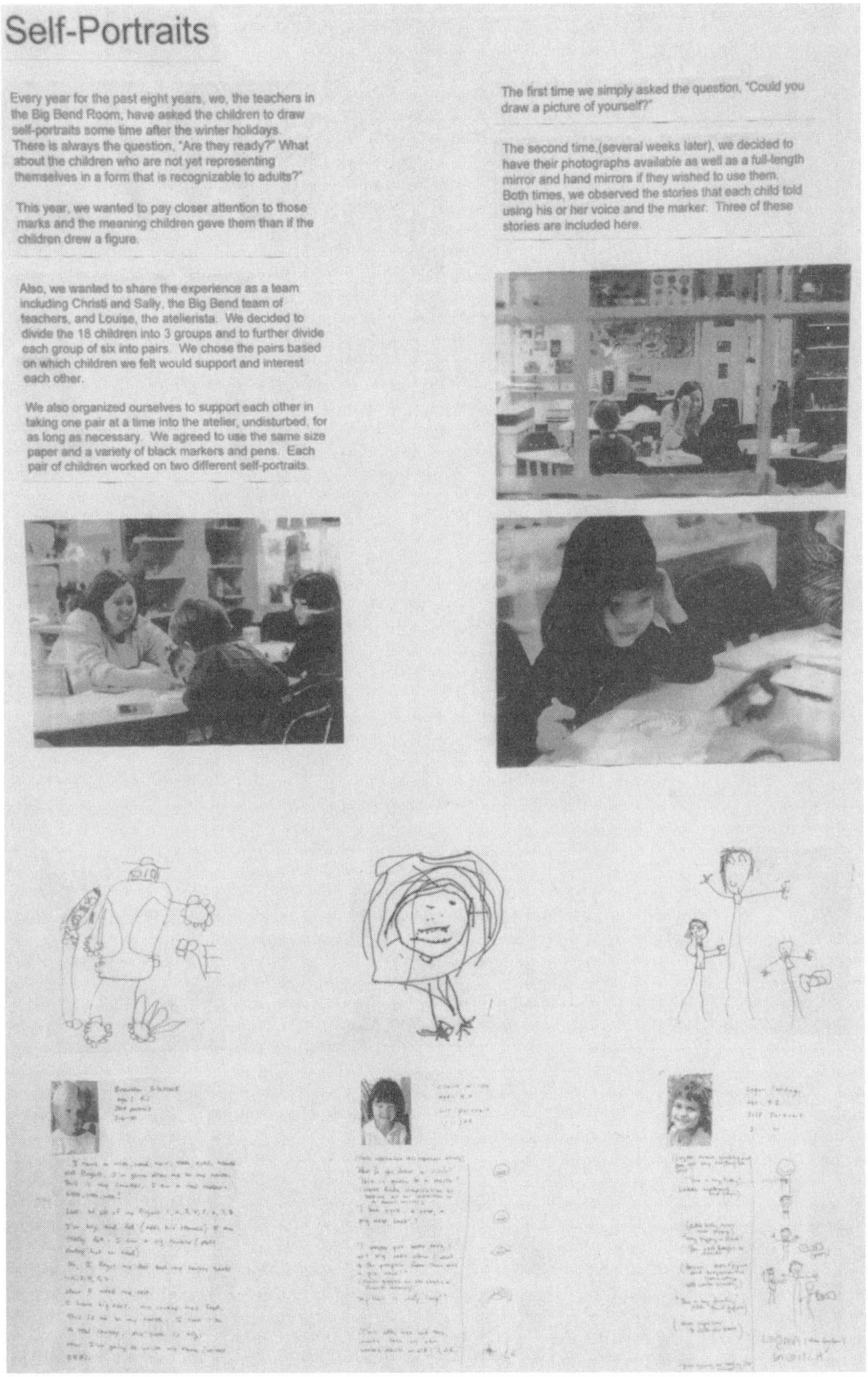

Self-Portraits

Every year for the past eight years, we, the teachers in the Big Bend Room, have asked the children to draw self-portraits some time after the winter holidays. There is always the question, "Are they ready?" What about the children who are not yet representing themselves in a form that is recognizable to adults?"

This year, we wanted to pay closer attention to those marks and the meaning children gave them than if the children drew a figure.

Also, we wanted to share the experience as a team, including Christi and Sally, the Big Bend team of teachers, and Louise, the atelierista. We decided to divide the 18 children into 3 groups and to further divide each group of six into pairs. We chose the pairs based on which children we felt would support and interest each other.

We also organized ourselves to support each other in taking one pair at a time into the atelier, undisturbed, for as long as necessary. We agreed to use the same size paper and a variety of black markers and pens. Each pair of children worked on two different self-portraits.

The first time we simply asked the question, "Could you draw a picture of yourself?"

The second time,(several weeks later), we decided to have their photographs available as well as a full-length mirror and hand mirrors if they wished to use them. Both times, we observed the stories that each child told using his or her voice and the marker. Three of these stories are included here.

FIGURE 3.8. The Process of Making a Self-Portrait: A Story from the Big Bend Room at the College School

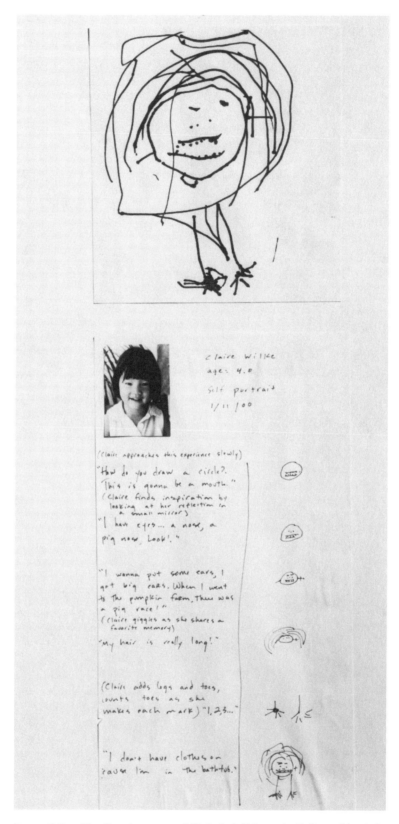

FIGURE 3.9. The Development of Claire's Self-Portrait, Followed by Sally

2. Because we know that families come to understand and feel roots in the place where they live together, and because collaboration with parents is vital to our work in school, we would like to offer parents more possibilities for partnership in the exploration of outdoor places in the city alongside their children. We would also like to encourage parents to help us in the documentation of these experiences so that our community can understand them in as rich a way as possible from multiple points of view.

Exploring an Open-Air City Landmark

To carry out our intention to visit outdoor landmarks in the city, Jennifer and Mark began to organize a mid-fall trip to Soulard Market. We thought about and planned for the many aspects of this trip together. Jennifer and Mark would talk with the children about the upcoming trip and gather their ideas: Had any of the children visited the market before? What did they think they would find there? What would they like to bring back? If parents came, what did the children hope the parents might do with them? As I write these considerations, I think, once again, of Amelia and her questions for us in 1994 about the way we organized field trips. She asked us, "How much do you involve the children in planning these trips? Are they involved in choices of where to go? Do they feel that they are researchers? Do they think with you about what equipment you might need to take along if, in fact, you are researchers in the middle of an experience?" Now, because we have become co-researchers with children and parents and have developed practical ways to organize ourselves to enact this role over time, the framework for making choices together is a part of our process for planning field trips.

Mark would be the digital photographer; I would shoot slides. I would follow one group closely from beginning to end, taking notes. Jennifer would encourage a large group of parents to join us and to lead small groups into the experience as explorers of a new territory. She would serve as a coach for the parents, encouraging them to become active agents in the children's experience and observers at the same time. She would invite the parents into partnership in the experience.

Both before we left and when we arrived at the market, Jennifer spoke with the parents, asking them to be companions to the children in searching for colors and textures, fragrances and tastes—to be real investigators alongside their children and to take notes on what the children did and said if there was a chance. If they could not write there, perhaps they would jot notes down when we returned to school to share with the children and the other parents. Some parents had brought along cameras and would also share photographs with us. (See Chapter 2 for the description of this trip offered by parent Jennifer Hillman.)

Soulard Market is the oldest outdoor market in the city. It is located in the heart of the old downtown area of St. Louis, close to the river. It is a big market with two long aisles lined with produce stalls and an indoor area with other food stores, including a well-known spice shop, a butcher shop, and a delicatessen. The vendors are farmers who come in to sell their wares. Soulard feels like old St. Louis, and it is. It has not been updated or upscaled. It becomes easy to go back in time, even a century, and imagine shopping for the day's vegetables and fruits here, wearing long skirts and carrying a basket.

The children were captivated by this place so different from the supermarkets that they usually visit. They became absorbed in selecting vegetables, counting money, and bagging plump tomatoes, crescent-shaped cucumbers, rosy-red Jonathan apples, and lime-green pippins. They began to play the roles of vendor and customer, considering, choosing, offering, counting, adding, packaging, carrying.

Later that week, back at school, many of them drew their memories of the day, focusing primarily on the stalls, stacked and bulging with rows of colors and shapes of fruits and vegetables. Jennifer's suggestion/invitation at morning meeting to remember through drawing was eagerly taken up by at least half the class.

In our team meeting the next week on Monday afternoon, Jennifer, Mark, and I discussed other ways we might encourage children to reflect on their vivid memories of the morning at Soulard and to bring the memories to life in their own way. Jennifer suggested that some children might want to paint at the easel, using their drawings and photographs of the stalls as references if they chose. She also mentioned that she would like to challenge a group to re-create the market in the block area.

Natalie's mother, Jennifer Hillman, had played a very active role with one group of children that morning. Perhaps one of us could interview her about her perspective. I agreed to do this, since I had followed her group. We decided at this point to include parents' voices and presence in every documentary panel that we constructed for the remainder of the year. And Jennifer Hillman was ready anytime to come to school to make applesauce with the children with the apples they had purchased. Mark volunteered to call Jennifer to organize her visit.

A Window into Girls' Work and Play in Blocks

Jennifer Strange's provocation to re-create Soulard Market in the block area was launched on Tuesday morning about a week after our trip to Soulard. We are not sure why it was that this idea intrigued several girls but no boys.

What began to unfold was fascinating in many ways. The girls staked a claim in the big block corner, an area that can be easily dominated by the boys. These girls not only built a market; from the beginning they had the idea that the market would be a collection of stalls that were actually "open for business" and that they would work as vendors. This would be an ongoing venture that would require them to run things, organize, advertise, open and close, supply, sell, and record sales. The big block area was transformed into a daily reenactment of the experience they had lived together during a lively field trip to the city. It became a unique blend of construction, dramatic play, literacy and numeracy experimentation, and early entrepreneurship.

Soon, the idea took on a life of its own. On many mornings, the girls chose to return to the place that they had made. Because the block area in the Newport Room is in an alcove, the stalls could stay up and be embellished and improved with new materials and new ideas as time went on. The market play continued in the block area for almost 2 months.

Mark became captivated by the particulars of these developments. In weekly team meetings, Jennifer encouraged him to observe, and together they planned time during the mornings when he would focus his attention on this activity. He photographed stages of the organization of the girls at work, observed them in progress, and took notes on what he noticed. Mark used some of his observations and photographs to prepare the daily journal on Tuesdays or Fridays, when he is responsible for this minidocument that we hope will engage parents in our daily life. (See Chapter 1 for a detailed description of the daily journal.)

In a February team meeting, Jennifer asked Mark whether he would be willing to organize his observations, photographs, and reflections about the development of

Soulard Market in the block area along with some of the other developments in blocks that had occurred earlier this year into a panel. He was eager to try.

In considering the weekly organization of our work, we chose times when Mark could revisit some of the episodes he had observed with the girls. He used photographs and his notes to discuss the history of episodes in blocks with the three girls who had been the central protagonists. He also spoke with Jennifer about developments in blocks in other years. The three of us looked at several panels about block stories in our archives, thinking together both about block construction and about panel building. Mark also did some initial research on children and blocks.

Several aspects of this extended experience surfaced as most intriguing. As had occurred several times in past years, a group of motivated children had caught the provocation of a teacher to make a connection with a specific experience and the block area. These children had designed and constructed a place in which an ongoing drama could unfold that became, for them, dynamic and real as well as imaginary and evocative. This year, Soulard Market was both constructed and managed by a group of girls. The girls developed a hierarchy of rules and procedures. They invented daily episodes and stories within the physical place and the elaborate system that they had created. The girls commandeered the place and were able to orchestrate its use in a way that engaged many of the other members of the class in buying and selling, keeping lists and records, and cooperating in a major venture. In *The Block Book,* Apelman and Johnson (1984) describe the naming of structures and dramatic play with blocks as the seventh and most advanced stage in children's development. However, the day-to-day functioning of the constructed market over time and the collaborative work that ensued among classmates seem to take the work to yet another level that is closer to the scenarios recounted in Elizabeth Dreier's chapter, "Blocks in the Elementary School," in the same book.

We speculate that, as in other years when children had created buildings and stories in the block area, the market continued to evolve because many factors nourished a network of significant relationships: the protected and alcove-like space where structures and props could remain for days at a time; the diverse collection of materials in the block area, such as stones, springs, shells, seed pods, pine cones, pieces of fabric, and small baskets; the provocation and the sustained interest of the teachers and the parents in the children's ongoing work; the observations and notes about the experience, contributed by both teachers and parents, that let the children see, think about, and project from their work.

To illustrate examples of the developments in the Soulard Market block adventure, Mark used excerpts from all the documents, data, and conversations mentioned above, in addition to selections from the photographs, children's drawings, sales records, notes and signs that he had collected in a large folder to begin to compose his first panel. Adhering to our joint commitment to include a reflection from a parent in every panel, he interviewed the father of one of the girls who had followed the development of Soulard Market in the blocks with great interest. Figures 3.10 and 3.11 illustrate examples from the collection of "windows" that make up the documentation panel that Mark prepared.

"Staying Alive"

In the cavernous, dimly lit ballroom of a convention center in Atlanta, I heard a string of words that made me strain to hear the speaker clearly through the whispering and

FIGURE **3.10.**   Farmers Recording Sales: "Lots of people come to Soulard. We were writing things down that they buy to keep up with business." Allie and Sarah

FIGURE **3.11.**   Closing Up Shop: "The girls have a tough job because people like to barge in sometimes." Justin

the background chatter, made me sit up in my uncomfortable plastic chair, made my mind wake up. The gentle voice belonged to Barbara Burrington, the head teacher in the lab school at the University of Vermont. Barbara said:

> Our passion for the chosen topic will motivate us throughout the documentation process. I suggest that we engage ourselves in our work across disciplines and view our teaching and our research as something inspiring, full of life, and phenomenal. We can frame our questions from infinite points of view . . . not only as researchers but as collaborators, advocates, intellectuals, artists working with found objects, activists, ethnographers, cultural geographers.

I love this idea that we see ourselves as possessing a collection of identities and dispositions, the first of which is not teacher, but rather inquirer, framer of questions that deeply engage us and that will help us be more equipped companions of children in our side-by-side research. My close colleague and friend Jennifer Azzariti, who worked as *atelierista* at the Model Early Learning Center in Washington, D.C., from 1991–1997, has a different name for this multifaceted way of being a teacher. She calls it "staying alive."

I think that Barbara and Jennifer describe the energy field that we tap into, the creative force that we have in us that is inspired and deepened while working with children and each other in this way. We feel a rush of excitement when we witness the birth of new ideas from children and adults, when we sense that we are on a collective journey, figuring out the way together.

I realize that seeing, noticing, observing, being fully present, paying attention, and creating, collecting, and sharing "documents" (lists, notes, photographs, writing, videos, notebooks, files, delegated tasks, shared processes) is now the central way in which we work. With this shared practice as our frame of reference, we are like anthropologists interpreting recorded observations, photographs, and collected artifacts. Then we become authors, found-object artists, editors, and producers as we assemble and compose our interpretations and data into accessible, irresistible forms that, as Amelia says, "make an impact."

We used to wonder what to document, what to follow, and how to do it. Somehow documenting was an extra, something that we did in addition to the rest of our work. Now, it is in the middle of everything, the centerpiece from which we move out, the hub of the wheel, the motor that drives the work. To say that it is in the middle of our work, however, is not to say that it has become easy to do.

In the midst of our complex lives, we share many practices, one of which is observation and documentation. In our commitment to this practice, we move along together. We travel, pushing each other, pulling each other, going somewhere, making meaning ourselves, discovering, looking deeply at children. We are amazed and excited every single day. This is what catches us and won't let us go.

GROWING AND CHANGING OVER TIME

I remember that when I was living in Reggio Emilia and spending my days at the Diana School, Loris Malaguzzi would sometimes just drop by. Although his title was "pedagogical director of the municipal preschools," his main job seemed to be philosopher/mentor/provocateur/political figure in residence.

He often came to the Diana School to see what was happening, to talk to Vea and the teachers, and to inject his ideas into the real-life laboratory of the school. He was a voracious reader. He read philosophy, psychology, biology, and the political theory of many different figures from different cultures. Then he picked out ideas that he related to the world of education, to research, to the child, to the school, to the place of the school in the world.

I have read some of the works that he and other Reggio educators read, like Bateson's *Mind and Nature: A Necessary Unity* (1979) and Maturana and Varela's *Tree of Knowledge* (1987). The ideas and theories of these authors are intriguing, dense, and, for me, sometimes difficult to follow. The ideas of all of them spiral around how we construct knowledge, how we are connected to one another and the universe, how we create our own realties, how there really is not an objective reality "out there" but rather a network of interconnecting patterns of which we are an integral part. The astounding thing is how Malaguzzi reinterpreted and reworked these authors' theories and ideas into a form that would enrich the real life and growth of the schools in Reggio Emilia.

Over the years a practice evolved, with Malaguzzi in the lead, of constantly stirring the pot inside the school by throwing in new ideas, fresh ways of thinking about the work or the significance of the work, innovative strategies to experiment with or new ways to interpret the children's thinking. The educational theories of Piaget, Dewey, Vygotsky, Montessori, Bruner, Hawkins, and Gardner were also read, analyzed, transformed, and used. One gets the feeling that these ideas were and continue to be almost chewed on, digested, and then put to use in the service of the continually evolving story of education in Reggio Emilia.

As a forward-looking, innovative, creative thinker, playing the role of agitator and partner, challenger and colleague, Malaguzzi set the stage and set the precedent for others to do the same. This all took place within a cultural context with a rich history of collaboration and political activism (Edwards, Gandini, & Forman, 1998).

Dialogue

Over the years the members of the educational community in Reggio Emilia have developed a practice that seems to lie at the heart of their work. This practice could be given many names—collaboration; thinking together; flow thinking; meaty, meaningful conversation; inquiry; inventing ideas together; or seeking and making meaning together. I am struck by how much the practice of dialogue that physicist David Bohm (1996) and William Isaacs (1999) describe resembles the way in which the educators in Reggio Emilia work together.

Isaacs describes dialogue as a conversation with a center, not sides. It lifts us out of polarization and into greater common sense and is a means for accessing the intelligence and the coordinated power of groups of people. In its most ancient usage, *logos* meant "to gather together." Dialogue is a conversation in which people think together in relationship. It requires that we relax our grip on certainty and listen to possibilities that grow out of being in relationship with others. We listen for an already-existing wholeness—a pool of common meaning that is capable of constant development and change.

Dialogue is different from *discussion,* whose root word is similar to that of *concussion* and *percussion. Discussion* literally means "to shake apart." Of course we know there is a place for skilled discussion and decision making. It is helpful to recognize the different types of conversation there are and the purposes they can serve.

Dialogue has a wholly different quality than discussion. Isaacs reminds us that this dialogic way of conversation is in our genes and as old as the human race, but in our modern-day life of fragmentation, busyness, and efficiency we have all but lost it and the richness of purpose and meaning it brings to our lives.

When I lived in Reggio Emilia, I was in the constant state of amazement that comes from living in such a generative atmosphere where ideas are flying and life is unfolding with words, in clay, with paint and gesture and voice. It was hard to hang on and know where I was sometimes—although, in spite of the excitement, it seemed exceedingly normal and sanely paced.

The idea of a container for dialogue is critical to Isaacs's (1999) work. He writes that a container is a vessel, "a setting in which the intensities of human activity can safely emerge" (p. 242). A container can be a physical space, but it also includes atmosphere. The environments and the way we are as teachers with children, with each other, and with parents create these containers. These spaces can be in our classrooms, in the natural world, out in our communities. It seems to me now that the whole way of living together in and among the schools in Reggio Emilia is based on this concept of dialogue that Issacs describes. The "container" that they have created is wide and expansive.

I have been feeling lately as if the context of our three schools in the St. Louis–Reggio Collaborative is one extended dialogue of rich possibility among the teachers, parents, and children. Now, through our years of working together as educators, we have grown into a similar state of being. It feels exhilarating to see seeds of ideas about materials, practices, parents, technology, subtle details about work with children and each other flying among the schools.

In the St. Louis–Reggio Collaborative we have slowly constructed a container in which we could grow as educators through actively coming to know one another and one anothers' schools, participating in large- and small-group meetings in both discussion and dialogue, hosting educators together, presenting together. This has all developed in dialogue with the Reggio educators and the Reggio Approach.

Groundwork

In our schools in St. Louis we feel as if we have been under construction for a long time and that we will continue to evolve for as long as we are together. This is the nature of the work. In some ways, however, we have emerged from the underground phase. We have done extensive groundwork together, not always understandable to us at the time, and not always pleasant. But now some things seem to make more sense in the light of day, and it is possible to reflect on some of our past work with a little perspective.

I like this word *groundwork* because the word itself is a metaphor. It means work that has to be done first, the foundation, the beginning, the solid base on which to construct further, a necessary clearing of the old and preparation for the new.

Part of the groundwork we have done is on ourselves, though we did not start to work on ourselves intentionally. We had no idea that becoming personally changed was part of this. We did know that we had been captured by the possible. We knew that we were in love with an ideal that we had seen, with an energy and truth and beauty that we recognized, and we wanted it for ourselves. With this shared longing, we formed a community of educators with a strong, shared intention. Carol Lee Flinders (1998) writes:

Life in an intentional community is like being inside one of those rotating cylinders full of water that the rock collectors use to polish their rough treasures. Little by little, over the years, a lot of the roughest edges get smoothed away. Maybe we even begin to shine a bit. (pp. 51–52)

Perhaps, because we wanted this kind of reality, we had to "rub up against each other's rough edges" enough and to the point that it hurt—sometimes a lot, and sometimes repeatedly—in order to begin to polish each other. There have been periods of personal suffering and tears and tension and unhappiness. Now, it is hard to remember all the scenarios that brought these emotions on. Slowly, it has dawned on us that if we wanted this truth, we would have to lose some of our personal righteousness and the need to be right. We would have to learn to listen and to adjust and to forgive and to know and accept each other as close colleagues.

By now, we have adopted codes of ethics that seem quite necessary if this is all going to fly. We deal with each other directly. We strive to handle little problems before they get big. We respect one anothers' rhythms. We recognize one anothers' strengths and help each other polish those as well. We balance our work. We pitch in and help. We accept and look for one anothers' constructive critiques. In fact, we ask for it. Over the years, we have come to realize that we must keep ourselves in check so that our work can grow deeper, so that the place we are building for children and parents can flourish.

I do not mean to imply that all this has become easy; it is still hard even on good days. We continue to face interpersonal and professional problems of all kinds. We always will. Yet we strive to listen, to respond to each other constructively, and to treat each other with great respect. To look back is to see that each one of us has been polished by the others, that we have changed one another, and that we have become much more humble in our work.

The Hindu god Shiva, Lord of the Universe, is most often depicted dancing with his four arms gracefully encircling his body. Balanced on one strong leg, he embodies strength and joy. Important to notice is the tiny human figure that his standing foot is crushing beneath him. This little human figure represents the ego, "the part of each of us that goes about stamping things mine and making interminable speeches about 'me' and 'what I need'" (Flinders, 1998, pp. 65–66). Shiva's dance represents the joy and ecstasy that we feel when we, even for a moment, are pulled out of this small, limited perspective on the world.

It is in dancing that we are able to become who we really are. We move, we float, we give and take, we become light on our feet, we are moved, and dancing with children is the highlight of our days. But dancing with each other, as teachers, makes this possible. And this takes grace. I guess you could say that it is a kind of grace that takes over when we let our little selves die and the dance begin.

CHAPTER 4

April

Living in a Place That Is Alive

Blooming
Masek
Crab
4/10/00

April 7, 2000. It is a shimmering spring morning. The white throat and the cardinal sing their morning harmonies. The green and gloriously fresh world outside pours inside through the east window of my study.

Before I begin to write today, I pick up my sketchbook and journal along with my coffee mug and wander outside to sit on a black iron bench on our front porch. Here, planted between the hedge and the house, a crab apple tree is coming to life. This same tree used to grow in my mother's yard a few blocks away. About 5 years ago, she asked John Masek, her longtime eccentric gardener friend, to plant it outside the windows of her bedroom so that she could see it through the seasons of bare winter, to blossoming spring, to fruit-bearing summer and red-leafed autumn. The tree is actually named Masek crab after her friend because he worked to create this particular hybrid. Once, after my mother had her stroke, John visited her in her reclining chair. He brought her a gift of crab apple jelly made from the tree. She could not speak; nevertheless, she understood, and she smiled.

Moving the Masek crab apple to our yard was a last-minute decision just before my parents' house officially went on the market. I was worried because we dug it out by hand and the root ball seemed small. The tree was not happy in the beginning. It dropped its leaves and stood uncharacteristically naked the whole first summer. John came by and volunteered to trim its spindly branches and told me he thought it would be fine. It was in shock. Not to worry.

Now, in early April of the second year after its move, the tree is fine. It is sending out buds, and the tiny leaves are opening. As I follow the contour lines of the emerging leaflets with my pen onto a page of my sketchbook, I smile at the tender babies so yellow-green and fresh and miniature. I remember the 5-year-old children of the Diana school in Reggio Emilia who said that to them, new leaves like these look as if they are still "lying in their cradles."

The flapping of large wings brings my attention up out of my sketchbook in time to see two geese fly low just above the barely budding branches of our front-yard oak, heading toward the southwest just across the axis of our house. They begin to call as they fly together. I often think of birds that fly nearby or call at moments like these as messengers from my parents, reminding me to be sure to stay awake and alive, to know that they are with me, that all is well, to realize that, as our Unitarian minister, Earl Holt, says, "Life goes on and love remains."

Slowly, I move inside and take my position in front of my new computer at my grandfather's old desk. The cherry drop-front desk includes multiple small cubbies, each housing a diminutive treasure that I have collected over the years—a soapstone Buddha, a glass elephant, a brass bell, a blue jay's feather. The iBook, from a different century, is sleek and snappy. It responds instantly to a light touch of the keys and the words appear. I appreciate the old and the new, the ancestral desk and the computer technology of these years that makes it possible for words to appear and disappear, shift and find better placement with the touch of a finger. No matter what the century, I imagine family members sitting at this desk thinking and wondering and composing their lives out of the pieces of their experience. Sitting at this desk supporting this word processor has become a ritual that has convinced me to listen. I am learning through writing to be a witness to the story that unfolds here and to the connections that reveal themselves that I did not anticipate.

ROOTS: DEVELOPING A SENSE OF PLACE

With Amelia's prompting and Jennifer's courage, we are off on a true adventure: a trip to the riverfront and the Gateway Arch. We will travel downtown by Metro Link. I am along as photographer. On our way there, we have a chance to walk through a little of the city. As we walk hand in hand, I feel Samantha's body twist and sway from side to side as she places her feet down in diagonal angles to match the pattern of the bricks in the old sidewalk. Then her hand wriggles free of mine, escaping. I recall other times like this one when a child has said everything with a gesture: "I need space. I have to see and feel this place in my own way. Let me go." The other children climb the steps and rails like jungle gyms, trail their hands along moldings of the facades of buildings as they walk along, stroke the head of a shiny brass statue of a woman reading a newspaper. They respond to the city viscerally. They mold themselves to it. They love it. I have never noticed this so clearly. The children are taking in the city with their bodies, with their whole being.

As we round the corner at the top of the street and enter the national park surrounding the Gateway Arch, we get our first glimpse of the towering steel structure. "There it is!" the children cry, jumping up and down, waving their arms, "There's the arch!"

They are voicing the same feeling I have when we first make out the distant form of this familiar landmark when we return home to St. Louis from Vermont every summer. The last stretch of our journey meanders through the low, rolling wheat fields of western Illinois. We can see the Gateway Arch, St. Louis's main tourist attraction and internationally known symbol of the city, from about 15 miles away. We leave Illinois as we cross the Mississippi River over the Poplar Street Bridge just south of the great stainless steel arch rising 632 feet above the river. As we drive by after our long day's journey, the arch welcomes us with a display of shooting flashes of silver as it reflects the setting sun in the western sky and the waters of the great river that flows at its feet.

On this trip today the children and adults approach the monument on foot. The ash trees planted in the park surrounding the arch reveal the tiny swellings of young spring buds. The arch gleams in the light of midday (see Figure 4.1). Jennifer stops the group of children and parents and asks them to gather around her.

"Louise just told me something last night that I think you ought to know. Louise, will you tell them your family story?"

I begin, "A long time ago, about 70 years ago, one day when my grandfather was coming home from Indiana, where he had been part of a ceremony to dedicate

FIGURE 4.1.   Children, Teachers, and Parents Approach the Gateway Arch

another monument, he was crossing the river looking out the train window. He saw that the riverfront was in terrible shape, with falling-down houses and a lot of mess and debris. He thought to himself that our city should have a wonderful riverfront and a welcoming monument to give significance to St. Louis and to commemorate the city as the place where famous explorers left for the West. After that he worked very hard for the rest of his life to help that dream come true. He never saw the arch before he died, but he knew that it would be built. His name was Luther Ely Smith, and he is sometimes called 'the father of the arch.' "

The parents look at me in surprise. This is not a story that I usually tell, though I feel deeply proud to be a part of this heritage and to be a descendant of this man who gave so much of himself to his city. From the horizontal slits of windows at the top of the arch, one can see a small park right in front of the old courthouse. There, a black marble marker dedicates the park to my grandfather. It reads, "This park commemorates Luther Ely Smith whose vision, dedication, energy, and love of his city and country brought into being the great Arch that symbolizes the nation's expansion west of the Mississippi River."

All of a sudden, Samantha is tugging at my elbow: "My great-grandfather built the arch, too!" she was saying. "He worked right on it."

Her mother nodded: "She's right. My grandfather was a steelworker. He was one of the men who worked to build the arch for 5 years."

My mind leaps to Charles Guggenheim's documentary film about the brave men who literally hung off this enormous structure as it grew, little by little, section by section. I think of grandfathers and dreams and hard work over lifetimes. And here we all are, almost 50 years later, approaching this graceful giant, a tribute to this city as the gateway to the West, the starting point of the adventures of Meriwether Lewis and William Clark, who set out from this very spot 200 years ago.

Jennifer adds to my reverie: "I didn't live in St. Louis when I was growing up. I lived in Indiana, but I remember this arch so well. Whenever we would come to visit St. Louis, this sight is the first that we would see."

Jennifer and I look at each other over the children, the wind in our faces, with the river rushing by like the flow of time and generations, with the arch rising in front of us. We understand our roots. We realize that this city belongs to us, and on pilgrimages like this one we are sowing seeds that will send down roots for the children who are here with us. We are part of something bigger, much bigger than a single field trip. Together, we are links in a long chain of events through time and space. We feel our common heritage and our shared responsibility to pass it on, right now, in these moments.

A place, the place where we find ourselves, the place where we live, nourishes us, if we let it. If we both value and contribute to the places in which we live together, they begin to reflect the best of who we are. In a way, we become what we surround ourselves with and what we pay attention to.

Antonella Spaggiari (2000), the mayor of the city of Reggio Emilia, introduces the new publication entitled *Reggio Tutta: A Guide to the City by the Children* in this way:

> All Reggio, then, where "all" is not the quantity but the quality of the city. A whole city to be seen, contemplated and lived in its wholeness. As a theme, the city is thus perceived and confronted as it develops, changes, and lives the selfsame life of its citizens: the women, the men, the children, and the elderly who inhabit the city, move through it, explore it, work in it, build it, love it. It is a wonderful message for all of us: to under-

stand and interpret the character and essence of a city like ours [for] these things are part of its history, inside its reality, and inside the people who have made the city and continue to make it what it is day after day. (p. 9)

When Amelia began to work with us, she was amazed that we did not have more in our schools that spoke of our particular identities in our unique schools in St. Louis, in the Midwest, living beside a great river, in the United States. She could not understand, at first, why our schools lacked what she called "identity." She explained that she felt this way in most of the schools that she visited in the United States. She discovered that because we all ordered from the same catalogs, the furniture in the schools all over the country looked the same. She could be in a school in Nebraska that felt the same as a school in New Jersey or New York. Where was our individuality? Where was our identity? Where were our roots?

These are big questions. At first, we were stunned by them, left wondering ourselves how this could be. Then, little by little, as we began to transform the way we worked together through questioning ourselves and searching for answers, we began to think of ourselves and our places and spaces differently. I think, as adults, we each wanted to reclaim our roots and to feel them more deeply as they support and nourish us and, at the same time, serve as companions to children as they find their own foundations in a strong sense of place.

In 1998 the educators in the three schools of the St. Louis–Reggio Collaborative made a conscious and collective choice to explore and discover our connections to our own city and our own context alongside the children. We began to rediscover our identities and our roots in our own community, our own parks, our own city. Somehow, alongside the children, these explorations have increased in significance. Now, we seem to take where we live and the part we play within the living system that supports us much less for granted.

At the Family Center, as a culmination to an investigation about where each family lived, after much joint research and planning by children and adults together, 3- to 5-year-old children and parents embarked on a day-long bus ride to visit one anothers' homes, following a map. They celebrated the end of the day on the roof of a newly constructed apartment building managed by one of the children's uncles to view "all of Clayton." As a part of this extended research, the children in Cheryl Breig-Allen's classroom each constructed a collage to represent their own house. These homes, hung together in a "classroom neighborhood," beckon us to look closely and admire the abundance of texture, shapes, and colors that each child chose to compose a whole.

At the St. Michael School, small groups of children, teachers, and parents went out to visit children's favorite places, like the local business, Fitz's Root Beer, and Turtle Park, a sculpture park near the neighborhood of the school. These experiences and these favorite places are now present in the school—in children's drawings and recorded memories, in clay sculptures of turtles inspired by the ones the children explored, in interviews with the employees at the root beer brewery and store, in the reflections of teachers and parents. These explorations of our locality are now a part of the history and identity of the whole community of the school.

After their trip to the city and the Gateway Arch, several children at the College School made a collage of the arch out of silvery transparent paper. It now shimmers on an entry wall of the classroom, surrounded by miniature copies of self-portraits in black pen drawn by all the children in the Newport Room earlier this year.

As we enter into our community and then return to our schools with these common experiences and memories, children, teachers, and parents begin to build a unique, layered, and shared sense of place. Our environments begin to reflect who we are and where we live. They begin to give us back our own unique identity. As children, teachers, and families, we begin to feel our common roots within our particular community.

TRANSFORMING OUR SPACES: TRANSFORMING OURSELVES

When I told Amelia that I wanted to write a chapter about the environment and that I planned to focus on the development of the *atelier* because it is the space that I know most intimately, she said right away, "Are you going to speak of the environment that is also outside the school? Are you going to address the larger meaning of environment?"

Until this year I had not put these two things together in such a direct way—sense of place and the environment in the school. Now, I see that the school is a microcosm of the larger world that we inhabit—a collection of bits and pieces of meaning fashioned together to create a layered, amiable, welcoming whole.

We build an environment based on who we are as individuals, and "who we are" is inseparably connected to where we find ourselves in space and time and what is important to us. Otherwise, we could live anywhere and we could be anybody. The school environments that we create are actually made up of parts of all of us and fragments of the world in which we live: children's words and ideas, teachers' and parents' words and ideas, fabric patches from 3-year-old Sam's baby blanket, my mother's button collection, papers of every imaginable kind from every family sorted and displayed for use on an accessible shelf, a miniature tea set from Jennifer's childhood, cups in a celadon glaze made by Sally on the *atelier* shelf holding tiny spools brought in by 5-year-old Erin, a piece of barn board from Jennifer's husband Mike's garage collection that frames the light table in the *atelier* where crystals from Missouri caves sparkle.

As I think about school environments, I recall the words of Carlina Rinaldi (1992): "The best environment for children is one in which you can find the highest possible quantity and quality of relationships." Our environment, the place that we have built over time, that is always changing and growing, is now made up of a high quantity and quality of relationships of all kinds among the materials, the space, and people of all ages. We have a better understanding of Carlina's words, which, for me, continue to be a little like a Zen Buddhist *koan*. A *koan*, as I understand it, is a mental puzzle expressed in a phrase or question that supposedly cannot be understood through logical thinking; its solution demands a higher level of insight, or, in Buddhist terms, enlightenment.

When I read *Children, Spaces and Relations: Metaproject for an Environment for Young Children* (Ceppi & Zini, 1998), a book that presents the collaborative research of Domus Academy Research Center in Milan and Reggio Children, I feel as if I am holding this idea—of a limitless quantity and quality of relationships—in my hands. In many ways, this publication stretches the notion of what most of us have ever conceived of as optimal learning environments. The complex network of ideas and possibilities represented in what the editors call "key words," along with the myriad images of children in space, of space itself, of current modes of thought in arts, science, and design, leave me at once terrifically stimulated and excited and mindboggled and overwhelmed.

Carlina suggests that we keep this book close by, read it, wonder about it, talk about it together, use it as a stimulus to our thinking about our space and our work here in St. Louis. She shared with us that for most people it is a work of enormous scope and challenge. In addition to this, like most of the work from Reggio Emilia, it is a gift to the rest of the world, a call to envision possible worlds of meaning and connection, value and depth, in our schools and also in our lives.

Development of the *Atelier* over Time

In *Bringing Reggio Emilia Home,* I told the first part of the story of how the *atelier* at the College School was created and, by 1995, transformed into a beautiful, functional space. In fact, the *atelier,* like all our spaces in the preschool, has been in continual evolution, and we have evolved along with it. The way the space functions and the way we act in it are somehow inextricably connected; it is a little hard to pull the two apart, but it is worth the exercise to try.

I love Malaguzzi's image of thinking with children as being a little like a game of tossing a ball back and forth. A child or a group of children have an idea or are drawn to something; and if we are listening, we notice. Then, perhaps, we want to play a game, so we "toss" them a twist, a provocation, a wide-open question about their idea. Then they respond with something marvelous that we did not anticipate, and the game continues. We don't know where the next ball will come from, but the game is fun and challenging for both child and adult, and we get better at playing it in many situations and scenarios.

I like to think that a space can be like this as well. It is actually alive (or dead, depending on what space we are talking about), and we can be in a living, nourishing relationship with it. If we live in a space and respond to it, little by little, fashioning each part of it into more of what we need and what is pleasing to us, then things continue to grow. We make a change; then the change alters the way we do things and new possibilities emerge. We are inspired to make another change, and so it goes. This is the way of an alive environment.

I am not referring to redecorating ad nauseam or change for change's sake or being obsessed with rearranging and redoing and cleaning. The idea is more about living in a space that you want to sustain and maintain in harmony with and in response to the changing, growing human beings who occupy it every day, month by month, year by year. As we all, children and adults, live and work in the *atelier,* we envision additions and/or transformations that will help us hold, organize, and continue to play and interact with collections of materials, children's work, our work, our history. The following are some examples.

Inspiration from the Diana School

At the Diana School, I have always admired the shelf in the *atelier* that runs along the vaulted window wall between the *atelier* and the piazza. It holds gorgeous assortments of seashells, stones, blocks of wood carved to make patterns on paper or cloth, even chunks of layered colors of dried paint from an easel that look like specimens of rainbow stone. It is an inspiring group of objects to look upon. I love this shelf of objects for many reasons: They are ordinary, but they are made extraordinary by their placement and diversity; through their primary presence in the entry to this intriguing room, they ask to be appreciated, examined, touched, discussed; they hold provocations for all who look into the room and enter; their presence here will evoke multiple responses from many different people of different ages and sensibilities, and, in this way, the collection gains significance over time; these objects become part of the place, part of the community, part of the scene—they are not extraneous. The collection changes over time—is added to, subtracted from, and rearranged. It evolves according to the influences of people and ideas. The collection is multisensory—spiky shells and smooth stones, myriad colors and textures offer us sounds, smells, and multiple sensations (see Figure 4.2).

Contemplating the identity of this shelf and the objects on it brings to life some of the "key words" that I referred to earlier, as defined and discussed Ceppi and Zini (1998). These words and their interrelationship, like the fundamental principals of the Reggio Approach, are, above all, a system of interconnecting values and ways of understanding and perceiving life that those of us who do not work in the schools of Reggio Emilia can use to ask ourselves: Are these values that we also hold? Are these ideas that make sense to us? Do these "key words" stand for aspects of life that we choose to support and sustain? Ceppi and Zini, after a "critical analysis of the cumulative experience of the municipal early childhood system of Reggio Emilia," identify the following "desirable characteristics of a space for young children":

> *Osmosis* . . . the characteristics of the space itself are hybrid, dense, "contaminated" by each other and the world outside . . . nothing is isolated.
>
> *Overall Softness* . . . means an ecosystem that is diversified, stimulating, and welcoming.
>
> *Multisensoriality* . . . the richness of sensory experience; investigation and discovery using your whole body. Sensory navigation that exalts the role of synesthesia in cogni-

FIGURE **4.2.**   Looking into the Diana School *Atelier*

tion and creation, fundamental to the knowledge building process and the formation of the personality.

Epigenesis . . . the school environment must be flexible over time and manipulatable . . . like a living organism must be able to change and evolve in line with the cultural project of those who inhabit it.

Community . . . is a form and quality of the space that fosters encounters, exchange, empathy, and reciprocity.

Constructivism . . . school as a place for research and experimentation, a laboratory . . . where the composition of knowledge does not take place in a linear way but as a developing network, based on dynamic interweaving of interconnected elements.

Narration . . . The environment generates a sort of psychic skin, and energy-giving second skin made up of the writings, images, materials, objects, and colors which reveals the presence of the children even in their absence. Self representation, the capacity of each space to narrate all the choices and references that generate the school environment, like in a hologram.

Rich Normality . . . A whole made up of different parts in harmony, balanced. Interaction of different elements (objects, situations, iconography, materials) that produces a tranquil result, a symphony of the individual parts. This effect of intense and interesting normality is not generated by a monologic environment, but the balanced combination of many different elements. (pp. 10–26)

Long before I had fully considered the complexity of the thinking behind these ideas, I dreamt of creating a shelf in our *atelier* at the College School that would echo some of the characteristics of the one in the *atelier* at the Diana School. Though it would be much smaller and lower, it could display changing collections on the top shelf and house papers and other materials on the lower shelves. My end-of-the-year request to Jan Phillips was granted, and Dan Masters, the carpenter/maintenance man, built this shelf in the summer of 1996. Like the one at the Diana School, it is flush with the glass windows that divide the *atelier* from the room on the other side. In the case of the Diana School, this room is the large piazza that connects all the classrooms, the outdoor courtyards, and the kitchen. In our case, the room outside the *atelier* entrance to the south is the entryway that we call the living room. In both cases, children and adults can peer into the *atelier* and see these inviting materials and examples of children's work.

Today, as my eyes meander around the objects from the natural world alongside children's work, I discover that it has become more than a delight to the eye; the objects encourage touch and play. Because the shelf is exactly at most children's eye level (the shelf at Diana is higher), and I noticed that children often wanted to handle the things on it, the shelf has evolved into a daily "invitation to interact."

In 1999, a group of children and I made up a matching game with some small clay shapes they had made out of coil, ball, cup, and other sculptural configurations. I shot a bird's-eye-view photograph of the shapes arranged in a grid pattern and then enlarged it. The actual three-dimensional clay "game pieces" placed beside the 8-by-10 photograph entice children and adults to handle the clay, to examine each individually sculpted shape, to find its match on the photograph, and then to place it on top of its twin. This seems fascinating to children of all ages. It could be a launching pad to invent new games out of different materials, games in boxes that could be transported anywhere in the preschool (see Figure 4.3).

FIGURE **4.3.**   Clay Game: The College School *Atelier*

Next to the clay game are two lines of stones that I have collected on trips—one a cascade of gradated sizes of gray, smooth stones from a pebbled beach on Lake Champlain in Vermont; the other, an angular puzzle of chunks of rust-colored granite from the rocky shore of the Maine coast. Both of these rock collections also invite handling, sorting, ordering, stacking, and reshaping into arrangements by children and their parents. One arrangement seems to call for a response from the next passerby, like an anonymous message left in stones.

Then, there stands the carved wooden puzzle of an iguana that a family brought back from Costa Rica. It is taken down by request, like a favorite treasure in a grandmother's sitting room, to disassemble and reform. Beside it, clay sculptures of lizards and frogs crawl on wide maple leaves brought in by children last fall. These creatures were born out of a desire on the part of a group of children to provide companions for the living creatures in the parent- and child-built terrarium in our living room.

Next in line, the paper sculpture of "Girl Land" made last January by Erin, Maggie, and Rachel curls and bends its way over the surface of the shelf (see Chapter 1; Plate 4). This, too, has movable parts and can be added to and played with. It also provides an inspiration for anyone who is looking to experiment and build with paper and other materials. These girls invented many ways to play with pearls and cardboard, wrapping paper and foil, that entice all of us.

This shelf is in evolution. It has a life. The way that the shelf functions takes its inspiration from the values that we recognize and aspire to within the Reggio Approach and, specifically, within the "key words" of the metaproject. This small piece of the environment reflects the whole of our particular ongoing experience, like a hologram.

The Archival Shelves

After several years of working on, recording, and composing both children's work and our reflections on cardboard display boards, the panels from past years were piling up in the back closet, and we were not sure what was where. How could we bring these panels back to life? How could they be made more immediately accessible? Again, Dan Masters helped solve the problem. We imagined what shape, size, and location a set of archival shelves might have. We studied solutions for this problem at the Family Center and the St. Michael School. In the end, we chose one of the only places that we thought would work to store our 28-by-44 display boards as well as panels of several other dimensions that we had cut to fit specific areas.

Dan Masters took the measurements in a space between the end of the sink counter and the wall in the northeast corner of the *atelier*. In the summer of 1997 he constructed floor-to-ceiling shelves, which now hold all of our archives organized by class, by subject, and by year. Now we are able to access our history, as well as specific examples of past work that we want to show children or parents, or study ourselves.

For example, in the fall, Sally, Christi, and I studied the identity panels from the past 5 years. We were able to look at the strengths of each year as well as the development of the ideas over all 5 years. We could use these panels to "teach" Christi what these were all about, but we could also use them to review our growth and the growth of the children who were now in the kindergarten through the fourth grade.

When Mark became interested in following the developments in the block area this year, Jennifer and I could find a series of examples of block panels from past years. We chose one that Joyce Devlin had worked on that emphasizes the connections between graphics and blocks; children had made block representations from drawings, and vice versa. Another panel told the story of a group of boys and girls who had built an "ice palace" out of big blocks one winter and had preserved it and inhabited it for several weeks. Reviewing these past episodes allowed us to revisit block history in the Newport Room and help Mark both support the children this year in this area, as well as prepare to organize, reflect on, and compose the block panels he was working on.

The Teachers' Work Area

The first computer and printer that appeared in the *atelier* came as a donation from another part of the school in the fall of 1998. Up until this point, we had either typed documents on our own word processors at home or been helped out by our kind faculty secretary. The documents I refer to are numerous, such as the declaration of intent; letters and fliers to families; some daily journal pages; conversations with children; reflections on all the ongoing projects; titles, introductions, and quotes of children and parents for panels or other communications.

The computer and printer arrived with a small, free-standing desk. The following year, we asked if we could update the whole system and have a long, built-in counter to hold both our new equipment and ongoing documentation that was in progress. Jan agreed to allocate funds to help us purchase a G3 Macintosh, an Epson printer, and our first digital camera. Mark, who knows quite a bit more than we did about computers, helped us to understand how we could use this new equipment to file and organize our work.

Our request for the built-in desk was also granted, and Dan worked again to build us a Formica countertop with turned wooden legs that is the right height for us to work at as a computer desk. We still use the vintage swivel desk chair that came with our first computer, but we have softened it with a red corduroy pillow.

The desk functions very well. Two or even three people, adults or an adult with children, can review digital photographs here, compose letters home to parents, transcribe conversations, or edit movies. We have various files for organizing and archiving written documents, still photographs, and video clips.

We store hard copies of written documents in several loose-leaf notebooks on a high shelf that is designated for these archives in the small alcove of the *atelier.* Sometimes, I forget what life was like before we had this equipment and this mutual work area. It has brought us up to speed with current technology and allowed us to communicate better with one another, with children, and with parents. It has also made the *atelier* more of a communal work hub that unites us as a team. Examples of the centrality of this aspect of our work can be found throughout the stories in this book.

Furniture to Support Painting

Replacing the rolling basket cart that held the paint jars was the first upgrade in the painting area of the room. In the fall of 1996, when we put out a request for help with carpentry, a father, Danny Harman, volunteered to build us two paint carts, one for the *atelier* and one for the Big Bend Room. A little later he also offered to construct a rolling wooden box to hold large portfolios, one for each child in the preschool. We had seen the paint carts in Reggio Emilia; the portfolio box was invented, as far as we know, by the St. Michael School team. We supplied Danny with the measurements and described what we hoped for.

The wooden boxes on casters moved both children and adults to another level of organization and possibility in painting. We can all count on flexible, movable, yet sturdy pieces of furniture to hold and organize paint colors and brushes by size in jars. The carts each have two shelves, so that we can store half-gallons and quarts of fresh paint on the lower shelves. They enable teachers and children to mix or uncap the paints in the cart next to the sink and then roll it over to the easels, which are located next to the glass west wall of the *atelier.*

The portfolio cart houses 24-by-36-inch gray cardboard folders marked with each child's name and photograph, alphabetized by first name. Now, each child can file his or her own finished pieces or work-in-progress as well as review past paintings, large drawings, or other work of this size with a parent or teacher. Some of the pieces that are stored in the portfolios cycle into visible documentation and displays. Some work serves as a launching pad for further work and development.

We were again inspired by the St. Michael School to replace our traditional early childhood easels with larger wooden framed easels, which we had all seen in Reggio Emilia. Chuck and a St. Michael School father, John Lesch, who is a furniture maker by trade, built two easels with leftover pieces of cherry wood over a weekend in 1997. In the summer of 1998, the same father agreed to help us with a similar project. Now two oak easels occupy the space next to the glass wall of the *atelier* that looks into the Newport Room. These spacious, well-crafted easels are taller than most of the children and give them a workspace that is equal to their size. A 28-by-44-inch piece of fresh paper seems big and wide, not limited in any way. They can choose to use some of it or all of it.

Children who are painting feel in touch with the rest of the children in the class who are busy with other things and other materials on the other side of the glass wall. At the same time, they are able to focus all their attention on the experience of choosing brushes and colors, and painting carefully and thoughtfully. The children in the Newport Room are also in touch with the painters through the gift of transparency. They can see paintings unfold, and they are often curious to come around to see them toward the end of the morning. Teachers, too, can catch each other's eyes and share moments of pleasure in what is unfolding on both sides of the glass.

Memories in Materials

Part of the feel of the *atelier* space, the irresistible quality that draws you into it, grows out of the pieces of the past made of many different materials, colors, shapes, and forms. Each piece was carefully constructed and lovingly made by one or several children. Gazing at these pieces today, I see their makers in my mind's eye—their freshness, their focus, their intent, their eyes, their hands. Along with the children come the parents and their appreciation, their amazement at their children's work, their growing partnership with us.

Our history and development as teachers sings through these works as well. For example, I can recall the year when we learned how to help children understand acrylic paints and use them for their own purposes. I remember our first attempts at gathering varieties of wire in different gauges—copper, steel, aluminum—along with metal washers and other bits and pieces from the hardware store so that children and teachers might discover an entirely new language with materials. I recall past projects through which our whole community learned how to follow children and how to lead in an open, fully focused way, not following one curriculum guide but rather our collective intelligence and our combined resources.

The Insect Mural

Yellow-green, apple, moss, lime, sunny yellow, golden, flaxen, straw, azure, robin's egg, sky blue, ruddy red, crimson, cherry, and scarlet: the colors of the field grasses and wildflowers, butterflies and bees, beetles and ladybugs that adorn a 5-by-6-foot hanging mural painted in acrylic on heavy clear plastic. These creatures of memory radiate down the hall from their central place in the *atelier* (see Plate 7).

The collaborative piece done with the class of 4- and 5-year-olds in the spring of 1997 still hangs from transparent fishing wire above the work area. Its size more or less matches that of the windows that now reveal the work and the daily life of the preschool community to the rest of the school, and vice versa. We can see out and they can see in. One thing that we all see immediately is a vibrant mural that tells the story of a year-long relationship among insects of all kinds and a group of 4- and 5-year-old children and their teachers: Jennifer Strange and Joyce Devlin; Mary Jo Wilmes, art teacher for older children at the College School; Louise Bradshaw, zoo educator/parent; and me.

The story of how the mural came to be is told in photographs and words in a 2-by-5-foot vertical panel located to the right of the mural. In this panel one can see that it all started with drawings of favorite insects that the children made throughout the year. Each child selected one drawing to enlarge, using an overhead projector. The collaboration with Mary Jo Wilmes is evident here in both the photographs and the words, as the painting project moved into her art studio so that we could have more space to consider each step of the process.

There, Mary Jo and I worked with groups of six or seven children at a time, first on enlarging their original drawings, then on composing the mural by moving the enlarged drawings around on top of the plastic "canvas" until a mutual decision was reached. We coached small groups of children first as we mixed a whole pallet of insect and field colors and then as they discovered how to use the acrylic paints, which were new to them. After each child painted his or her insect onto the plastic, a group of four girls who had fallen in love with this part of the project volunteered to finish the field of grasses and flowers and sky that made up the insects' habitat.

The last step was to unveil the finished piece for the community and the parents, who were astounded by the effect of the whole. In a short segment about a project about poppies with 5- and 6-year-old children in Reggio Emilia that was aired on PBS in 1991, Loris Malaguzzi is interviewed standing near a mural that the children had painted about their experiences in the nearby poppy fields. He says something like this: "Children need the opportunity to work alongside one another, supporting and weaving around one another, as in a symphony, creating a whole, harmonious, beautiful sound with their individual voices." This mural of insects tells the story of our strivings toward a full, vibrant sound in St. Louis.

The Children and the Garden

A composition of photographs—children watering new sprouts in a sunlit window, a boy and a girl pulling a cart down the hall laden with potting jars nurturing tender seedlings, collages of tissue papers in greens and yellows, delicate drawings of seeds and first shoots of bean plants emerging from the soil—this is a collection of memories for me and for all of us from the first year of the *atelier* alcove, pre-reconstruction, in 1992. It hangs inside one of the modules of windows near the easels. The pieces come from several of the first panels that we ever made at the College School, reconstructed now on a piece of clear acetate.

These memories are a reminder of our starting points, the best of our beginnings. I keep them here as chosen pieces of my particular experience, of our shared past, of the history of this place. The children in these photographs smile out at me, as do their drawings and collages, to remind me of where we are and whence we have come. These children—Milla, Dan, and David—will graduate as eighth-graders from the College School in 2002.

Small Remembrances

From the ceiling more remembrances hang in mobiles—a cylinder of chicken wire, woven with wooden beads, ribbons and bells, and colored wire from spools made 5 years ago. Hanging at an angle, it jingles and tinkles in the breeze of the overhead fan. Next to it, transparent plastic boxes filled with feathers, beads, and shapes of shiny papers twirl from a series of descending dowels in a hanging sculpture made by a group in 1998. Whatever can be strung or hung, woven or glued, can be made into a piece of sculpture for hanging. All these moving ceiling pieces that float and spin in the *atelier* alcove make us want to look up and help us to take ourselves lightly (see Figure 4.4).

To the right of the door hangs one of my favorite small pieces from the past, a birthday gift the Big Bend children made for me in 1996 with their teacher, Beth

FIGURE 4.4.   Mobiles at the Family Center

MacIntosh. Postage stamp black-and-white photographs taken by Joyce Devlin are each glued on the front of a mouse-sized window that opens to surprise the viewer. Inside each window there is a minicollage (see Figure 4.5). The one I am looking at now by Madison resembles a little bouquet—a sprig of diminutive pink wax flowers, shiny sequins, a ruffle of yellow daffodil petals, reflective silver patterned paper, a soft pink seed pearl. Each child is represented in six rows of three windows, all smiling at me from their diminutive collection of treasures. They are just above the light switch. Every time I touch it, I notice their collages and remember the children.

Mementos from Reggio Emilia are assembled on the 3-foot section of the east wall near the sink: a drawing of a cat with arched back and speckled coat and wide eyes drawn by children at La Villetta School; tigers in pen in all manner of positions and moods prancing across a 9-by-18-inch paper drawn by children from Neruda School; watercolors from my 1991 journal in Reggio Emilia of the lions in Piazza San Prospero and the view from the window of our apartment. All these were framed in glass with clips by Melanie Redler, a mother who volunteered her time and the materials. These are selections of favorite pieces that take me back to Reggio Emilia. They also take us all forward. They support us and give us confidence, hope, and inspiration. They encircle us; they are a part of us.

Like a patchwork quilt, all these pieces are in some way held together in space. They wrap themselves around us and sustain us in memory and in joy. They saturate the room with meaning and significance, creating an irresistible desire to follow suit, to

FIGURE **4.5.**   Window Collage at the College School

play, to connect, to reach, to search, and to invent. The place is alive with possibility and potential. The children and the teachers who have lived their lives here have created this living quilt.

Clearing Clutter

When we were in California in early March, I visited my niece and noticed a book on her kitchen table entitled *Clear Your Clutter with Feng Shui* (Kingston, 1999). I bought it as soon as I got home and read the small, neatly organized volume the same afternoon. Kingston has created her definition of clutter in the form of a list. It is as follows:

- Things you do not use or love
- Things that are untidy or disorganized
- Too many things in too small a space
- Anything unfinished (p. 17)

She also describes in brief detail some of the major reasons most of us hang onto clutter. The list is so apt for teachers that I want to include part of it here:

- Keeping many things just in case they might be useful "someday"
- Holding onto things because somehow our identity is tied to them

Plate 1 The Corridor Leading to the Preschool at the College School

Plate 2 Looking into the College School Atelier from the Living Room

Plate 3
A Palette of
Materials

Plate 4
Making
"Girl Land"

Plate 5
Materials at
Clayton School's
Family Center

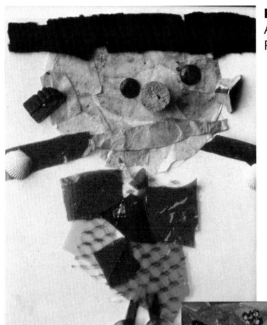

Plate 6
Allie's Self
Portrait

Plate 7
The Insect Mural

Plate 8
The Light
Table in the
College
School Atelier

Plate 9 "The Smells are Dancing," the St. Michael school

Plate 10 The Ring of Energy, from The Curtain, Reggio Emilia, Italy

- Territorialism, the feeling that someone else might get it if we don't
- A belief that more is better
- "Scroogeness" (pp. 18–21)

She explains that the word *clutter* derives from the Middle English word *clotter,* meaning "to coagulate." She equates clutter with stuck energy. Kingston has seen over and over again that "sorting out your life by sorting your junk results in a tremendous renewal in your life force energy" (p. 11).

If we take this to the level of the classroom, we can get "down and dirty" quickly. When we started our work at the College School in 1992, years' worth of accumulated clutter and stuff surrounded us everywhere we looked. Spring brings with it the strong urge to open up the doors, let in the light, let in the fresh air, and clean and sort. Maybe the first spring of the new millennium has a thousand years of accumulated spring-cleaning energy behind it. This is the kind of energy that we need to capture as teachers to begin to see our classroom environments and our school spaces with new eyes.

A basic, underlying principle that the educators in Reggio Emilia have incorporated into their classrooms and piazzas and dining rooms is school needs to be comfortable, pleasant, orderly, inviting, and homelike. Children have a right to a place like this, as do teachers and parents. All of us have the right to spend our days in school surrounded by places and spaces that will enhance our lives, support our growth, and hold us in respectful ways.

We, as teachers, administrators, and parents, have to create these places. Little by little, we can examine the spaces that we have and shape them into more livable and amiable rooms. I like to think of the whole space in terms of Kingston's first point about clutter: "Anything that you don't love or use." We deserve to love our classrooms, every corner of them. For us to love them, they need to breathe the life of everyone who inhabits them and not be containers of stuck energy.

As teachers in the St. Louis–Reggio Collaborative, we strive to look at our classrooms with critical and observant eyes as often as we can. We ask ourselves

What is tattered, broken, unloved?
What needs care, repair, a new coat of paint, a sparkle of light, a splash of
    color?
What needs to be passed on in order to make room for new life energy and
    new ideas?
What aspects of ongoing experiences are unclear or left unexplained or
    empty of meaning?

At the three schools of the St. Louis–Reggio Collaborative, one rule of thumb is that everything be out in the open so that we can see it and use it. On the high shelves in the College School *atelier,* there are Lucite boxes of fabric and ribbons and twines and raffias of all colors. On nearby selves are collections of clear folders of sparkly paper, patterned papers, handmade papers, white and cream-colored paper curls. On the low shelves transparent jars of shells, buttons, beads, wires, tiny pine cones, dried rose petals, sequins in the shape of flowers, and spiral shavings from colored pencils reflect the light and reveal their enticing contents to both children and adults.

Children know where things are and can find them. So do the teachers and so do the parents. The environment is useful and plentiful and organized. What is here is being used and loved. This atmosphere seems to attract more energy, ideas, connection, and possibility that propel us all in a positive direction.

Things are recycled, have an order to them, have surprises inside them, are reconsidered always, are alive. There are so many eyes now working on this, so many hands, and they are in concert. This is what is meant by developing a culture. It is a culture of people age 3 through 73 who are living the same values.

The children here used to dump blocks in piles. They used to empty little Lucite boxes of sequins on the light table or mix things up to be a bit mischievous or to see what would happen. Some even used to draw on the walls or color on the tables on purpose. Now, this rarely happens. Why? The children are part of this culture, and they know that the order, beauty, and abundance of materials exist for them and for all of us. The materials wait like treasures to be touched, explored, transformed, composed; to hold stories, inventions, and layered ideas. Now, the children actually teach each other to care and respect the many aspects of our complex environment. Now, these values, these living, growing guides to life, keep taking us farther and deeper toward richer possibilities. Gradually our eyes have been completely reeducated, and our hands as well. Our standards and expectations have been significantly raised. We have established, slowly but surely, with children and parents, a culture of respect, appreciation, interaction, care, and love of the space in which we live. It is astonishingly beautiful and comfortable to live in. The way in which the materials are displayed and used parallels the way in which ideas flow and circulate, gathering energy, excitement, form, and shape whether among children or adults. This phenomenon generates an atmosphere that feels electric and alive.

There is something to this idea of *feng shui,* the awareness of energy in things and in inhabited places. If we pay attention to it, the energy becomes another force behind our ability to dance in our work and in our lives—who knows, maybe even fly.

ATELIER ROOM PARENTS

As do many schools, we ask for two parents per classroom to serve as "room parents" for the year in all the grades at the College School. As mentioned in Chapter 2, these parent volunteers help teachers to organize sign-up sheets for various events, coordinate field trips and class parties, and reach out to the other parents to help with needs that may arise during the school year. The drama, music, physical education, and art teachers also have room parents to help them with a variety of things. Each specialist works with the volunteer parent to create an appropriate role. In the first years after the construction of the *atelier,* it did not occur to me to ask for an *atelier* room parent. In retrospect, I think this is because, as a team of teachers, we were working hard to build my role as an integral part of the preschool team rather than as a specialist. In many ways, I was and still am "attached" to the classrooms.

A Fresh Eye to Organization

One day in the fall of 1997, Joni Ridgway, a mother in retail who had an abundance of talent for organizing and displaying materials, asked me if I would like her to tackle and reorganize the two sets of shelves that housed most of the collage materials in the *atelier.* I accepted with pleasure. In my opinion, the shelves were not in such bad order, but they needed sorting and cleaning. Usually, as I clean, my tendency is to put things back where they were rather than to envision a new system. I was eager to see what a fresh eye and hand would do with the materials and the shelves.

Together, we chose an afternoon when Joni was free and I could be in the *atelier* with just two Newport children, including Ashley, Joni's daughter. We arranged this with Joyce and Jennifer, the Newport teachers. We wanted to include the children as assistants in this process but chose not to ask a big group. I wanted to ensure that we had the time and space to fully benefit from the gifts Joni had to offer. We talked about this with all the children. This inclusiveness engaged both the children's and teachers' anticipation and excitement.

That afternoon, the children and I watched Joni as she studied the jars, investigating what was in each one, then standing back and considering the shelves as a whole. She then took every jar and basket off the shelves, placed them on the octagonal table, and began to sort them by color and sometimes by texture and type: white tissue paper balls, next to snow-white feathers, nesting near cream-colored curls of paper and a petite jar of pearly angel-wing shells. She talked to us as she worked, now asking if the girls would sort out the buttons by color. We could see from what she was doing that the white buttons belonged here.

Two-inch sticks from the oak tree on the playground upright in a basket slid over to seedcases in a tiny wooden dish and dried yarrow and straw flowers in a 2-inch-diameter, low, gray card octagonal box. The natural materials seemed to attract one another, and the containers were changing, too, as Joni worked, putting natural materials in baskets and wooden receptacles, white things in transparent Lucite and glass.

The colored beads and buttons, bright feathers, glistening sequins, and tufts of multicolored embroidery floss joined together in complementary containers and jars. The girls, still enjoying sorting buttons into baby food jars—blues, greens, yellows, metallic, bone, corals, and reds—looked up to see the shelves wiped down and the jars and baskets ready to find a new home.

"Can we help?" the girls chirped hopefully.

"Of course you can. Where do you think the whites should live?" asked Joni.

At morning meeting the next day, the two girls shared their experience with the class, showing off the newly sorted buttons with pride. All the children were anxious to see the new shelves and to get their hands on the materials. They would need encouragement and support in maintaining the new system, as all of us would. Yet they had all taken part in the new organization in some way and were proud of it. They could see that this new organization would help them; it was for them. A parent had contributed her way of seeing and her abilities to enhance their space and their lives. This meant a great deal to all involved. Other parents noticed what had transpired. News went out both in the daily journal and in the weekly newsletter.

Even a very small event, as small as sorting buttons, became like a stone thrown in a pond. Many ripples grew out from this one afternoon: I asked Joni if she would continue to help me that year as my first *atelier* room parent; new ideas for organizing materials emerged; the quality, variety, and organization of classroom mini-*ateliers* and message center materials increased; children's respect and care of materials was strengthened; all of our imaginations were sparked and teased just in viewing and handling the materials; ideas about what to make with these treasures and how to proceed seemed to flourish; other parents began to think more about how they might contribute to the life of the school and the life of the community; the tapestry of our community was enriched in myriad ways.

New Spaces: New Possiblities

In the spring of 1999, Kathleen Sprong, whom I introduced in Chapter 1, asked me if she could be the *atelier* room parent. I could not believe my good fortune. Kathleen, like Joni, lives and breathes both an understanding and a pure enjoyment of "beautiful stuff" (Topal & Gandini, 1999) and how it might be organized and used. She has a well-developed aesthetic sensibility about everything: choosing fabrics for her house, determining paint colors for ceilings and walls, designing gardens, selecting and preparing food.

One of the first things that Kathleen did last fall was reorganize and renew the shelves over the sink—the ones that have been rearranged and sorted and renamed and redefined so many times. One day I found Kathleen standing in front of them with her chin in her hand, her hip to one side, gazing at them with a pensive look. "I think these could be better; I think they could be more functional," she mused.

"Go for it," I encouraged her, "whatever you want to try."

It happened one morning when no children were working there. She took everything down. Everything. She emptied the shelves onto the tables and looked at all the contents. She reconsidered each thing and its purpose and function. Section by section, some of it went back. Now, a clay section takes shape with slip (a mixture of clay and water) in small glass jars and wooden clay tools in a gray mustard crock near collections of stones of different colors and sizes and shapes. Now, a collection of polished gray and ochre marbled stones fills a goldfish bowl. A spiral bisque-fired snail made by a child several years ago creeps along the second shelf in front of the stones. A painting section follows with brushes in a low, wide-mouthed, yellow ceramic vase. The vessel leaks but is perfect to hold a variety of fat-handled brushes.

After Kathleen and I had worked together for 6 months, over our spring break in March of this year, I started to dream about making the *atelier* even more available to children, more "user-friendly" than it ever has been. I thought about arranging separate trays of collage materials, drawing materials, and wire, respectively, so that both adults and children could access and move these things easily to whatever place they wanted to work. I also envisioned mini-areas in the room—a construction area; a small shadow screen; a smaller, lower light table than the one we now used; a drawing area; even a reading area. How we would manage all this and where we would locate the areas I did not know yet. In fact, I didn't know if it would be possible.

When we returned to school after break, I explained my ideas to Kathleen and we began to think and imagine together. We also began to experiment right away and to try out ways to make these dreams come true. The following is a late-year declaration of intent that I composed as a way of organizing my thoughts and of communicating them to my team and the Parent–Teacher Committee.

> The *atelier* is taking on a new look and a fresh way of offering itself to children. Over the break I dreamed of making materials of various types more accessible and "user-friendly" to children. I want them to envision the *atelier* as a place to play with and explore many media, as a kind of playground for materials, yet also a place in which serious and imaginative dreams can take shape. To this end, Kathleen and I have started working to transform various parts of the room.
>
> 1. There is now a *drawing tray* equipped with several types of soft- to hard-lead pencils; several types of black drawing pens; colored pencils

arranged in cool, warm, and neutral colors; thin and thick water-based markers. There are also many different types, sizes, and shapes of paper on which to draw that are accessible to children in drawing baskets.

2. There will be a *collage tray* as well. This is in development. Both Kathleen and Elise McBride will help to keep these trays supplied with materials, exciting and provocative, changing, evolving, and ready to use.

3. The four shelves under the windows facing south toward the living room are going to be equipped with different media. There is now a *paper sculpture shelf* and a *weaving shelf.* We plan to have a *wire sculpture shelf* as well. These shelves will also grow and change and evolve during the course of the year. I envision them growing out into the classrooms as well if the interest in independent work grows and space allows.

4. We are planning a *small construction area* big enough for three children at the most. There will also be a small overhead projector, which I am purchasing out of the *atelier* budget, for projecting light images onto the wall to create a *mini-area for projection and play with transparent media and objects.* We will hang some kind of curtain/screen that can be opened and shut to change the quality of the images. We are planning a reading shelf with art and photography books for children to look at. There will be a *tube to whisper through running from one side of the alcove to the other.*

5. Mike Strange has constructed a *light table* that is now in the corner immediately to the left as one enters the *atelier.* This is big enough for two or three children to work at. Shelves nearby and above the light table will house both transparent construction and drawing and wet media for the light table.

6. The papers for *painting* are either on one of the shelves under the sink (half-easel size) or in the first shelf to the left of the sink (large easel size).

7. *Clay media* and boards are on the shelf under the sink to the left. Tools and slip for now are on the shelf above the sink.

I teach three full days a week at the College School, Monday through Wednesday, so Kathleen and I agreed to schedule two workdays together on Thursday or Friday to create the new mini-areas.

Workday 1

Kathleen and I meet early, at 8:15, with coffee in hand. We begin sitting close together on child-sized chairs, surveying the room and thinking out loud.

"What about under the shelves?" Kathleen is saying, "what if we just take out all the lower shelves, which are pretty low anyway, and make the areas in there?" I nod, thinking while Kathleen gets up and begins taking things off the shelves so that she can remove several of them. "Let's just see if this would work."

She starts in the southeast corner of the *atelier* alcove on the shelf next to the glass wall that looks into the Big Bend Room. She places the baskets of yarn and ribbons, twine and string that are currently there out on the table.

"Where is that Plexiglas shelving you ordered last year? If you can find it, we could use it here. I have an idea about what we could use to support it," Kathleen says, disappearing from the *atelier* and heading toward the back closet that all of us share.

I look on our archival shelves, where I had stored the piece of Plexiglas that was slightly too small for our needs last year.

"Here they are," she says, returning with two 8-inch-square, gray metal boxes. "I picked these up because I thought they would be good storage for message center materials, but no one wanted them." Kathleen kneels down and assembles her idea on the floor in the alcove. She balances the Plexiglas on top of the metal boxes and rattles it to see if it is sturdy. She has created a low, transparent surface on which to build. It looks as if it had been planned. It looks built-in. It fits perfectly (see Figure 4.6).

"Will you hand me some blocks," Kathleen asks, "and some shells?"

She sits cross-legged on the floor facing the newly installed, mini–construction area, building a playful sculpture with small blocks and balancing shells. I scoop up two clay lizards from the shelf nearby and hand them to her. She slides one under the opening of a small conch shell.

"What do you think?" she asks.

"How could we go wrong?" I answer.

We are tempted to go get children to show them the brilliant new setup and see what they do, but we don't. We move on.

"OK, let's keep going with this idea of under the shelving, don't you think?" Kathleen queries.

"Definitely," I nod. We have made a great discovery about the space in this room.

"What about this one?" Kathleen asks, pointing to the adjoining built-in shelves on the same side of the room. There is a big, boxy 3-by-4-foot-square free-standing shelf

FIGURE 4.6.   Mini-Construction Area in the *Atelier* of the College School

on casters pushed into the wall under the shelves in this area. We use this deep shelf, inherited from the art room, to store colored drawing paper and tissue papers.

"What about this for the little shadow screen? We'll have to relocate this paper shelf or get rid of it."

"I don't see why it wouldn't work," I say, getting excited at the thought of a shadow screen all set up and ready to go within the *atelier.* I used an overhead quite a bit last fall and had noticed that children loved to play with transparent and semi-transparent materials on what, to them, seems like a miniature light table. The only available place for this arrangement last year was in an area of the room, between the archival shelves and the teachers' work area, that was crowded already.

We pull the box shelf out into the room, freeing up the area for the coming shadow screen. "You know," Kathleen says, "I have a white tea curtain at home. It has a little embroidery on it, but I think it would be perfect for this space. I also have an expanding rod that I'm sure will fit. I'll bring it tomorrow and we can try it."

"Great! That sounds perfect," I confirm. "I've researched and found the overhead that I want. It's small and compact. We can store it behind the curtain/shadow screen."

"Now, shall we move over to the other side? What do you envision over here?" asks Kathleen. We are flowing with the energy that we are discovering today. It is as if the two of us are entering into dialogue with the space; we become like an experienced trio improvising and experimenting as we invent new songs.

Kathleen begins to empty and pull out shelves, leaving the lowest one nearest the floor in place. I get a clean sponge and wipe it down. Kathleen finds a gray cardboard rectangle and puts it down as a blotter, then adds a small jar of drawing pens and one of colored pencils.

"What about this?" I wonder, reaching back onto a teacher equipment shelf on the opposite side for a Lucite brochure holder that can hang on the inside of this mini–drawing area.

"That's just right," Kathleen says as she pulls cut paper scraps from a basket on the top of the paper shelf. She knows what I am thinking before I explain. I hammer the little holder in place, and she adds the paper. Lastly, Kathleen reaches for a standing clock in a red-painted birdhouse frame. Under a feathery bird on the bottom is written, "Tiffany, December, 1999."

"Tiffany and her mom, Terri, made them for each of the teachers as a gift," I tell her.

Kathleen positions the clock in the back of the new desk.

"The red clock reminds me of my mom's red gardening chair that I loaned to the Big Bend Room children," I say. "I'll get it."

The 2-foot-high, slat-back red chair that my mother used to sit in while she weeded the front brick walk fits perfectly under the newly created shelf/desk. The whole setup looks as if it has always been there (see Figure 4.7).

"What next?" Kathleen looks at me.

"Where will we put this paper shelf?" I ask.

"Let's try it over here by the new light table." Together we slide the shelf over to a potential new location next to the 3-foot-square light table box that Jennifer's husband, Mike, built out of weathered gray wood. The old paper shelf fits perfectly in its new spot, liberated from the crowded shelf complex where it had been stuffed for 4 years. Now, the top is clear and available for paper trays of different sizes and shapes.

FIGURE **4.7.**   Drawing-Area Desk in the *Atelier* of the College School

Both the children and I have been enjoying this small light table. Jennifer and I traded light tables this year. She wanted a bigger one and I wanted a smaller one. The smaller one that Mike built just happens to fit perfectly in the niche between two of the glass modules on the north window wall of the *atelier.* The sill, which falls right above the top of the light table, makes an ideal shelf to store things to play with here: colored Plexiglas squares, rounds of smooth blue malachite from the West, bubbly blue Lucite cups and bowls, feathers, red and yellow theater gels.

Kathleen continues, "I know the perfect stool for that little light table. And I have a mirror at home we could hang above it that I think would be great. We can try it. And I have an idea for a big tray for some of these jars of collage materials that we've just removed from the shelves that we took down. I have to go to Target to get it, though. Will you go to the hardware store to find the tubing and funnels for the whispering tube telephone? How about we call it a day and meet same time tomorrow?"

Workday 2

On Friday morning Kathleen arrives with bundles from home and from Target. First out of the bag: a white, fake-fur, round stool, about a foot high.

"Do you think it's too much?" she asks, laughing. "I just thought it was perfect for the light table. And look at this."

Out of a canvas bag, wrapped in a towel, emerges a gold-framed mirror with a swooping top that reminds me of a small version of the magic mirror of the wicked witch in Snow White.

"Mirror, mirror on the wall," I chant.

In truth, both of these additions to the light table area and the room are wonderful surprises. Who would ever expect a white fur stool with a barn board–framed light table under a gold gilt mirror? But somehow it all works, and the combination brings so much fun to the already enticing corner (see Plate 8).

"I'm so thrilled that you're able to come to Reggio Emilia with me this spring! We'll have such a wonderful adventure!" I can't help thinking of how much Kathleen will see and learn from this upcoming trip. I feel like pinching myself because we will be able to travel there and learn together.

"I know; I just can't wait," she answers, looking at me with excitement in her eyes.

"What else do you have in that bag?" I ask expectantly.

"Well, here's the curtain I was telling you about." Kathleen holds up a gauzy, white, scalloped curtain and the spring rod to hang our first *atelier* shadow screen.

"Let's try it," I say, heading out the door to borrow the overhead from the kindergarten.

When I return we sit on the floor together and play with a box filled with light table toys: pink Plexiglas; plastic hair combs; a pale-blue, transparent, fish-shaped soap dish. The colors and shapes flash onto the curtain and curve as it curves. A troupe of Big Bend children are peering in through the window wall amazed, faces to the glass. One of them is John, Kathleen's son.

"Can we try?" John appears at the *atelier* door with Ryan.

"Sure. Doesn't this look like fun?" Kathleen says as she gets up.

The boys begin to play and talk excitedly as they experiment with the brand new setup (see Figure 4.8).

FIGURE **4.8.**   Mini-Shadow Screen in the *Atelier* of the College School

"Now, for the last thing," says Kathleen, pulling a huge, flat, oval basket with loop handles at each end out of an oversized bag. "This was a little bit of an investment, but I think it might be worth it. It'll be my donation, if you like it. I think that it will fit on this shelf and that it will hold a lot of these jars of all the collage materials." Kathleen slipped the basket into the shelf. "It hangs over a little but I don't think that matters too much." Kathleen is thinking out loud.

Together we begin to arrange the jars on the handsome tray-like basket. She is right. It holds a lot, and it shows all the materials beautifully together, like a carefully composed hors d'oeuvre tray. Joni would approve, I mused, as I recalled her day here and her thoughtful contribution.

Layers, I think to myself—layers of ideas, daydreams, visions and viewpoints, personalities and talents, time and care, respect and knowledge. All this beauty and energy, potential and possibility growing over the years in this one central room surrounded by glass and infused with love.

ATELIER METAPHORS

Lately, I have been daydreaming about what the *atelier* has become for all of us—for the children, for the teachers, for the school, for the parents, for the visitors, for the community. It seems impossible these days to fully describe it literally. That is why I often fall into metaphors. The *atelier* becomes a metaphor for the whole school, the whole school as laboratory, as workshop, as studio in which to marvel at all of life, to make sense of things over and over, always new, in a community of friends, in a community of practice, in a place that supports us as we support it.

I chose to focus on our *atelier* here because it is in this place that I personally have been transformed along with the space. But the processes that I have described have taken place in all of our spaces in one form or another in each of the three schools in the St. Louis–Reggio Collaborative. In fact, similar stories are unfolding all over North America and throughout the world.

Here I have followed the process of growth and change of one space and one group of people over time. But this particular story becomes an example of transformation that takes place anywhere that vision and dogged commitment take hold.

In myths and legends, the phoenix is a great magical bird with feathers like a rainbow that rises out of the flames of its own destruction. This is our *atelier* at the College School. It is a phoenix rising and taking all of us with it as it soars. In flight, the phoenix transforms itself into another metaphor: a beacon of light, hope, possibility. I heard my friend and colleague, Sonya Shoptaugh, speak of this idea, and I love it because it is true. In this work, as we work everywhere in the world, we become sources of light and inspiration for one another.

While riding in a friend's car I once heard a taped interview Bill Moyers conducted at the Geraldine E. Dodge Poetry Festival in 1995 with poet Gary Snyder, who said something like, "You go to poetry when you want to say what really happened and how you really feel. You start with the imagination; that is what takes you. You start with images. It takes work to write poetry but also a lot of play. You have to be loose as a goose with language and then throw away the excess." With his words in mind, and with the idea that, metaphorically speaking, the *atelier* is like a seed from which to grow a school and a vision, I let myself go and follow my imagination. The *atelier* is like:

The hub of a wheel. A center from which other parts radiate out to other spaces, other places, other connections, other ideas. It is like a wheel hub that supports movement, traveling, and discovery.

A meeting place. A welcoming space, a generous space, an evolving space, a place in which to fall in love with materials, to fall in love with human intelligence and creativity.

The treasure cave of Aladdin. A place to become rich with ideas, colors in your hand, light in your mind. For both children and adults, the *atelier* is a place potent with possibility, openness, limitlessness, expectation, excitement, focus, engagement, dialogue.

A microcosm of the world. A container of small pieces of everything—metal and wood, earth and fiber, pigment and ink, shadow and reflection. It keeps things both translucent and opaque, opalescent and matte. It holds feathers of gossamer lightness; stones, heavy and cool. All together, it becomes a puzzle of pieces to fit together.

Layers. Layers of experience, of respect, of atmosphere, of a way of being in this place. The space relaxes the people who enter, puts them in a mode to be open, to play, to wonder, to breathe.

Freedom. A place that inspires flying, soaring, turning inside out with ideas, entering the domain of invention.

A place of dreams. The *atelier* beckons us all to play with the stuff of the world and to imagine and reimagine ourselves and what we might become together.

CHAPTER 5

May

What Are the Children Learning?

This morning flickering light falls through the high southern window at my back and onto the worn walnut hutch table in the alcove of our kitchen. My simple breakfast waits before me.

I love the rhythm of preparing this solitary meal. The ritual of grinding the coffee beans, so earth brown, shiny and pungent, packing the small metal receptacle with the finely ground, powdery coffee, and securing the handled cup under the steamer requires complete attention. I turn the knob to the right and the machine begins to hum loudly enough to be heard on the second floor as the coffee flows out in two thin streams into a small espresso cup. Next, I turn the knob to the left, holding the shiny steel pitcher of cold milk, and listen to the hiss of compressed hot water shoot out of the metal tube. Slowly, I pour the frothy white liquid into the rich dark coffee and notice a lighter, gentle color emerge; I witness the blending of deep brown and pure white.

I toast a wheat bagel in mom's old toaster oven, the one whose door is missing a spring, which causes the glass front piece to bang onto the counter when opened. We keep this old (I calculate about 30 years) appliance because it still makes good toast and the bell sounds a terrific, authoritative ring when its work is done.

The last detail—I butter the crispy bagel, watching the pale yellow disappear into the rough brown surface, anticipating the flavors and textures of both.

With bagel and coffee in front of me now, I remember the blessing of Vietnamese Buddhist monk Thich Nhat Hanh (2000):

> This food is the gift of the whole universe, the earth, the sky, and much hard work.
> May we eat in such a way as to be worthy to receive it.
> May we transform unskillful states of mind and learn to eat in moderation.
> May we take only food that nourishes us and prevents illness.
> We accept this food in order to realize the path of understanding and love.*

Buddhist monks and nuns don't drink coffee. Strictly speaking, it is not the healthiest beverage. But, so far, I still savor and appreciate its taste, texture, and aroma. I have given up attending to any other activity while eating alone in order to practice being present with the whole universe that has come together in this meal—the sun, clouds, rain, seasons, fields, heat, cold, people, and animals that have worked to produce this milk, coffee, and crisp, round bagel. This solitary time is a gift—a small morning pleasure that I enjoy on this bare table with the sun, the sounds of morning, the spring air, and my full, undivided attention.

"THE PATTERN THAT CONNECTS"

On my first day as an intern at La Villetta School on February 5, 1992, I climbed the three flights of stairs to the top floor of the school to see Giovanni Piazza in the *atelier.* His is a marvelous space: a garret-like, real studio under eves and supporting beams, with square windows near the floor looking over the meadows behind the school.

There, on Giovanni's door, I found the first stanza of a poem in Italian. I recognized these lines from Walt Whitman's "There Was a Child Went Forth":

> There was a child went forth every day,
> And the first object he looked upon, that object he became,
> And that object became part of him for the day, or a certain part of the day,
> Or for many years or stretching cycles of years.
>
> The early lilacs became part of this child,
> And the grass and the white and red morning glories, and white and red clover, and
>   the song of the phoebe bird,
> And the Third-month lambs and the sow's pink faint litter, and the mare's foal and
>   the cow's calf,
> And the noisy brood in the barnyard or by the mire of the pond-side,
> And the fish suspending themselves so curiously below there, and the beautiful
>   curious liquid,
> And the water-plants with their graceful flat heads, all became part of him.

I stopped and thought a moment. How wonderful to find this poem in this place on the door, an important message at the threshold of a room. This, in part, is what it said to me: Remember childhood, all who enter here, our childhood, the once-upon-

---

*Reprinted from *The Path of Emancipation: Talks from a 21-Day Mindfulness Retreat* (2000) by Thich Nhat Hanh with permission of Parallax Press, Berkeley, California.

a-time when we became what we saw as a natural state of being, when we lived in synchrony with life in the moment, minds and bodies together. Remember this. Cherish children for this. Listen to them and their way of being. Learn from them. Learn alongside them.

Another idea behind this poem has to do with patterns of experiences that connect to one another and to us over time. Having read some writings of Gregory Bateson (1979), who is known for his research and writing about what he calls "the pattern that connects," I searched to find out more about him on the Internet. I came across a draft of an article for the Italian journal *Alfazeta* entitled "Gregory Bateson's Notion of the Sacred—What Can It Tell Us About Living Constructively?," by Vincent Kenny (1998). At the end of the article, Kenny tells a wonderful story about a child that I will paraphrase here.

The author was on an almost-deserted beach in Sardinia observing a mother, father, and baby girl. The girl had just realized that she could almost walk if, after getting to an upright position, she threw herself forward for a few steps before she lost momentum and fell down. She was totally absorbed in this cycle for some minutes before she noticed that her hands and feet left marks in the sand as she fell and that she could make all kinds of interesting indentations in the wet sand on purpose. She was busy with this until a wave swept in and washed the marks away. She was amazed!

Next, she began to combine all these things: getting up, lunging forward, making marks, and waiting for the waves to take them away. Then something new arrived! A single piece of seaweed was left at her feet by a wave. She picked it up and gazed at its luminescent, glistening colors.

Then, she almost ran the few steps toward her parents, screeching with joy at her discovery. Kenny writes, "But it seemed that her father had already seen seaweed." He took it and threw it down, put her in her bright floating ring, and waded into the water with her for a little swim.

The girl strained back toward the beach and couldn't wait to get back to the sand and her piece of seaweed, which, this time, she showed to her mother, who became engaged in the immediacy of her astonishing discovery.

Kenny explains that he tells this story so that we might see an image of what he calls the "sacred in action," which he describes, in the case of this 13-month-old baby girl, as "being able to spontaneously live her amazement of being-in-the-world, discovering exciting connectedness between her and everything around her." Kenny goes on to say, "If we are lucky (as adults) we retain this ability to be occasionally amazed, astonished, in awe of the whole system within which our living is embedded."

Kenny's words bring to mind comments Vea Vecchi made one morning in the Diana School *atelier* in the spring of 1992. Marina Mori came in with two detailed and beautiful messages that had been made that morning by several 5-year-old girls. Instead of being for classmates or their mothers or fathers, the messages were written to Mil. Mil was their adopted apple tree, which lived outside the school near their classroom. The adoption was one of the last chapters in a year-long project about trees and plants (Cadwell, 1997). The girls' spontaneous messages were somewhat unusual and very exciting to Marina and Vea. I did not write down Vea's exact words, but she she said something like this:

> If you and the children go deep with something, almost anything that captures the imagination of both children and adults, eventually the children will begin to bring in everything, make connections you never dreamed of.

It is as if when you investigate in depth, uncover more and more layers of meaning, the roots go down, and the tentacles go out, and the children begin to see how this one thing is actually connected to everything. Here, they understand sending messages as a way to further extend their relationship with a tree they know and care about. That is what we hope will happen. That is what we want to happen for the children and for us. Aren't we all compelled by the tapestry of life and the relationships among things, rather than by fragmented pieces of knowledge?

WORLD-MAKING

It seems that we are born with a powerful desire to connect with the world, to interact with it, play with it, get to know it, and leave a trace on it. In a way, these marks on the world give us back who we are like a mirror. They become like a vital, new kind of umbilical cord to life, which carries with it our potential to create our own relationship with our experience and to make our own meaning. We need marks, images, words, dance, and voice to do this. These first marks are our voice in its earliest development. They are our lifeline.

I have always remembered Rachel Carson's (1956) words from *The Sense of Wonder* when she writes that, in order to fall in love with the natural world, to become a steward of earth, and to understand our connection with it, a child needs at least two things: an adult companion who has deep connections to the natural world as a guide and a lot of free time to roam in the outdoors, to play with it as a friend.

For me, a strong connection with the world is wedded to a fundamental human drive to shape that connection, that bond, that vision that we, each as a unique human being, feel and understand in our own particular way. Words, songs, gestures, the shape of our bodies in movement, pens and papers, paint and clay offer us the chance to mold ourselves into being so that we can then see ourselves in relationship to that which is vital to us. Judith Burton (1991) reminds us that we do not so much represent things in our works in materials as we represent our particular relationship with those things. Thus, we are not drawing, sculpting, or painting objects. Rather, we are drawing and sculpting our relationships.

I remember a conversation that Chuck Schwall and I had with a group of visiting educators. Several teachers asked Chuck to talk more about the drawing games he played with the children, about which he had spoken earlier that day. The game works like this: Chuck asks a child or several children whether they would like to play a game with him to make a drawing. He suggests that they each take turns making lines. "You make a line; I'll make a line," Chuck says.

"The child might make a very energetic back-and-forth mark, and then I might make a slow, meandering line. The children and I have fun exploring all the possibilities there are in making lines. The children here needed some support in their drawing, and this is one way I have discovered to give it to them."

The teachers asked honestly, "Isn't that interfering too much with their way of working? Is that game developmentally appropriate?"

Chuck and I both described our take on this question. For us, playing with the qualities of lines and the possibilities of marks on paper is a natural and grounded activity. It is at least as natural for us as writing letters, maybe more so. This is part of who we are. We believe, as teachers and as adults who share our lives with children, that we have this to offer them—this naturalness, this fun outlook, this freedom, this process of discovery. We likened this relationship to that of a parent with a young toddler learning to walk or to talk.

Think of all the games adults invent to play with children about sounds: we sing, we coo, we imitate the babies, we talk nonsense syllables to them, we read to them, we tell them stories. Most attentive adults surround children in a playful, loving way with sound, with language, and with communication. And the babies absorb it all. We hope that they emerge with their own strong voices and their own unique ways of speaking and communicating.

Chuck and I, and the teachers with whom we work in the St. Louis–Reggio Collaborative, believe that we are offering children the support they deserve in playing and working with lines and paper, clay or paint, blocks or letters with the same kind of enthusiasm, joy, and engagement with which parents embrace their children with language. We do not show them how to make lines or how to draw, but rather how we love lines and are intrigued by what a pen or pencil can do in our hand and on the paper. Then, when this game begins, we learn from the invention, grace, lack of inhibition, and freshness of the children with whom we work.

The following stories speak to the relationships among many elements: the context of a layered, well-understood, and well-equipped environment; the dance of teacher and child together in search of meaning within shared experiences with materials; the power that materials give to children to both make discoveries and to shape meaning; and the time given over to these events.

Live Action in the *Atelier*

After the transformation of the *atelier* described in Chapter 4, many children who had seen the work in progress were anxious to get into the new mini-areas. It was almost as if they had anticipated the arrival of these new spaces before we even thought of them. The children, by now so familiar with both the materials in the *atelier* and the potential for invention, concentration, and play that the place holds, were immediately able to transfer this knowledge and expectation directly into the mini-areas. They seemed hungry for these small spaces, well equipped and beautifully organized just for them (see Figure 5.1).

For several mornings in a row, I introduced the areas to a small group; then each child would choose where to start, and things would evolve from there. I observed what the children did as much as possible in these first weeks of use. I was intrigued by the children's strong attraction to the places, and I was curious to see how they would use them.

"Can we turn the big lights out, please, Louise?" asks Chase. "Then we can really see the colors on the shadow screen."

"That's a good idea, Chase; let's do," I say as I reach for the switch and turn out the bright lights beaming down from the ceiling. In the meantime, the children and I turn on the collection of lamps, which are recent additions, located in various places around the *atelier:* a gooseneck desk lamp on top of the relocated box shelf that houses collections of papers; a clip-on lamp above the construction area; a small, battery-operated lantern in the desk area; and a brass bedside lamp near the computer.

Today, when we turn on the overhead projector and the light table, the whole room fills with an incandescent glow. It feels warm and a little mysterious without the

FIGURE **5.1.**   Alcove with Mini-Areas in the College School *Atelier*

usual brightness that illuminates every detail. I think of the section on "Light" in *Children, Spaces, and Relations* (Ceppi & Zini, 1998) and the photographs that draw one into the possibilities of lighting and light as play. Now we are in half-light, or what the editors call "semidarkness." They write: "Light, in fact, is one of the great emotive components of our aesthetic perception . . . and the plasticity and richness of an illuminated space depend on the modulation of the light" (p. 46). I put on a CD, Handel's *Water Music.* It spills into the space in cascades of liquid harmonies.

Chase and Luke kneel down on the soft Peruvian area rugs, loaned to us by Kathleen, next to the overhead projector. They are picking out a number of things to put on the light surface and project onto the curtain.

"Look at this, Louise," Chase says in an excited voice. "Isn't this cool?" The boys have arranged feathers in a grid pattern and are putting red, yellow, green, and blue geometric Plexiglas shapes in patterns in between them. Dark, feathery shadows peppered with colored shapes appear on the shadow screen.

"I wonder why the colors of the feathers don't show up?" I query.

"I don't know," says Luke with a questioning tone in his voice.

The boys change the arrangement, sweeping off the first one and beginning again. This time, they are building with transparent blocks on top of the overhead projector surface. They do not seem to pay much attention to the projection this time. They are captured by the intense glow of light refracting up through the clear colored blocks. This whole picture reminds me again of the section on lagoonal lighting in *Children, Spaces, and Relations.* The light source shines from underneath the children's faces, from below rather than above. This is a new way to perceive light that both the overhead and the light table offer.

This morning at the light table, Allie and Sarah work quietly, almost in a dream state. Allie stands a tall, green Plexiglas water glass upside down. Sarah balances a blue transparent bowl on top of it. Sarah turns a lavender bowl upside down. It glows like a great jewel in the center of the square table of light. Allie places a tiny rubber giraffe on top. Sarah picks up a scallop shell and puts it between the bowl and the giraffe. The giraffe on a half-shell, like Botticelli's Venus, now seems to floats in midair.

Brewster comes over from his place at the little desk. "I need some tape, Louise. I need to make a portfolio."

"What?" I ask, surprised to hear him say this word at this point in time. "Why do you need a portfolio, Brewster?"

I follow him over to the little desk, where he shows me his growing collection of drawings. He has used three pieces of the 2-by-3-inch paper in the hanging Lucite container. "This is my dog. And this is me. And this is some writing. And I'm not done yet. I need a portfolio to put my things in."

Brewster has drawn lines in orange fine-lined marker. His dog is a rectangular-shaped body with an attached head placed horizontally on the page. It has four long-legged lines with turned ends for the paws. His portrait is similar, except the body is formed with an upright rectangle placed vertically on the page. The "writing" is a series of squiggly lines. "It's a message for my sister," Brewster clarifies. "It's a secret."

I hand Brewster the tape, which should, after all, be on the desk in the first place. Brewster walks over to the box shelf to choose the appropriate paper for his portfolio. He chooses brown construction paper, which he finds on one of the shelves with other neutral-colored paper. He sits down again at the desk and begins cutting the construction paper.

I am just amazed at how much the children in all three classes seem to love this little, solitary desk. There is really only enough room for one child, but sometimes two try to squeeze themselves in and work side by side. However, for most children, the prize seems to be the chance to be there alone. I think this place provides a corner of privacy for engaging in individual work that children must really need from time to time.

Working here last week, Justin produced a book on tiny squares of paper. He created a collection of strong designs and geometric patterns. He used little squares of cream-colored tissue paper for the pages. Children in the Newport Room have been making books all year. The idea of creating sequences and series is now part of their repertoire of ideas. Bookmaking was not an idea that I had suggested. It was what he wanted to do here when he sat down.

A few days ago, I had a hard time convincing Nicholas to leave this spot to get ready for lunch. He cut strips of paper and then taped them together in three rows. On the collage tray he found some crinkles of brown packing shreds of paper and a yellow feather, which he taped to the first configuration. On it he wrote "Mom, Dad." "It's for them," Nicholas beamed (see Figure 5.2).

My thoughts are broken by Noah and Ryan shouting at each other through the just-installed talking tube. An 8-foot piece of clear plastic tubing, with blue funnels poked firmly in each end, hangs on 1-inch cup hooks and stretches across the window wall that separates the *atelier* alcove from the Big Bend Room. Noah and Ryan have been building a block and shell castle in the nearby construction area, and they have been pulled away to play with this new feature of the *atelier*.

"Boys, there is a rule about that. Remember? It is for whispering so no one else can hear you," I say.

FIGURE 5.2.   Examples of Messages and Drawings Made at the Desk in the *Atelier*

The boys turn and look at me with reluctance. "OK, we'll whisper," says Noah as he turns back to put his mouth up to one funnel and Ryan puts his ear to the other one. Something secret begins to be exchanged.

Suddenly, everyone's attention is grabbed by the goings-on at the shadow screen. We all gather round. Chase and Luke have been layering pieces of transparent acetate one after the other—ocean blue, sky blue, grass green, ruby red, sun yellow. The edges of the overhead lamp blaze with color. The center is dense and dark. The boys have put a collection of small zoo animals on the overhead standing upright, but they do not show up on the screen. I can see Chase thinking, looking at the screen and down to the overhead and back again. In another instant he has figured out the problem, and he and Luke are turning all the animals so that they are lying on their sides. Now, on the projector they look as if they are sleeping on a rainbow of light, but in their shadow shapes they are galloping across colors on the screen.

The animals have come to life! It reminds me of a jungle dream. The boys have created a fantasy out of the interplay of the materials, the light, the projection, and their own thinking.

Things need to be turned on their sides sometimes to show up, or upside down, or who knows which way. The right way is not always what it seems. The shadow screen as puzzle, I think. Or as a place to tell stories, to push and pull sense out of thin air, out of fugitive colors and light!

I notice that it is 11:00. How could it be time for lunch already, I wonder. The mood in here will change when the lights turn on and the music goes off. The space is flexible and accommodating. Nevertheless, I hold back briefly and take in the scene of the moment with joy and gratitude. Then, on go the lights.

"Time to straighten up," I say. "You can leave your constructions; just put away the unused things in the right places. Brewster, you have some scraps to put in the recycle basket."

I see that Brewster has made a little pocket portfolio that resembles a library card pocket in the back of a book. In it, he has slipped a self-portrait series of four, his dog drawing, and several pieces of writing similar to the first described earlier.

As I move toward the door to go find my own lunch, I notice the light table. It is arranged in a palette of colors. The girls have put all the blue objects together, all the reds, all the yellows, all the greens. White feathers lie on top of a clear plastic plate surrounded by ice cube–like blocks of Plexiglas: azure marbles in the translucent blue bowl draped with blue theater gel; red blocks, ruby acetate, fire-engine feathers in a garnet glass. A palette of objects, a rainbow of shapes, a composition of light created as in an improvisational duet by two girls in a morning.

Our collective experiences here with each other and with the environment have generated a sense of what Mihaly Csikszentmihalyi (1990) has called "flow con- sciousness," a psychic state when we are both challenged and completely focused, totally concentrated and deeply engaged. In this state, we have the sense that time and other distractions disappear and feel joy in the moment. It is the environment in all its complex manifestations and our mutual respect for and appreciation of its pos- sibilities that have made this quality of experience possible. I remember Renate and Geoffrey Caine (1994) writing:

> Brain research establishes and confirms that multiple, complex, and concrete experi- ences are essential for meaningful learning and teaching. Optimizing the use of the human brain means using the brain's infinite capacity to make connections. . . . Every complex event embeds information in the brain and links what is being learned to the rest of the learner's current experience, past knowledge, and future behavior. The pri- mary focus for educators, therefore, should be on expanding the quantity and quality of ways a learner is exposed to content and context. (pp. 5-6)

When I read that passage, I was excited to come upon a version of Carlina's challenge—"The best environment for children is one in which you can find the high- est possible quantity and quality of relationships"—in a book on brain research and teaching. I reflect on the scenes of the morning. Two girls constructed a system of rela- tionships among colors, their unique creation of the spectrum of the color wheel with multiple transparent objects. A group of boys conducted experiments with objects and shadows within a narrative using tools (the overhead projector) and materials (theater gels, toy animals) in unusual ways. One child made a sequence of representations using pens and papers, drawing and writing, and finally constructing a well-thought-out, care- fully crafted container to hold his important collection. Another group of children con- structed a narrative using small blocks and other objects, thinking about and calculat- ing weight and balance, parts and wholes, composition and story. Each child and each group were aware of the others and what was evolving in their peripheral vision, yet each child was completely focused on what he or she was doing. A "group conscious- ness" emerged that produced and added to the high quality of the *flow* that we all felt.

Worlds in Clay

We have observed that children tell stories almost continuously—in the sandbox, in the housekeeping area, in the block area, with paint, with clay. Within the telling they seem to string together pieces and parts of their personal histories, their knowledge, their intuitions, and their current wonderings about life as they might select a variety of beads to loop onto a flexible copper wire.

Over the years, among the most intriguing tales are those that have emerged in clay. As such, bisque-fired and strong, these "clay stories" have remained for a time in the *atelier,* reminding all of us of the vitality of the medium and of the freshness and the depth of the narratives that clay can hold.

Emmy's Garden

We have decided in our teacher meeting on Monday afternoon that I will return to work with children and clay for the next few weeks of the month of May in the outdoor *atelier.* Today is Tuesday, and it is about 1:45 in the afternoon. I touch base with Jennifer to see which children are finished with their rest and would be available to work outside.

"Let's see. What about Emmy, Natalie, Justin, and Greg? That might be a good start. What do you think?" she asks.

"That sounds fine," I say, "I'll get them."

The five of us head down the black metal staircase that hugs the north side of the brick building and through the gate of the low wooden fence that surrounds the decking of the outdoor *atelier.* This outdoor room was constructed in the fall of 1996 by Sally, Mike Strange, and a group of parent volunteers. The area where it is located used to be a bare patch of ground with no real function. I think it was originally Jennifer's idea to transform it into an outdoor space that would be both beautiful and functional. Her husband, Mike, volunteered to help, as he has so many times.

The committee of parents and teachers, with Mike at the lead, built an 8-by-8-foot deck, with a 3½-foot fence to border it. They placed 7-foot beams at each corner. These beams support a square of 2-by-4s that, in turn, hold cross-wires for grape vines. This arrangement gives the illusion of a roof while still being open to the sky.

A year later, in 1997, our maintenance man, Dan Masters, added a corner, built-in easel and a rectangular table, large enough for about six children, with benches on either side. Every year since then, parents have helped to both maintain and improve the space. One year, a mother found a perfect speckled linoleum to cover the wooden surfaces of table and easel that were damaged by the weather. Every spring, parents volunteer to plant pansies in terra-cotta pots; in the fall, chrysanthemums. This is an outdoor space that we can use in good weather as an additional place to work in small groups in conversation or with materials.

Today is breezy, warm, and delicious. Justin helps to carry the red clay in a clear plastic bag. There are about 12 pounds left in a new batch delivered early this month from Krueger's Pottery just down the street from the school. Emmy and Natalie carry the boards, 2-by-2-foot squares of plywood covered with canvas and stapled underneath. Greg carries the crock of clay tools, and I balance several jars of slip and my notebook on a clay board and my camera on one shoulder.

"How about if you build onto slabs today? You've done that before with me and on your own but not for a while now. I thought it might be an interesting way to begin. What do you think? I'll help you roll them out, and then you can use the rest of the clay to build with the slip whatever you would like."

"I like to roll the clay, Louise. I can do it all by myself," Justin offers.

"Great!" I say. "Let's get started."

The children, who are all enthusiastic about this starting point, take turns helping as we roll even, half-inch-thick slabs of the moist clay. The clay seems to breathe with a fresh and inviting quality as we remold the angular chunks we slice off into flat slabs.

"Why don't you choose what shape you would like to work on. We can cut any shape," I suggest.

Most of the children choose a rectangle, and together we use the wooden-edged tools to shape the slabs. The children begin to talk happily about all sorts of things as they work. They each take small pieces of clay from the block in the middle of the table to build onto their own slabs. They shape these small pieces in their hands.

Each child has a different style. Justin takes big chunks of clay and begins to build long, tall shapes on his flat slab. He leaves them rough, with the marks of his fingers in them. Natalie works with a similar zest, attaching many pieces in rather short order. Her pieces take shape on a more horizontal plane than Justin's vertical sculpture. Luke works slowly and carefully, stroking and smoothing each piece of clay before he attaches it (see Figure 5.3).

Emmy uses a variety of techniques. At first, she makes a collection of small balls about the size of marbles. Then she smoothes several flat pieces of clay in the palm of her hand. Next, she rolls a coil on her board about 3 inches long. She begins to attach some of these pieces to the slab with slip.

"I'm making my grandmother's farm," Natalie announces, leaning over her clay. "This part is where we make jam. It's the barn in back. This is the garden," she says definitively, pointing to various lumps of clay that she has grouped together.

"Well, this is my garden in back of my house," says Emmy. "And this is my favorite tree, and this is my swimming pool."

FIGURE 5.3.   Working with Clay in the Outdoor *Atelier*

FIGURE 5.4. Emmy Working on Her Garden Sculpture

The breeze blows hard, and some of the new, tender oak leaves blow down and land right on the outdoor *atelier* table. Emmy picks one up and attaches it to her sculpture at the top of the thick coil that she has positioned vertically at one end of her garden.

"Look, now the tree has leaves," she smiles, glancing sideways at us, looking very pleased.

"Maybe the tree here is sending you leaf messages for your tree at home," I wonder out loud.

Emmy gets up and wanders out the gate. She bends down and picks up several of last fall's acorns and some small sticks.

"Could I pick just one pansy, please, Louise?" she asks with her pleading voice.

"Sure you can, Emmy." How can I resist?

She returns to the table with her collection of natural materials to embellish and furnish her sculpture. Emmy continues to speak as she stitches clay pieces and meaning together (see Figure 5.4).

> This is a little path. It goes to where my cousins live. This is where I live. There are two trees. This is where I want to put my other leaf message that came down to me from the big tree. These are stores here. And this is the Kirkwood Pool. This is my car, right here. This is my neighbor's car, and this is one of their apple trees.
>
> This whole thing is my yard. I can tell you about the secret clubhouse with a door on it that we made. I have some real tall trees. And I made a secret tunnel with a door on it. This is actually my front, back, and side yard,

FIGURE **5.5.** "My Garden," by Emmy

and my neighborhood. Now, I'm going to put this little feather in my yard that I found. I like to build feathers into my collages if I find one [see Figure 5.5].

I watch in delight on this windy spring day in the outdoor *atelier* as Emmy constructs her own outdoor place in clay and natural materials from her memory and her imagination. After Emmy's garden is fired to a bisque terra-cotta, she reattaches the acorns, leaves, and feathers that were removed during the firing process. Emmy chooses a title and spells it out on a standing card: "My Garden, by Emmy." The sculpture and the card are now on the interactive shelf in the *atelier* under the window.

In making her garden sculpture, Emmy drew on her experience of home as well as her sense of her neighborhood and surrounding, close community that make up her immediate world. Her sculpture does not resemble a garden, a backyard, a home, or a neighborhood in any literal sense. The pieces of clay that she assembled here take on that significance for her because she imbues them with her own personal meaning.

In *Bringing Reggio Emilia Home,* I refer to a story told by Seonaid Robertson (1963) in *Rosegarden and Labyrinth.* Robertson tells of a similar sculpture of a magical rosegarden made of a circle of lumps of clay formed tenderly by a young girl. Somehow, clay seems to offer children the chance to embody ideas of great importance to them. This is true even though we cannot see the things that they say are in the clay. In some way, the children are capable of seeing beauty and significance, power and meaning in what, to us, look like abstract forms of clay, random marks in pencil, or sweeping gestures of paint. As authors of myths do with words, children have the ability to put together the stories they want and need to tell through working with a medium that invites them into this realm.

Remembering Other Children's Places in Clay

The clay landscapes made today remind me of several sculptures made by 4-year-olds in 1998 that stopped me in my tracks. Though we had worked with clay often and in a variety of ways since 1992, that year we made a decision to study clay with more intention as a team. My colleague Sally is a working potter with her own studio. She brings her knowledge and love of the medium to all of us and to the children. Jennifer had become more and more interested in clay over the years and wanted to focus on learning more about both the material and children's response to it. In a team meeting in the fall of 1998, we determined together how we would begin the year with children and clay in the Newport Room. Our colleague Brenda Fyfe, who sometimes joins us as a curriculum adviser, was with us. We considered these questions:

> How many children should be in a group?
> How will we decide which children will participate in each group?
> Should we meet with the groups in the *atelier*, the classroom, or the outdoor *atelier*?
> Should we have slip available for the first experience or not?
> Should we have natural materials or some other material available or just the clay?
> What kind of shape would the clay be in? Would we prepare it with children?
> Which teachers would be with which groups?
> Who would take notes?
> Who would be responsible for the audiotape?
> Who would photograph?
> When would we consider the work of the children together?

As a group we decided to begin only with clay for this first experience of the year. On reflection, we felt that perhaps, in the past, we had offered too many choices. We wanted to see what would happen with clay alone. We decided to prepare the environment so that each child would begin with a piece of clay of similar size and shape—a 3- or 4-inch block sliced off the rectangle that the clay is delivered in. In this way, we could better see in how many ways the children might act on the clay from a similar starting point. We came up with a very simple question to begin with: "Can you change this clay? How can you change it?" (Cadwell, Miller, & Strange, 1999).

We really didn't know what to expect. This was more clay than these children usually worked with. It was a particular shape. We did not often start with such a specifically worded question that was born out of collective intentionality on our part. We felt butterflies of excitement fluttering inside us.

A first group worked with Jennifer facilitating, while I documented in photographs and with notes.

Taylor's Home. I remember that morning clearly. Taylor was sitting at the large, adult-height table with Jennifer nearby. We sliced the clay off the block like a huge piece of cheese. The children loved it. Then they tried to cut it. Holding the thin wire at two ends, they pulled it toward them through the moist, earth-red clay.

When each child was face to face with this sizable piece of clay, Jennifer asked with excitement in her voice, "Do you think that you can change this clay? How do you think you will change it?"

Taylor, a new student that fall, had never worked with clay before in her life. "Yeah, I can change it," she said in a quietly assured voice as she pulled a piece off her block about the size of an orange. Right away, she began to smooth it and shape it in her hands, gradually curving it into a shape like a big section of peel off a grapefruit, rounded and thin. She pulled off a second piece, and began to do something similar but left this piece a little thicker and flatter. Then she placed the peel-like piece perpendicular to the flat piece, which she had placed on her board, creating a slab. She joined the two pieces using her fingers to smooth them together.

At this point, she began a process that I have observed other children engage in but not in the systematic fashion that Taylor now used. She began to pinch off little bits of clay and flatten and smooth each of them in her hands, echoing the first gestures she had made with the clay. Then she started to attach these pieces in rows, one after the other, overlapping, row by row, one on top of the other, onto the standing, curved piece of clay.

Up until this point she had worked mostly in silence. Now she began to talk about this cave-like piece as her home. She added little pieces, similar to the ones on the back of the "wall," as she called it, inside the curved structure. Taylor explained that these were couches in her den, her bed in her bedroom, and her mom and dad's bed in their room.

When she was finished, after an hour and a half of work, she said this about her sculpture:

> I started with this big wall back here. I didn't know what it was at first. Then I got this little idea and I started tearing off bits and pieces of clay and attaching them underneath. Now it's like my house to me. My bedroom is inside and my mom's and dad's bedroom, too, and here's the den and the couch in the den. Those are the little shelves and stuff. There is a gate door to go in and out [see Figure 5.6].

What Jennifer and I observed that morning about Taylor's way of working on the piece was absolutely unexpected and astounding to us. In discussing what we had seen, and using our notes, photographs, and reflections, we surmised that Taylor was certainly supported by the surrounding children and their confidence with the material; by the focus and intention of the experience; and by the anticipation, shared by both children and teachers, that something exciting would happen that morning.

We also discussed her unusual technique and where it might have come from. To me, it seemed similar to the way a wasp builds a nest with overlapping pieces of paper-thin layers. Jennifer saw an innovative, quiet, and pensive side of Taylor that she had not seen before. Sally and I had seen vessels made with a similar technique by Paulus Berensohn (1972) in a book entitled *Finding One's Way with Clay.* Apparently, ceramic artists have used this technique for centuries, but Taylor knew none of this. She invented it for herself. The structure that she built with this unusual technique is a protected place, a shelter, curved and smooth like a shell. As she worked, it became her home in her imagination.

William's Eagles' Nest. On another morning William joined his group in the *atelier.* This morning I was alone with three children as they worked and Jennifer came in and out of the *atelier* so she could to follow what was happening.

This was William's third year at the College School. He was comfortable with clay and already knew that he could invent many things with this malleable medium.

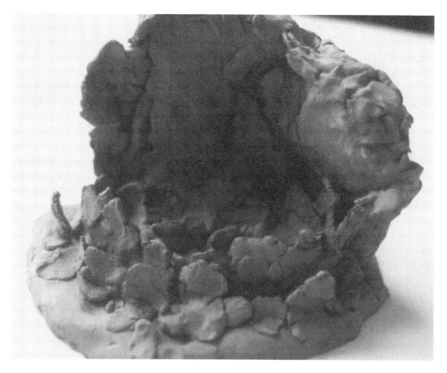

FIGURE **5.6.** "My Home," by Taylor

When asked if he could change the clay, he said right away, "I am going to take this apart." William began to tear the original block into many pieces, arranging them in what appeared to be a random way on the board.

Next, he began to shape some pieces a little more, using a squeeze technique to make a kind of "coil with fingerprints." He formed other pieces into block-like configurations. It looked to us as if William had taken the whole big piece apart so that he could then reassemble it in pieces. In the end, he used every bit of the original piece to construct a square full of other shapes, all defined by his clay coils and blocks. As he worked, he began to talk about eagles and the nest that he was making for them (see Figure 5.7). The following are a sampling of William's comments as he later explained the process and significance of building the nest to us:

Louise: Do you remember what you started with? What shape the clay was to begin with?

William: It started out as a block. This high and this fat (showing with his hands about a 6-by-6-by-4-inch block).

Louise: How did you get the idea to make this eagle house?

William: Well, when Nathan and Adam brought their clay sculpture to meeting— it was a school or a house or something—I got the idea from them. They said that their sculpture was for eagles.

Louise: Even though you got the idea from them, yours is completely different from theirs. How did you start?

William: Well, I started with the eagles: the mommy, the daddy, and the guest. The guy in this room (pointing to one section) is the guest. And in the middle there are the eggs. This is the nest room (pointing to the middle section). Actually, this is all a nest. The whole thing. The middle is the very special egg room. I put this guy over here in the guest room so he could have some privacy.

Louise: Would you explain more about the house/nest and the eagles?

William: Well, the eagles are kind of like airplanes (flying a piece of clay around making sound effects). And they have friends. And if they have nonflying friends, they come in this door (pointing to an opening). You know the eagles were pretty smart to build this house!

Louise: William, did you have a plan when you started?

William: I didn't know it would look like this. I didn't know what to do in the beginning. I just started. I was going to add on, but I decided to stop. You can just pretend all these pieces are twigs and sticks. And that's how birds really make their nests. I just thought of that right now. I think that I should count the rooms again: 1, 2, 3, 4, 5, 6, 7, 8, 9, 10, 11, 12, 13, 14—14 rooms! I keep on rearranging them. But you don't have to move them too much. You just play with the eagles. I have a rule. You can't have anything touching.

Louise: Do you think clay was a good thing to make the eagles' nest out of?

William: Yes. I didn't want to make it out of blocks. You can't pinch them [blocks] like clay. You can take clay apart. You know the eagles are celebrating. They are getting three new babies. They are having lots of guests, not just kids, but kids can come. I made a nest room for the babies in the center because it's safer for the babies like that [see Figure 5.7].

As a team, we were as stunned by William's work as we had been by Taylor's. First of all, both Taylor and William seemed to have a strong idea that came from somewhere inside them, drawn out, we surmised, by the shape and quantity of the clay, the provocation, their personal experiences, and their strong, instinctive drive to shape materials into forms and in the process to imbue them with meaning. They had each used many different techniques. For example, they constructed slabs, coils, blocks, attachments, arrangements, rearrangements, dramatizations, animations, story and sequence in an hour and a half out of what started out as a block of clay.

Like Emmy's garden, these clay pieces themselves would not appear to have much significance. It is the way in which Taylor and William had formed the structures and given them significance that intrigues us as teachers and keeps us questioning. The following are thoughts that William's work provoked in us.

The way in which William arranged his clay pieces on the clay board is reminiscent of a mandala shape—one that appears often in children's drawings and paintings. It has a clear center and the rest of the parts radiate out from that center. What impulse leads children to give this shape to materials? Why do children of all cultures seem to do this (Kellogg & O'Dell, 1967)? In William's case, it came from his imagination, not from any model he was observing.

The center has special significance to William. It is the most interior room—the room where the babies and the eggs will be most protected. Why is the imagery around babies, eggs, and being born so strong in children? It seems to show up over and over again and is often given special, magical significance (Cadwell, 1997).

William's composition fills the board perfectly. Did William do this instinctively? Is this his "style"?

William's nest looks like a geometric pattern of shapes. The whole configuration is about parts and wholes. The square shape is made of "rooms" that fit together.

<small>FIGURE 5.7.</small> William Explains the Dynamics of the Eagles' Nest

Is this geometric sense instinctive to William, or has he done this before? To our knowledge, he invented this way of working with clay for the first time on this day.

William used the clay as he might have used blocks, lining pieces up in configurations and making shapes out of shapes. In addition to being a structure, William's eagles' nest is a puzzle that can be taken apart and reassembled.

His nest holds an enchanting dramatization about a family of eagles with a mother, a father, babies, and guests who visit. This is a complex, interactive, and ongoing story. This clay configuration invites play, change, new chapters, new inventions. It is not a static, finished object. William's clay structures and story are open to continual evolution.

What Did Emmy, Taylor, and William Learn Through Building Places in Clay?

All the children brought many things into these experiences with clay: their unique qualities and personalities; their knowledge and/or intuition about the material and its potential to hold many forms, ideas, and feelings; recent episodes and emotions in their lives that bubbled up as important when they came in contact with the medium of clay; the capacity to integrate multiple pieces of experience as well as pieces of clay into a satisfying, complex whole. These capacities testify to what the children had learned before they sculpted their places. And yet we might not have known these things about the children—and the children might not have discovered these qualities and abilities in themselves—had they not met the clay in this way. I doubt if these clay places would have emerged in such clear and surprising ways if we teachers had not thought carefully about and organized the most supportive environment we could imagine. Further, neither the teachers nor the children would have discovered the lasting significance of these events if the teachers had not listened and documented the children's processes of working with both curiosity and complete attention (see Figure 5.8).

When I observed each of these children sculpting what turned out to be a place, I felt that I was witnessing a kind of birth, in the sense of something new coming into being that did not exist before—a birth in that many elements were coming into new relationships and thus unfolding into fresh meaning. In bringing these places into the world in a context in which both creator and creation were fully supported and valued, I am sure that Emmy, Taylor, and William understand themselves as composers and inventors of important artifacts and ideas. As they compose and invent in clay, they are learning to trust a medium to hold and communicate the complexity of their ideas. They are learning to transform a neutral material into a symbol that stands for many things yet is in itself a whole. They are learning to create a system of relationships. They are also learning to enter into and enjoy an open dialogue both with their experience in the world and with a particular material.

THE SCENT PROJECT

During the 1998–1999 school year, a young woman named C. C. Tompkins became an *atelier* intern in our schools. C. C., who had just graduated from the Chicago Art Institute, fell in love with the Reggio Approach after reading *Bringing Reggio Emilia Home.* "This is what I want to do with my life," she said. "Where can I go to learn how?" We suggested that she intern for a year at the St. Michael School, since she could work in the before- and after-school program there and balance a small paid position with

FIGURE 5.8.   William, Jackson, and Jackson's Father Admire the Story of William's Experience

a learning one. Chuck Schwall agreed to have her work alongside him every day to learn the ins and outs of the role of the *atelierista*.

During the fall, C. C. attended our St. Louis–Reggio Collaborative meetings and read more books and articles about the Reggio Approach. She visited and worked with me at the College School and observed at Clayton Schools' Family Center. Little by little, she began to absorb the ways of our work and to contribute more and more to the context in which she found herself.

In the winter of 1999, Chuck and C. C. began to share their excitement with teachers in the St. Louis–Reggio Collaborative about a project that was developing on scents and fragrances. Many of us were intrigued and were eager to hear how this project would grow. Since then, I have had the privilege of assisting Chuck as he presented this project to an audience using the framework of the Harvard Project Zero protocol described in Chapter 3.

When I saw it presented for the first time, I was a member of a group of four from the St. Louis–Reggio Collaborative presenting at the National Conference for Constructionist Teaching in St. Louis in May of 1999. That day, Brenda, Jennifer, Lori, and I worked together, taking different roles as recorder, facilitator, and dialogue leader. Chuck was the "presenting teacher." We were stunned by the effect of the whole. To me, it is one of our strongest examples of project work in St. Louis. I will share it with you now from my perspective as an outside observer and great admirer of this story of learning.

Initially, I will describe the sequence of events in the manner of the presenting teacher, using transcripts of the children's work. Following the protocol framework, I will describe what happened without interpretation. At the point at which we would engage the audience, I will offer some of the responses of the participants who have taken part in this process of thinking together with us. You might think to yourself as you read the descriptions:

> What do I notice about what the children and teachers do and say? What questions do I have?
> What do I speculate that the children are learning?
> What implications for my work might any of this have?

The Beginnings

When the holidays arrived, C. C. decided to give the children in the 3- and 4-year-old class an oil burner and a collection of scented oils to burn. She studies aroma therapy and was eager to share her enthusiasm about fragrances and their positive effects with the teachers, Frances Roland and Susan Bradshaw, and the children.

In January, the classroom filled with unusual and delightful scents. Small groups of children took turns choosing a scent for the day: lavender, tangerine, rosewood, jasmine, ginger. Then teacher and children together would light the burner, pour in drops of the oil, and wait to be enchanted by the chosen aroma and the power of their noses.

As all this was taking place, the teachers, Karen Schneider and Melissa Guerra, and the children in the 4- and 5-year-old class were becoming fascinated with the fragrances that permeated the environment. They joined the experience after several weeks, and the two classes began to share the oil burner. The teachers began recording some of the children's comments about the fragrances and about the oil burner and how it might work. In early February, Karen, Melissa, Chuck, and C. C. decided to devote a team meeting to the delight and curiosity about scents that they noticed brewing in the children and also in themselves.

The following is a list of beginning questions that emerged during their dialogue in this first formal meeting:

> How do children perceive scent?
> What are ways that children might discover to communicate their perceptions of scent?
> What role does scent play for children in their understanding of the world?
> What languages and materials can support children's explorations of scents?

This group of four teachers also made a decision to launch an intentional, organized, and collective study of these questions. They were excited, and they were a little nervous. They had a shared feeling that they were about to begin an unusual adventure in discovery alongside the children.

In order to begin, they chose to initiate small-group "smelling sessions," in which groups of four children from both classes would have an opportunity to smell scented oil on a cotton ball and, in another session, smell dried materials, such as herbs, spices, and leaves. The teachers envisioned the scents as provocations that would stimulate response and conversations among teachers and children. As teachers, they would ask the children to make associations with each scent. What did each scent smell like to them? What did it remind them of? Where did they think it came from?

The teachers chose the two different approaches for several reasons. Oils were the original scents that they had been smelling in the classroom; therefore, the children had some experience and connection with them. In spite of the classroom experience, trying to make an association with a scent when there is no visual clue could be challenging. The teachers liked the idea of this kind of challenge, and they hypothesized that the isolated scents on cotton balls might push the children to invent unique and far-reaching connections to the smells.

They decided to include the experience of smelling the sources of these scents (herbs, spices, leaves) in order both to note any differences in the children's responses and to give the children more of a link with real things in the world that have fragrances. These teachers could have started their investigations with the children in any number of ways. At the time, as a group of four, they chose to begin this way.

Smelling Sessions: Oils

Each group of four children smelled four different oils on separate cotton balls that had been dipped into small jars of oil. Some of the oils that they smelled were strawberry, vanilla, cucumber, chamomile, rosemary, lemon, and grapefruit. The groups of four met in the studio with Chuck or C. C. over a period of several weeks. Chuck and C. C. recorded the conversations on a tape recorder, transcribed each one, shared them with their colleagues, and kept them in a collective notebook they had started for this project. The following is an excerpt of one such conversation about the scent of strawberry with Aisha, Ann, Gabriel, and Pete.

Chuck: Can everyone see the little bottle and how there is something inside there?
Aisha: Yeah.
Chuck: Well on the inside of the bottle is oil like the oil you have smelled in your classroom. The oil smells like something, and you will be able to use your nose to really, really, smell it.

Aisha: You can't put your hands through it.

Chuck: No, you can't put your hands through it. OK. Everyone look carefully. C. C. has these little eyedroppers, and I'm going to put a little drop of oil on the cotton and give each of you a jar to put the cotton ball in. (Chuck passes out the jars.)

Aisha: It kinda smells like something.

Chuck: What does it smell like to you?

Aisha: You know what it smells like to me?

Chuck: What?

Aisha: Cotton candy.

Gabriel: You know what it smells like to me?

Chuck: What?

Gabriel: Oil cotton.

Chuck: It smells like oil cotton?

Ann: It smells like four frogs drinking.

Chuck: Did you use your nose, though? Gabriel, did you use your nose?

Aisha: It smells like cotton candy. We go to the circus together and we got cotton candy. She [my sister] liked it but I didn't.

Chuck: OK, let's hear what Pete says. Pete, what does it smell like to you?

Pete: Ice cream on a cone.

Chuck: Gabriel, use your nose and tell me, do you have any other ideas?

Gabriel: Cotton oil.

Chuck: Would you all like to try another one?

Ann: This one smells like ice cream, and it looks like ice cream.

Smelling Sessions: Herbs

The dried materials that the children smelled included rosebuds, eucalyptus, cloves, peppermint, oregano, cinnamon, cocoa, orange peels, coffee beans, lavender, whole star anise, sage, yellow mustard seed, and Jamaican allspice. The following is a collection of children's responses from different groups to peppermint, eucalyptus, and sage.

Peppermint

Aisha: It smells like a candy cane and everything in the whole world.

Gabriel: It smells like grass.

Hannah: Stars up in the sky falling down at my house and grown-up toothpaste.

Isabella: Like a toothbrush.

Eucalyptus

Hannah: It smells like a strong smell.

Jack: Yuck!

Lunsford: I don't like this. I think it's poison ivy.

Nicole: It smells like an elephant.

Sage

Annie: It smells like sunflowers.

Ann: It smells like a person with no bones.

The Bloodhound Game

After their initial smelling sessions, the children seemed eager to mix some of the dried materials to create new scents, which the teachers encouraged. Several children wanted to name and label their potpourri, and this labeling desire grew among other members of the class. It seemed that both the children and the teachers began to notice fragrances, even subtle ones, with a heightened sensitivity. Several children began to sniff objects around school to see what kinds of smells they might find. When one child shared her knowledge that dogs, especially bloodhounds, were experts at smelling, a game was born. This shared knowledge and excitement seemed to encourage the children to pretend to be bloodhounds. The children began to smell what seemed to the teachers to be very unlikely objects: desks, chairs, doors, shelves, the telephone. They asked if they could go on bloodhound tours throughout the school. The teachers were fascinated by this strong desire on the part of the children to smell all kinds of things. After a team meeting, the teachers decided to invite the children to play the bloodhound game in small groups outside.

Outside, the teachers were detectives following the child detectives as they searched out what to smell. Singly and in pairs, they smelled, among other things, the bark of trees, branches, flowers, ivy, bushes, cars, and bricks. The teachers photographed the selections and the children smelling, as they had recorded this experience from the beginning, in digital photographs and slides. They also recorded the children's comments, such as "The bricks smell like clay" and "The leaves smell like the sun."

Response to the Work So Far

This is not the end of what happened in the Scent Project. When we present to a group of parents or teachers using the protocol developed by Project Zero, we have adopted the practice of stopping at a certain point in the project that seems roughly like the middle so that we can engage in a reflective process about what is happening.

We pause when it seems that the children and teachers have come to a turning point in their investigations, when a new kind of anticipation begins to flicker around the edges of the experience. When this happens, everyone seems to ask, "What next?" "Where can we go now?" "How can we take the investigation father and deeper?"

The following is a sampling of responses at this point in the presentation to the questions about the Scent Project: What did you notice? What do you wonder or question? What do you speculate the children are learning? These responses were collected from educators in Oregon, Ohio, and Pennsylvania who were attending workshops about the Reggio Approach. They are taken from notes written by a scribe as participants called out ideas. (Refer to Chapter 3 for the fuller, conversational nature of the actual experience of moving through the process of Project Zero's protocol for examining children's work.)

What Did You Notice?

Initial planning by the teachers
Children in small groups
Teachers taking notes and tape-recording
Children outside of their classroom
An investigation initiated by a student teacher

Natural materials

Children found scent in everything

Response to curiosity by the children and teachers

Connections to real experiences

The initial phase of the scientific method—observing, questioning, hypothesizing

Exploring the world

A process developing over time

Risk taking on the part of the teachers

Children speaking freely

Poetry of the children; emotions in words

Teachers gave no answers or "correct" theories

Invention of an idea by the children: the Bloodhound Game

Children and teachers listening and observing

Enchanted children

The teachers' questions encouraged children's listening to different perspectives

Different facial expressions

Smells evoking memories

Teacher as facilitator and supporter

Children receiving validation

What Are Your Questions and Wonderings?

Was this part of the curriculum?

Did this project carry over into the personal lives of children and teachers?

Does the teacher ever give the right answers?

What happened to the cotton oil comment?

Was the mechanism of smell followed up on?

What were the parents' reactions?

How were the groups chosen?

How long did this all take?

Was there parent involvement?

What were the other children doing?

Were "bad" smells addressed?

Did the teachers notice the effect of different smells on children?

Did different smells influence their behavior?

Did the Bloodhound Game transfer to other animals?

Did the children refer to the teachers for answers?

What happened to the potpourri?

Did you explore smells in relation to other "languages"?

Did you go into other senses?

Where did the project go?

What Do You Speculate That Children Are Learning?

They are learning to discriminate in an area that is not prominent; we don't pay much attention to smell.

They are putting scents together with their memories and using many descriptive words to do so.

They are learning that scent is not talked about much but that it is very
  present.

They are learning about scents as a "language."

They are exploring how smell works.

They are beginning a study of physiology and anatomy.

They are learning about cause and effect.

They are isolating one sense and "thinking" with it.

They are learning to discover through one sense.

Smelling is hard. Making associations is often subtle. They are learning to
  do it.

They are using other senses to help them, like the visual and tactile. It is
  hard to isolate one sense.

They are learning to stretch using language, to use descriptive words and
  metaphors.

They are feeling valued.

They are learning to be comfortable expressing their own ideas.

They are learning to learn in a group; they are building on one anothers'
  ideas.

Drawing the Way the Scent Moves

The next phase of the project was launched following another meeting of the teachers. As part of a declaration of intent, Karen, Melissa, and Chuck had included a mutual
curiosity about children's theories: How might the teachers elicit children's theories?
How could teachers support children in formulating and articulating their theories
about how some part of life works?

Already they had played with theories in the scent explorations. Children and
teachers had stumbled on them. Was this the time to ask the children about their ideas
about scent and how it comes to be or how the nose works?

Chuck wanted to involve the graphic language in the mix of experiences. He
had a feeling that the children might sneak up on theories through using pencils and
pens to follow scents. He was not interested in asking children to "draw" fragrances.
He wanted to provide a context in which children might discover more about their
experience of smell. He and the teachers thought carefully about how such a context
might be created, what it might look like. After brainstorming together, they dreamed
up the following game.

Chuck and/or C. C. would again work with groups of four children at a time.
They would use flowers with a distinct fragrance as a provocation. The children and
the teacher would place a vase of flowers on a central table in the studio. Then, the
group would move to the door of the room farthest away from the flowers. Chuck
would ask, "Can you smell the flowers?" The group would then move a little closer
and stop. Each time they inched a little closer, the teacher would ask, "Now can you
smell the flowers?" When they finally got to the table, the teachers would ask, "Can
you show with your pen the way that the scent moves?" What follows is the story of
one day as I have heard Chuck tell it.

Chuck always begins by saying, with a longing laced with thrill in his voice,
"I have had many exciting days in the studio with children, but this is one of the most
amazing to me. I would die to have a video of the morning, but since I don't, I will do
my best to convey what happened to you in slides and with the children's words."

I had a group of girls, including Lindsay, Nicole, and Samantha. A parent had volunteered to purchase a bouquet of flowers from the grocery store: pink-and-yellow-striped alstroemeria, white and lavender chrysanthemums, and pink carnations. I began with the girls in a circle in the studio around a table covered with white butcher-block paper and the flowers. As we had asked many times by now, of different things in different contexts, I said, "How do these flowers smell to you?"

Lindsay: They smell like honey.

Samantha: Strawberries.

Nicole: Sunshine and grapes (referring to the purple chrysanthemums).

Samantha: Cream and strawberries.

Lindsay: Garden berries.

Chuck: Do you think if we stand way over by the door we will be able to smell them?

Girls: Yes!

Chuck: Well, let's go try. (Chuck and the girls walk excitedly over to the door.) Can you smell the flowers from way over here?

Girls: No. (Disappointed but very thrilled just the same, they inch a little closer, a company of one teacher and four small girls moving in synchrony with their curiosity led by five noses.)

Chuck: Now can you smell them?

Samantha: No, here we go again. (They creep closer.) Now we can smell them! Now the smell is here!

Chuck: How do you think the smell gets from the flowers all the way over to your nose?

Nicole: The breathing comes all the way over here and comes all the way back. (She gestures to her nose and breathes in and out as she walks to the flowers and then back to her original place as she explains her idea.)

Lindsay: The smell stays over here (pointing to the flowers on the table). Our smells go over there and bring the smells back. And if you put the flowers in the middle, it goes here and here (pointing in two directions). If you put it to the side, it goes this way. The smell goes sideways and backwards and frontwards.

I was so taken with what the girls were saying. They were all talking about breath moving out to get the smell and bring it back and about the flowers smelling us as well as us smelling the flowers! Their ideas seemed connected to one another and somehow cyclical and reciprocal. It was as if they were feeling their way into the sense of it all as they moved around the flowers and the fragrances.

I asked them if they thought they could show with the pens and pencils on the paper that covered the table on which the vase was placed how the scents moved. I was full of excitement and anticipation myself. I think that they could feel that. The girls began to draw lines of all kinds in fluid, flowing gestures, using markers and pencils. They wanted to fill the whole paper with lyrical lines, and they did. They began to dance and to sing as they drew.

Then, this is what Lindsay said, as if in a reverie: "What goes around (making circles around the base of the vase in a duet with her friend) is bows, and ribbons and clay and blankies. To the rest of your life should be the colors. And these kinds of colors make around and around. The pink and the purple go together; as long as you can breathe they go together. And now the fun begins—the smells are dancing" (see Plate 9).

I was just stunned at this point. I watched as the girls decided to go and get pastel chalks from the shelves. I had not anticipated this or even thought of pastels for this experience. Yet, familiar with the studio, the girls knew where they were and how to use them. I think they instinctively felt that they needed a softer material to show the way the fragrances move. Lines were not enough.

Theories Take Shape

Chuck and C. C. continued to work with small groups playing this game of asking and showing with materials how the scents moved out and around from real flowers. Within this process the children continued to speculate about breathing, scents, air, and the connections between their body and its capacities and the world and how we know it.

The four teachers met again to review all that had happened in the graphic experiences with Chuck and C. C. They all felt that the children might be ready to formulate theories about how smelling works. Karen, however, felt that she wanted to give them one more strong experience of isolating the sense of smell. She proposed that she would like to play another kind of game with the children in small groups. It would be a blindfold game, in which she would ask the children in the group if any of them would like to put on a blindfold and to try to guess what she was doing.

When she introduced the game to the children, most of them wanted to participate. Those who did not want to play could participate by observing. In fact, the children who observed participated in the conversation and were an integral part of the experience. The following is an excerpt from a transcript of one such experience with three children: David, Eliza, and Sara. At this point, David was blindfolded and the other two children were observing the situation. Karen began cutting an onion in front of him.

Karen: What do you think I'm doing?
David: Yuck. What is this? It's an onion. I smelled it.
Karen: How did David know that it was an onion?
David: Because I smelled it.
Karen: How does smelling work?
David: The smell comes in your nose and comes out.
Eliza: It comes in your nose and out your mouth!
Karen: How did the smell get from the onion to your nose?
David: It comes out of the onion to my nose.
Sara: A tiny germ!
David: The smell just got there.
Eliza: Maybe a piece of onion goes into your nose.
David: I didn't feel it.
Eliza: Then it comes out your mouth!
Sara: A tiny, tiny, tiny piece.
Karen: How does smelling work?
Sara: I have no idea.
Eliza: I guess onion pieces come into your nose and say, "Hello! This is onion!"
David: "This is Mr. Onion Head!"
Eliza: Maybe the onion says, "Hello, hello, hello."

After all the children had experienced the blindfold game in a small group, more discussion and opportunities to both draw and verbally narrate theories ensued. In small groups with Karen, the children began to develop ideas and flesh out theories as they continued to respond to questions that were, by this time, their own questions. How does smell get to your nose? How does smelling work? Does everything have a smell? The following five theories illustrate the kind of thinking that the children engaged in during this process.

Robbie invented two theories. The first includes a figure drawing and a looping line from the nose to the outside of the figure and back again (see Figure 5.9). Robbie explains:

> The smell goes into your mouth. It goes to your tummy, then it goes out of your legs, and then it goes back in your mouth and up through your nose to your brain. The brain memorizes what went into it. The brain tells you that it can't forget unless it goes to sleep. Your brain does not go to sleep.

In a second theory, Robbie follows his first line of thinking about the brain (see Figure 5.10). He narrates how the brain and smelling are connected:

> This giant thing is a brain. All the words like *food* and *old school*—these are memories. The memories are locked in my brain so they can't get out. The number 3 boings down and boings into your legs, and your brain tells your mouth to say, "It smells like lemon."

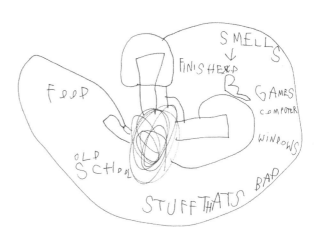

FIGURE 5.9. Robbie's Theory 1   FIGURE 5.10. Robbie's Theory 2

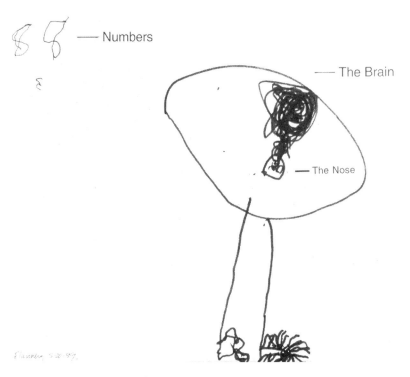

FIGURE **5.11.**   Flannery's Theory

Flannery develops another complex idea with words and images (see Figure 5.11). He explains:

> The smell goes up into the brain. The brain goes in circles and circles around the eyes until it remembers the smell. Then it goes ding and you remember it. The place in your brain where memory is is right between your eyes. You have to smell real hard to get the smell out of it. The one you already smelled goes out of the nose, and the one that you are smelling goes in the nose. These numbers are how old the smell stays. It can stay for 8 months and then you have to smell it again. Not 8 months for tunafish— forever for tunafish, because I love tunafish. I think the brain is made out of some kind of plastic. The nose is made of skin and bones. Smell is made out of fruit and everything else that I smell.

Like Robbie, Lindsay develops two different yet complementary theories. She explains the first in this way (see Figure 5.12):

> The air is trying to find the particular smell of the lemon. It touches the lemon. The smell is running through the lemon. The air is trying to find the juice. The air is dropping the juice into your nose. You can't see it and you can't feel it because it is teeny, tiny drops. The air takes the teeny, tiny drops, and it brings the juice up to your forehead to get smart. Then the

drops go to your head and your muscles and your heart. You are strong once you smell the lemon.

In her second theory, Lindsay elaborates her ideas about the connection of smell to the heart (see Figure 5.13). She explains her thinking this way:

The bottom lines are the air. The little lines above it are in my body, and they go up and down when I breathe. If you don't breathe, you can't smell. The air goes right across to your lungs. There's a bone there (touching her breastbone); you can feel it. Then the blood picks up the smell and takes it to your heart.

"This is air."

Lemon

FIGURE **5.12.** Lindsey's Theory 1

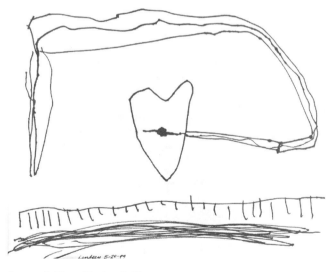

FIGURE **5.13.** Lindsey's Theory 2

As a culmination of this project, the children and teachers compiled a book about the experiences that they had lived together. The book includes transcripts of conversations, explanations of the sequence of events by the teachers, both color and black-and-white photographs, and at least one theory of each child rendered in graphics and in words. Each family was given a copy of the book on the Scent Project at the end of the year.

The children, along with C. C. and Chuck, planned another gift for their families to accompany the book. Each child chose among various dried fragrances to compose a potpourri that was placed in a small bag and tied with a ribbon. Each child made a clay potpourri pot that was fired in the kiln. These were wrapped in boxes with a card made by each child to give to his or her parents on the last day of school. The year following the Scent Project, the teachers at the St. Michael School composed a small in-house publication about it that is for sale at the school.

Meaning Making

As you read earlier in this section, when hearing about the Scent Project educators and parents often ask questions such as "Did you tell them the right answer?" "Did they ask you for the right answer?" "Isn't it misleading to leave them with multiple theories and not tell them the right answer?" These questions are as unsettling as they are completely natural. They come out of our familiar, mechanistic, rational, "teacher has the knowledge" worldview. In relation to the children's scent theories, these questions put us in a state of disequilibrium. When we read the children's theories, we sense multiple worldviews that have emerged in a context that is rich with authentic questions, provocative experiences, and deep listening; that is, the theories have evolved in an ecological context. They represent "networks nesting within other networks" (Capra, 1996, p. 35). The theories are small pieces of the "systems revolution"!

In regard to the "right answer" question, I cannot resist quoting Capra again:

> What makes it possible to turn the systems approach into a science is the discovery that there is approximate knowledge. This insight is crucial to all of modern science. The old paradigm is based on the Cartesian belief of certainty in scientific knowledge. In the new paradigm it is recognized that all scientific concepts and theories are limited and approximate. Science can never provide any complete and definitive understanding. (p. 41)

To follow Capra's thinking, I looked up *smell* in an encyclopedia. I found these phrases used: "physiologists think," "it is thought that," "perhaps," ". . . is not yet known." It is fascinating to me how much about smell was stated as provisional and uncertain. So, what is the "right answer" to the question "How does smelling work?" It seems that there isn't one.

Add to this apparent open scientific question the following observation. In the chapter "Characterizing the Osmic Dimension," Ceppi and Zini (1998), write:

> The olfactory sense communicates with the most "ancient" part of the brain (the rhinencephalon) . . . therefore, [our] deepest and most direct emotions are associated with smell. The perception of an odor has strong evocative potential, as it can immediately awaken the image and memory of place. (p. 84)

With all this in mind, isn't it even more astounding how grounded the children's theories are? They intuit and wonder about the elements that must play together in order for us to smell, about the role that memory plays in smelling, about the evocative nature of fragrance in our lives, and about the way bodily and environmental systems interact and function. Their theories are rooted in their personal experiences, in systemic thought, and in their willingness to put together, often exuberantly, a collection of very different, cohesive theories. Because the context was fertile, their thinking was alive. Because they felt a surrounding sense of safety, energy, and possibility, they became a team of scientists, composers, performance artists, authors, and inventors. They could live with the idea that they had different theories, and that fact enriched everyone's thinking about the question. Lindsay and Robbie each had two theories. The second time, they each elaborated and focused in on one part of their first theory. Given the context, why wouldn't they want to keep going deeper with ideas, beyond first thoughts? Why not keep envisioning possibilities in ever-new combinations out of the elements of one's experience?

Throughout, the children and the teachers were creating relationships with the questions. I see each episode of this project as yet another context in which to create relationships with the questions, with the experiences, with the smells themselves, and with each other. The relationships come to the foreground. The separate parts and players recede to the background. The children are on a quest for meaning, for ways to make sense of their shared experiences and investigations. The teachers are on a similar quest, thinking and wondering about what they witness and thinking again about how to continue.

I love Carlina Rinaldi's definitions of *to learn*. They lure us toward a new way of thinking. I have heard her say, "To learn is to change, to be changed." To me, this implies that real learning is more than accumulation or assimilation; authentic learning pulls us toward evolution and transformation. Another of Carlina's definitions is this: "to know something is to love something." A friend writes that, "When I first heard Carlina Rinaldi say this, I thought that it was the oddest definition of knowledge that I had ever heard. I now understand it to mean something like, 'without deep attachment, an impact on identity, there is no such thing as knowledge.' Or, 'information without a commitment of mind is useless.' "

I think it is fair to say that every child and adult involved in the story of the Scent Project has constructed a deeper, more complex, more wondrous, more informed, more poetic, more curious relationship with smells and fragrances and with one another than they had before. I remember Vincent Kenny's observation of the little girl on the Sardinian beach and Vea Vecchi's comment about the girls who had written messages to their adopted tree, Mil. I remember Walt Whitman's words about our vivid sensory relationships with the world as they become part of us "for a day, or for a part of the day, or for many years or stretching cycles of years." I marvel at the far reaches of the connections that Lindsay makes as she shows the way the fragrances of flowers move with pen and chalk as she sings and dances:

> What goes around (making circles around the base of the vase in a duet with her friend) is bows, and ribbons and clay and blankies. To the rest of your life should be the colors. And these kinds of colors make around and around. The pink and the purple go together; as long as you can breathe they go together. And now the fun begins—the smells are dancing.

CHAPTER 6

June

Returning to Italy

I feel fortunate to be traveling to Reggio Emilia this spring with my good friend and *atelier* room parent Kathleen Sprong. I am thrilled that she will be able to see the school environments, see the children in action, meet the teachers, and meet Italian parents. I wonder what it will be like to experience all these things through her fresh eyes.

On many other trips to Reggio Emilia I have happily accepted the responsibilities of interpreting and organizing logistics for groups of educators, most often with colleagues from St. Louis. Every one of these trips from St. Louis has carried gifts of its own, moved us forward, challenged and enticed us to continue on our own journey to grow as American educators. I expect the week that Kathleen and I will spend in Reggio Emilia will be filled with surprises and delights as well as challenges and that both of us will return with treasures to share with the parents, the teachers, and the children. Though I am honored to help in any way I can with visiting groups, I relish the chance to feel more free on this trip, free to focus on our experience as a teacher and a parent learning in partnership.

DAY 1: MEETING THE TOWN AND THE GROUP

After our overnight flight, we arrive in Milan in time to catch one of the buses at Malpenza airport that will transport the 250 participants on this unusually large study tour to Reggio Emilia. Along with most of the rest of the people on the bus, Kathleen and I sleep during the better part of the hour-and-a-half journey. I open my eyes just as the bus pulls up in front of the Hotel Astoria, the central location for presentations during the week. Suddenly, I realize where we are.

"That's where I lived!" I point up to the apartment building across the street from the hotel. "Look up to the third floor with the skinny balcony," I say to Kathleen, who is stretching as she slowly opens her eyes, "And there's the fruit and vegetable lady, Teresa, and Francesco, the barber, in those shops underneath that open out to the piazza. I'll introduce you to them later."

We shuffle off the bus with other passengers to greet Paola Ricco, one of the coordinators of the study tour. "Ciao, Luisa!" she exclaims, smiling, handing us our packets for the week inside yellow canvas bags emblazoned with the Reggio Children logo—three child-rendered galloping horses in profile in red and blue. Because we registered rather late in the spring, there was not a room inside the city for us this first night. Kathleen and I are staying in a small hotel just outside the center of town that Paola Ricco suggested.

It is 12:30 P.M. Italian time when we arrive at the hotel. Though tired, we are too excited to rest and head for a restaurant right next to the hotel. We are directed to one of the many tables covered with white tablecloths, and our young waitress explains the choices of the day because it seems there is no written menu. She tells us that we could have *cappelletti in brodo,* a local specialty featuring ground meat and cheese inside half-inch curled triangular twists of pasta floating in a slow-cooked broth. There are also *tortelli verdi* or *tortelli di zucca.*

"I'd like to try the *cappelletti,*" says Kathleen, looking at me and then up to the waitress.

"*Prendiamo tortelli verdi per me e cappelletti in brodo per la mia amica, due insalate verde, e vino bianco, mezzo bottiglia,*" I say in anticipation, as my mouth shapes itself around the Italian syllables. I relish this—our first meal in Italy, celebrating our safe arrival and the opportunity we have before us.

When the food is placed before us, I love looking at Kathleen's face as she tastes the tender *cappelletti* and the clear, flavorful broth. I share her delight as I enjoy the first morsel of *tortelli.* These are the tastes that I dream about when I am in St. Louis.

After lunch, we wander into town on foot for a tour. It is around 2:30 now, and the streets are quiet because the shops are closed for the afternoon. They'll open up at 4:00 or so. We stroll in the public gardens, which are filled with the heady fragrance of the tigli blossoms on the trees that line the ample paths that border the several-acre green space. The temperature is pleasant. I show Kathleen my route from our apartment in Piazza Valdisneri through the Astoria parking lot and the park, which the Italians call the Giardini Publici (public gardens), to the Diana School. I remember the first time that I discovered the school on my first trip here on a similar quiet afternoon. Here it is in the middle of a city park, low-roofed and almost camouflaged, unassuming under the arching branches of a stately cedar.

Today, there are official-looking men in black suits outside of the school and several shiny black cars. We find out later that the U.N. Committee on the Rights of

Children is meeting here. They have come to view firsthand the exceptional schools that have gained such international fame.

We wander in and out of quiet streets. Every once in a while a solitary biker rides by, tires thumping on cobblestones. We stop in Piazza Fontenasi, with its black-and-white square tiles and shade trees planted in a grid pattern. We eat lemon sherbet cones sitting on the benches in the afternoon sun, watching a group of children play hopscotch on the squares. Time seems to float and suspend itself inside the sunny, quiet afternoon and the sharp taste of citrus (see Figure 6.1).

That night we are greeted by Amelia Gambetti and Paola Ricco in the huge conference room on the basement floor of the Astoria. They explain the week carefully and enthusiastically. I find some friends that I am delighted to see—Jeanne Goldhaber from the University of Vermont; Susan Lyon from Mills College in Oakland, California; Angela Ferrario, liaison for delegations to Reggio Emilia, who is helping to organize our week; Penny Fahlman from Shady Lane in Pittsburgh; Judy Graves from Portland, Oregon; Lilian Katz from the University of Illinois; and other educators who have visited our schools in St. Louis. Amelia and Paola give us the warmest of welcomes to their city and to the schools. All 250 of us are thrilled to be here and glad to be together. We anticipate the week ahead with excitement and gratitude.

DAY 2: A NEW VIEW OF SCHOOL

Kathleen and I sleep very well in the room on the outskirts of town. We begin the day in the breakfast room downstairs with yogurt; fresh, warm croissants with strawberry

FIGURE **6.1.**   Roof Line, Reggio Emilia, Italy

jam; and cappuccini in thick, white china cups. Again, we are treated to the delicious custom of a simple Italian meal. At 8:30 we take a cab to the Astoria with our bags.

The morning begins in the Astoria conference room, which will be the home of the big group for the week. Amelia greets us all with a warm, friendly smile, "Good Morning. Did you sleep well? Are you ready for the day? This morning we will hear from Sergio Spaggiari, the director of the Municipal Schools in Reggio Emilia."

As Sergio begins to speak, I think of my first encounter with him in his office in the spring of 1991. I was asking permission to come to Reggio as an intern for the year in 1991–1992. I had written an official letter in the fall of 1990, but this was our first face-to-face meeting. I remember that he seemed reluctant to agree. I told him that I was good at being a fly on the wall, that I would not ruffle the environment or be intrusive. He responded immediately, "But we don't like flies on the wall. We feel we might like to swat them!" Much to my surprise, shortly after that alarming statement, he informed me right then and there that I could come with my family for the year.

Over the years I have not spent a great deal of time with Sergio, though my impression is that he has become more and more articulate and passionate about the work he supervises. His address to us today is a good example of this. He greets us and begins to speak in Italian with no notes in front of him. We can feel the intention and emotion in his voice as he develops a comfortable pace with the interpreter. He tells us that he believes humanity has greatly undervalued the extraordinary strengths and potential of children. He quotes Dewey ("Knowledge is research, not accumulation") and Bruner ("Meanings are constructed, not received"). He calls us to become an indispensable support for children to make meaning for themselves.

He quotes Plutarch: "The job of a teacher is not to fill sacks but to light fires." Again, Sergio call us to keep this fire alive inside us "almost like an obsession—the fire of curiosity, amazement, wonder, fascination, passion." He reminds us that we are still ignorant and that we have much to learn. One way to learn is to know what Saint-Exupery's *Little Prince* knew—"what is essential escapes our view." Through paying close attention to children and what they do, we find pleasure and joy, wonder and curiosity in the new things that come out day by day.

Sergio continues with a second theme—solidarity and cooperation. His tone invites us to think of a new way of being in school. "It is through dialogue and exchange that we become more curious and desire to learn more. Where we do not work together, we waste our energies and our strength." He cites Bateson's work on systems.

Sergio concludes his speech with this powerful provocation:

> Be like the bees. They do not copy. They go to the flowers for what they need, but they make honey in their own home. Make honey in your own schools. If you want to be like us, don't copy us. We have never copied anyone. If you want to be like us, be original. (Spaggiari, S., 2000)

Spontaneously, we rise to our feet and clap. We are moved by Sergio's words, by his direct and heartfelt delivery, by his call to action. His speech provides a terrifically energetic beginning to the week. I am struck to hear what seem like the essences of the Reggio Approach distilled and presented so succinctly in these pithy sentences. Also, I appreciate the short, to-the-point references to Dewey, Bruner, Plutarch, Bateson, and Saint-Exupery. Sergio draws on the wisdom of scholars from the distant past as well as recent thinking across disciplines. I am challenged by Sergio's last statements. I think to myself, "What does it mean to 'copy'? Are we 'copying' the Reggio Approach in St. Louis? What would it look like to be inspired by these ideas and be completely original?"

Clapping along with us, Amelia steps up to the podium. As we settle, she thanks Sergio and asks us to go to the discussion groups that we have been assigned to. She suggests that we introduce ourselves; tell something about our background; and share impressions of the town, of one another, and of Sergio's speech. This afternoon we will meet back here to go off to various schools to tour environments and meet with teachers.

Dialogue Groups

I make my way to a small room crowded with chairs arranged in a circle on the third floor of the Astoria. We take our seats and begin. As we all introduce ourselves, we realize that our group of 25 represents a huge range of geographic and professional affiliations. Together we span the continent—from Alaska to Manhattan, from Vermont to California, from Wisconsin to Georgia. In many different career tracks, we are politicians, *atelieristi,* art teachers, administrators, elementary and preschool teachers, special needs teachers, graduate students, teacher educators, educational coordinators. In age we range from 22 to 72. We teach in public and private schools, in Head Start programs, and in universities.

As individuals begin to speak, the following issues emerge: We need to have courage to take action and to put some of these ideas into effect; we need to realize our own image as powerful; we need to take that power into the political arena; we have a responsibility to be visible, to transform our undervalued image of ourselves and make our new image public; we need to acknowledge that teaching is a political and moral act. Are we repressing children's thinking, or are we supporting it to the fullest extent? We continue with questions. What are the essences of this approach? What does it mean to use Sergio's analogy of the bees in our lives as teachers? As a collective, we are energized, telling stories of both frustrations and triumphs from our personal experiences.

The hour goes by quickly, and we are asked to return to the large conference room to share briefly with the whole group. One by one the facilitators speak from the podium, sharing a few important thoughts from their group dialogue. I begin to synthesize the energy that Sergio elicited in our group to take on a powerful identity as educators and see our role as change makers. I shared our questions: How do we see ourselves as bees creating our own honey, as educators taking inspiration from powerful values and ideals that we, too, embrace and living them within in our own context?

Next, Jeanne Goldhaber suggests that we might think of the stories, ideas, and experiences of the week as individual beads that we might string on a metaphorical power bracelet to take home with us. She names a few of the beads that her group has already strung: one stands for the idea that it is worthwhile to take one's time, to ponder, to reflect, to imagine, to enjoy; another stands for wonder as an essential part of being alive; another proposes that what is possible for children in Reggio Emilia might also be possible for adults.

Judy Graves summarizes the ideas of her group: These are real people here, who speak from their hearts; we wonder what it is really like to be part of this community; we see that teaching here is a political act, that everyone's voices are heard.

Lilian Katz explains that her group considered the idea of listening. What is the difference between hearing and listening? If you are listening to children, what are you listening for? How can we begin to listen effectively and to share what we discover with our colleagues?

I like the idea from Jeanne's group of creating metaphorical "power bracelets" to take home. This image works well. I can see that Kathleen and I will be stringing thoughts, ideas, and questions together in order to make a collection of bracelets to wear and to share with our teacher and parent colleagues in St. Louis. We have had a full morning, and we are all still a little tired from traveling. Amelia thanks us all and suggests that we break now for lunch. We will resume at 3:00, when we will venture off in different directions to visit schools after the children have gone home.

Scuola Allende

Kathleen and I board one of the large, comfortable buses that are headed toward several schools; each of us is going to a different school so that we can compare notes later. I join the group of 15 that will tour Allende, a school that I have never visited before. After 10 minutes or so, we arrive at the school, which is on the periphery of town in the center of playing fields and what looks like community gardens. We are welcomed by several teachers and parents and invited to look around the school at our leisure. We will gather for a snack later in the afternoon.

It feels good to be inside a school and to wander freely in the physical space. It breathes with openness and care and speaks of the teachers, children, and families who live here. On the inside the building is crafted with natural wood, more so than I have noticed in other schools that I have visited. I imagine that it has the feel of a school one might find in Scandinavia or Switzerland. In several rooms there are natural pine dividers that define smaller areas within the larger space. In others, sturdy wooden lattices hang from the ceiling, marking the space of a mini-*atelier*. In some classrooms, polished, unpainted oak shelves hold natural materials of all kinds, and decorative half-shelves displaying clay figures hang on the walls. In addition to wood, I notice raffia and grasses, seeds and leaves, wicker and baskets. The school reflects the surrounding environment, open and textural in muted colors of buff and chestnut, umber and auburn.

In my notebook, I begin to sketch ideas about the space and the materials that I do not want to forget. I am savoring this time to look and to see, to notice and to take note, to be quiet and reflective, appreciative and slow. My eyes travel around the room that I am in (which I think belongs to the 3- and 4-year-old children) and stop to rest on a mobile hanging from the ceiling. With my pen, I loosely render the triangle of heavy wire that supports four thin copper wires about 2 feet long from which various configurations of what one might call "sculptural collages" are suspended. Working from top to bottom, I sketch a circle of brass wire with metal nuts strung on it, a collection of finger-sized fired red clay coils, a steel wire strung with pearls of different colors, a nest of wire, and balls of fired clay. All these pieces gently twirl in the breeze that drifts across the room from the wide-open waist-to-ceiling window in the corner.

I continue making simple drawings and adding descriptive words and phrases. As always, the process of seeing and drawing enables me to notice the way things hang together, the actual curve of a wire, the simple sheen of metal, the matte of terra-cotta. Following the particular shapes of things and the connections among them with my eye and pen allows me to fix these things in my mind's eye. I know that these simple lines, along with the descriptive phrases that I jot down, will bring these experiences back when I revisit them, perhaps much more vividly than a photograph.

I wend my way to the back of the school into the room of the 4- and 5-year-olds. What an irresistible scene I come upon as I enter the space. A door, open wide to the outside, allows the sun in and the afternoon breeze to circulate. Near the open door, in a circle of sunlight on a raffia rug, a small wicker table is set with a blue-checked tablecloth. Matching napkins, silverware, china cups and saucers, and a tiny *caffetiera* (a stove-top espresso maker) are arranged on the table. Two wicker chairs welcome whoever would fit into them to an afternoon tea party. I wish I were small enough (see Figure 6.2).

In this same room a mirrored table in the corner reflects a glass vase of red field poppies and a collection of inks to paint them with. Variegated philodendron stems and leaves cascade down from the pots on the rafters on which they perch. My attention moves toward cool shadowy shapes that illuminate the middle portion of a center wall. I look for the source and find blue and green bottles placed on their sides on an overhead projector. Along this same wall I gaze at a dressing table housing a collection of diminutive glass bottles in many warm and cool colors. Glass beads hang on the corner of a big mirror, about 3 feet by 4 feet, framed in dark mahogany above the dressing table. Several educators drift in and out as I sketch these things. The atmosphere is hushed, the pace relaxed.

With the time remaining, I go to find the *atelier*, where I find more spaciousness and natural materials displayed and used in unusual and pleasing ways. An oversized loom made out of bamboo poles is woven with grape vines from local vineyards and twine strung with dried lemon slices. Fresh pink-rose and deep-cherry peony petals spread across a glass-topped table. On the floor, a square wooden-framed box with low sides is filled with yellow corn meal, small pieces of bark, hazel nuts and chestnuts, gray-green leaves and smooth white stones. These natural elements are arranged in mandala forms spreading out from the center of the square.

The door opens out to an outdoor *atelier* terrace. The same large windows that are in the other rooms swing open to let in the light and fresh air. For a moment I feel

little round table with wicker chairs in open door. Set with china cups, spoons and coffee maker. On raffia rug, with linen table cloth ..

FIGURE 6.2.   Sketch of Wicker Table Set for a Tea Party at Scuola Allende

as if I have come upon a Zen garden. All the elements complement one another. There is plenty of space in which to think and imagine. The whole scene feels at once calm, provocative, and peaceful.

I think about our *atelier* at the College School. Is it too full? Is there enough space to think, to imagine, to dream? I will take this place back home with me and consider my own with new eyes. I remember Sergio's speech from this morning. I will be like the bees. I will collect the images and atmospheres here as the bees take pollen from flowers. I will use them to make honey in my own home with my own hive of bees.

DAY 3: THEORY AND PRACTICE

We begin the next day feeling more rested and grounded than we felt yesterday morning. Amelia greets us again with her usual good humor in front of an audience. She cajoles us, talks to us, makes us laugh, and then she introduces Carlina Rinaldi, now pedagogical consultant to the Municipal Infant–Toddler Centers and Preschools.

We are ready for Carlina. Many of us have heard her before, and she is always provocative. She creates a wide context for the work we are witnessing and the concepts behind the thinking of the Reggio educators. It is not always easy to understand the ideas that she presents. They sometimes sound simple, yet they are far-reaching and profound. Carlina begins by reminding us that when we say that we "understand" something, it means that we have developed a theory. She says, "Our theories are really satisfactory explanations that provide answers to the 'whys' of daily life, and all theories are temporary; they can be continually expanded" (Rinaldi, 2000a).

She explains that it is critical to ask children questions because in doing so we are "offering them the possibility of collecting and to putting together all the thoughts and questions that are there in mind, perhaps, to date, unexpressed" (Rinaldi, 2000a). Carlina continues to help us see that adults' and children's search for answers fulfills an aesthetic, intellectual, and emotional need that we are born with. She echoes and extends Sergio's thoughts from yesterday: Our job as teachers is to learn; we must transform our schools from schools of teaching to schools of learning. Carlina tells us that in order to listen we must "welcome difference and uncertainty and welcome many truths." This means that if we truly listen, we will change. Carlina ends her speech with these comments:

> All we can do in life is to offer our interpretation of events. And we need the listening of others in order to do this. In listening to each other, it is as if we create an invisible connection between us that allows us each to become who we are. The threads of listening among us form a pattern that connects us to others like a web. Our individual knowledge is a small part of the meaning that holds the universe together. (Rinaldi, 2000a)

When Carlina finishes, we rise to our feet and clap. I remember her speech earlier this year at Mills College. These ideas are connected to those that Carlina spoke to us about in March in California when she told us that the educators and the community members of Reggio Emilia have chosen to value subjectivity and differences, participation and democracy, play, enjoyment and emotions, learning and continual personal and professional development. Today, as we struggle to understand the full meaning of what Carlina has said, every person in the room feels inspired by her dedication to share with others these complex and very real ideas that drive the work here even as they continue to evolve in theory and in practice. I take one sentence, in particular, to string on my metaphorical bracelet: "Our individual knowledge is a small part of the meaning that holds the universe together." This is another of Carlina's Zen-like *koans*—not a logical thought, but rather an idea for contemplation.

Vea Vecchi—Theater Curtain: The Ring of Transformation

This afternoon both Kathleen and I have signed up to hear a presentation by Vea Vecchi. She will present the story of a group of children and teachers as they meet the challenge of designing an image for a curtain in one of the town's principal historical theaters, the Ariosto. I am eager to hear Vea and to see the images that she will share with us. I am also ecstatic to be able to share this experience with Kathleen.

There are nine other presentations for this afternoon, making the group size for each about 25 people. This part of the organization of the study tour amazes me. It strikes me as a distinct privilege to be part of a relatively intimate group in this setting with Vea. I am sure that the other members of the delegation feel the same way. The pace and rhythm of both big- and small-group events is skillfully orchestrated; we feel part of small-group experiences, and, at the same time, feel a part of a big, powerful body of educators.

After lunch, we find the appointed room for our group on the ground floor of the Astoria. Vea arrives, and we greet each other warmly. The interpreter soon strikes a good rhythm with Vea, who takes off at a rapid pace in Italian, giving us the background to the project. Vea explains that this project grew out of many years of collaboration among community members, institutions of the city, and the schools. She tells us that a recent interest on the part of teachers and children in attending local plays and performances in the nearby theaters had coincided with an idea that perhaps a group of children from the Diana School might be able to design a curtain for the Ariosto Theater. Local artists had designed other curtains; maybe the children could also make a contribution. Every year they celebrate the birthday of Loris Malaguzzi with a special event. This could be a marvelous gift presented at the celebration from the schools and the children.

The teachers realized that this adventure would be full of challenges, but they decided to go ahead. They started out with all 25 5- and 6-year-old children at the Diana School, although toward the end a group of 8 children worked as the final authors of the curtain image. First the children explored the outside of the theater in small groups. The teachers observed their exuberant movement—running in between the great columns, "feeling the rhythm of the architecture with their bodies, the empty spaces and the full spaces, the light and the shadow." Vea reminds us that if we understand children's autonomous strategies of understanding, such as this one, then we, as teachers, will be able to use them when other situations present themselves. Then the children and teachers entered into the silent theater, which was illuminated just for them; the children were enthralled. Remembering the children's way of exploring the outside of the building, Vea suggested that they follow the circumferance of the theater as well, feeling and following the shape of the whole room with their hands and bodies. The children called it an egg shape, an arch shape, a welcoming shape. When Vea proposed the idea of designing a new curtain for this theater, the children were at once amazed, incredulous, and excited.

After they had taken plenty of time with the exploration of the theater's space and the idea of designing a curtain, the time came to gather their ideas for a subject for the curtain. Back at school, the teachers asked the children what they thought would be appropriate.

The children suggested that they should draw things that are beautiful, important, and interesting, like plants and flowers; perhaps the sun, moon, and stars; maybe grasshoppers and dragonflies; maybe happiness and peace in the world. Vea took this opportunity to stress that when drawing from life, it is important to her that children have enough time and concentration to understand the relationships and connections among the various parts that come together in one subject as well as to establish their own relationship with what they are investigating. This thought reminds me of the work of Victor Lowenfeld (1964) and also of Judith Burton (1991). Vea cites Gregory Bateson, who accuses schools of misinforming students if teachers take away the pulse of life and relationship from things. She asserts, "When children draw from life, our attention should not be focused so much on the likeness to the subject they are drawing as on the fact that the children feel the pulse of life and the vital connections with everything that surrounds them."

Given the perspective of their teachers, the children were supported in envisioning these beautiful and important things that they had suggested as suitable subjects for the curtain, in relationship with one another. As they drew their first renderings, the children could consult books and photographs and, when possible, observe the actual objects they had listed. The children and teachers had collected these resources from around the school.

Vea explained to us that as they were drawing, one boy exclaimed, "My plant is in a phase of transformation; it is getting transformed into something else," as he drew an eye appearing in the middle of a leaf. Vea said, "From time to time, certain comments made by children influence the course of a project and orient it, and this was one of them." I will continue to describe the course of the project through my notes of Vea's words:

Where did he get this idea? Perhaps from games and toys that the children have that transform. They themselves, growing, are in a phase of transformation. Perhaps from television shows where the characters transform. Perhaps from fairy tales. Transformation is halfway between biology and magic. It is very present now in our culture. This is a fascinating idea to us as teachers, too. Colors, forms, and structures do pass on information between living species, the vegetable and animal world, between us and our environment, creating a continuous link among all things.

We asked the children, "What is transformation?" They debated among themselves and then decided, "You need two different things. One thing becomes another thing." Then, after thinking together, they added, "The subject decides when it will transform, and it can decide to go back to its original identity if it wants to." In their drawings we noticed that small parts of the original identity of the subject remained even through the transformation. This seems to indicate a strong intuition on the children's part about energy and matter in the physical world.

Things became difficult and delicate at this point. We had so many drawings that the children had made. How to put them together with sense and significance? We suggested that both groups experiment with two different ways to organize the drawings: one that has become a traditional way for us and one that is relatively new to both adults and children. Using the familiar way of working, they could move their drawings around on a common surface to search for a composition that made sense to them. Using a new way to compose ideas, they could use the computer and the programs of Photoshop and Pagemaker to compose their composite of drawings of beautiful things.

In this period in which we are all trying to understand whether and how digital technology modifies learning, I believe that it is worthwhile to reflect seriously on the process that traditional education permits and facilitates as well as the processes supported and nurtured by digital technology. Only in this way can we investigate an area that is yet unexplored: that of the connections that are created by weaving the two together.

Again, with the computer, it was not so important that we "teach" them how to use it as to observe their strategies for learning. This compares to what we did when they explored the space of the theater. As I said earlier, if we recognize and listen to the strategies that children use in a certain context, we can often make use of those same strategies in other contexts. This way of working transforms our proposals so that they are more in harmony with children's ideas and natural ways of being. With their scanned images of grasshoppers, moons, and galaxies, they pushed the limits of the program. How big could they make the grasshopper? So big that they could only see a small portion of the drawing on the screen. But they discovered that they could manipulate the controls to move it around in order to see other parts of this monster grasshopper. They said, "Come on, get really big! We are looking inside you."

How small could they make the grasshopper? As small as a dot. Could they still see all the parts? How many times could they multiply the image? Many times, they discovered. A multitude of insects crowded onto the screen. And could they overlap them? Yes. The grasshoppers appeared in multiple layers.

We noticed that they constructed little stories as they worked, putting their subjects in relationship to each other. In fact, this way of telling mini-stories as they worked on arrangements and compositions was a similarity between the two groups. Narration was a link between them and a basic support for both.

The teachers made notes at this point and tried to follow the processes of the children in both groups so that we could discuss these things with colleagues later. At this point, we did not know where to go. We actually felt in the dark. We had interesting things, but how were we going to put them on a theater curtain?

It is important to remember that it is not the teacher who conducts the children. The adult lets him- or herself be conducted by the children. During the course of a project, we often find that we need other colleagues' perspectives in order to clarify our ideas. When Malaguzzi was with us, we often asked his opinion in a meeting or even on the telephone. When you see documentation composed about such an experience, it looks streamlined; somehow the sequences seem to flow with ease, and it looks easy. But I want to emphasize that it is not easy. You might take off on a path, and the children are not interested. Sometimes, it feels as if we are in the dark with a lantern trying to understand which way to go.

After much deliberation, we teachers decided to push the accelerator toward narration, the principal avenue that both groups of children had used to put their subjects together. We suggested that one child start off with a story about their subjects, and then another child would continue. We tape-recorded these narratives.

Up until this point, all the children in the class had worked on this project in small groups. We decided, at this juncture, to continue with a smaller group of eight children, four boys and four girls, whom we chose for their interest, skill, competence, and diversity. (We have learned through past experience that to exceed this number means handing over the role of director to the teachers and the role of performer to the children.) The rest of the class continued to work on a book about rules at home and at school, which was a subject that interested them very much.

As we observed the group of four boys tell their story, they began to whisper, "Once there was a butterfly who entered into the sun's energy for the entire winter. Then he changed into a smaller butterfly, and he went to cool off in the moon's room of energy. The energy was so powerful that he changed into a grasshopper. Then a rose transformed into another rose and then into the sun. It is a chain of transformation. A ring of transformation. A ring of energy." We have this on video. It was another moment in which all the waiting and the sequences of experiences and processes seemed to come together. They had arranged all the elements in a ring, all connected and circling. Where did the circular form of the final image for the curtain come from? The circular form of the internal space of the theater, the painting on the ceiling. The strong spatial symmetry of the theater undoubtedly left traces in the children's memory. I would add another hypothisis: How much might the game of ring around the rosy or the repeated rhythm of nursery rhymes have led the children to represent a chain of transformation?

The girls had made an arrangement that was more like a texture. All the plants and animals, sun and moon were separate and lined up, making a pattern. The boys said they liked their own composition better. The girls were not completely happy with this and wanted the whole class to vote between the two. But soon after, in a discussion among themselves, they decided that, indeed, the boys' ring of energy was dynamic and a better choice for the curtain. This seemed an intelligent thing to do, and we teachers were impressed with the girls' choice.

Vea continues to describe with her words and her slide images the next chapters of this project, in which the children worked together in small groups to transfer the design to paint and to a large format that would be used to create a screen print for the actual curtain. They were able to work in a large room on the top floor of the theater itself. When it came time for the celebration of Malaguzzi's birthday, the teachers and children and community members planned a great unveiling with all the children, the artists of the other curtains, town officials, families, and members of the community. The celebration took place on a Saturday, with short commemorative speeches, lots of applause, and, of course, refreshments (see Plate 10).

When Vea finishes her story, all of the educators in the audience sit as if stunned by this work and this presentation. There is no time for questions. Vea tells us that she spent a whole day on this topic in Stockholm earlier this spring and that it is a challenge to condense it into several hours. She also tells us that eventually there will be a book and a video documentary of this project called *Theater Curtain: The Ring of Transformation*.

What does this ambitious project about the curtain offer us? I am enthralled with Vea's emphasis on the difficulty that the teachers faced in choosing which way to go, on her clarity about how in the dark they had felt, and on the necessity of waiting for the children. I am intrigued with the way that the teachers went about studying the children's exploration of the space of the theater and their discoveries of what the computer could do with their images. I think about the kinds of proposals we make to children in St. Louis. I wonder whether we have this intention in the forefront of our minds—to discover children's strategies of exploration, to dedicate ourselves to this, to pay attention.

The final result—the children's ring of energy—presents us with an extraordinary example of children's intuitions about the deep connections among all the parts of the world in which we find ourselves. The circle of energy reminds me of the Buddhist concept of "interbeing—nothing can exist by itself, all things exist as part of an interconnected totality" (Badiner, 1990, p. 242). The ring of energy makes me think of chaos theory in physics, in which physicists describe how all matter and energy are linked together in a cosmic dance thoughout time. It reminds me of mandala forms, and the ancient image of a spiral, and of my son's physics teacher, who explains that we are actually all made of stardust.

Vea's presentation of the curtain is a marvelous illustration of Carlina's speech this morning. Carlina spoke theoretically and passionately about how we all need to formulate and express theories that answer questions about life—interpretations that others will listen to. Vea told a real story about a group of children who have formulated a universe theory, a scientific theory, a fantastic theory that satisfies their emotional, intellectual, and aesthetic needs as vital young explorers of the world.

Now their "answer," in the form of a collective childhood theory, hangs huge in one of the oldest and most beautiful theaters in their city. What will this mean to them as they grow up here? What does it mean to them now? What does it signify for the citizens of Reggio Emilia that these children's answers to life questions—their "ring of energy"—hangs in a significant place of honor among them? As Carlina reminds us, their ring of energy is "a small part of the meaning that holds the universe together." I think of Loris Malaguzzi and the cycles of birthday celebrations that come around each year in his honor. His energy and creativity will continue to live within the children's circle at the Ariosto Theater for many cycles of years.

DAY 4: GOING DEEPER

This is the day when we will travel to the schools in which we will spend the morning observing children and teachers. The afternoon will be a kind of open house, when buses will circulate among the 10 schools that the 10 different groups are visiting this morning. Once again, we are divided into groups of 25, making the visits to schools manageable for the children and teachers and also very pleasant for us.

The Diana School

Kathleen and I have signed up to visit the Diana School. We enter the school and make our way to the *atelier*, where we meet Isabella Meninno, who is the *atelierista* now that Vea has changed roles. As it turns out, Vea's name is also Isabella, but she has been called Vea since she was a little girl. The new Isabella is charming and speaks English very well. When I ask her how she is doing, she tells us that she never imagined the job would be as difficult as it is. However, she says that she loves it and that she was interested in it for a long time. Vea is still helping her, as are the teachers. She understands a little more every day. By this time, other delegates are arriving, and Vea, who has emerged from the small office after finishing a telephone conversation, suggests that we all gather in the *atelier* for a few minutes for a brief orientation before we go off to observe.

We gather around the large square table in the *atelier*, some of us sitting, some standing. In the middle of the table a ceramic, child-made coil pot holds feathery crimson field poppies. At the base of the vase, clay creatures of all kinds crawl on fresh hydrangea leaves, looking like frogs on lily pads. We are surrounded by color and form in clay, paint, photography, graphics, shells, wire, wood, and words.

The exterior door of the *atelier* is open to the schoolyard and the public gardens. Windows continue up from the glass door to the peak of the ceiling. Outside we see the yellow-greens of new leaves on shrubs and the blue-greens of the needles of the cedar of Lebanon sweeping down to the roof of the school.

Vea greets us with warm words and gestures that invite us to freely explore the school. She tells us that there are three classrooms, each with 26 children and two teachers. The ages of the children in the three classrooms are respectively 3 and 4, 4 and 5, and 5 and 6. There is one special needs teacher who works most often with small groups of children in addition to any children with special needs attending the school.

I feel so happy to be in this school with the freedom to wander and enjoy the physical, real world that we heard about in the speeches of Sergio, Carlina, Vea, and the other presenters yesterday. I feel so at home in the Diana School, the place in which I spent much of my internship in 1991–1992. I realize that the organization of the space, the way the morning light falls into the central piazza, the ease with which the teachers and children move around the school, the rhythm of the day—all are a part of me as my memories come flooding back.

The Entryway

Kathleen and I decide to begin together by returning to the entryway of the school, where the information about the school and calendars are located. We want to reconsider our similar Parent Board at the College School. We also think that all the teachers of the St. Louis–Reggio Collaborative will be interested in the organization that we find.

We walk back across the school piazza to the 8-by-15-foot corridor that leads from the public gardens to inside the school. This entry room has glass doors on both ends. One door leads outside; the other, into the school. Posted on a white bulletin board to the right of the entry is a large Community–Early Childhood Council calendar laid out on a large piece of graph paper. The council is made up of a group of elected community members and parents of each school in unlimited numbers as well as the teachers and staff of the school, who attend meetings on a rotating basis. The council's task is to promote co-responsibility of the school families and the community in educational issues and to promote participation of all families. We see that the times and topics of monthly meetings, which are open to the public, are listed here.

Next we study a calendar that is dedicated to events of the Diana School. This calendar is alive with photographs of meetings that have taken place next to the dates on which they occurred. We see that there were three meetings with parents in February, one for each class. Black-and-white, postage-stamp-sized prints from the evenings line up next to the dates.

On March 16 there was a council meeting to which everyone had received a special invitation. They were celebrating the imminent publication of *Reggio Tutta: A Guide to the City by the Children* (Davoli & Ferri, 2000). On March 27, Vea gave a presentation on "The Curtain" to parents from all the schools.

Kathleen and I both have our notebooks open, and we decide who will record what we both notice. "It's interesting that they use contact sheet or small snapshot photos right on the calendar. It connects the dates to real events, and it highlights parent participation. I really like that idea. It brings a calendar alive. It makes it something that looks forward to events as well as a document that records history," Kathleen says as she sketches.

"Making the calendar live. That's an idea to take back on our 'power bracelet of ideas' that Jeanne Goldhaber's dialogue group conceived of," I agree.

Below the calendar information, whimsical black-and-white photographs of the teachers and staff dance across the board, and a nearby mirror invites whoever enters to play with facial expressions as well. I remember that the mirror strips at the College School entrance were inspired by these.

The Room of the 3- and 4-Year-Olds

We decide to move on to the 3- and 4-year-old room, Section A, as there are not too many other visitors there. Just outside the classroom, I am struck by the bold yet simple documentation of a project called "The Sun and the Apple Tree," in which the children adopted a schoolyard tree. I take time to read Vea's introduction to this piece, which is entitled, "Listening." Vea describes children's natural, empathetic relationships with all things and their "ability to grasp the pulsing of life and the connections between living organisms of Earth and Sky." She asserts that, as teachers, we wish to nurture this precious resource of children and to further its development toward an "ecological way of thinking," which she suggests requires "creating vital bridges between elements that are only apparently separate, and the ability to engage in and develop reciprocal listening." Throughout a series of experiences and conversations with words and materials, teachers have posed questions like these to the children: Can you make friends with a tree? How do you do it? Does the tree have friends? Who are they? What do you think the apple tree likes? What doesn't the apple tree like? Are the tree and the sun friends? Why? What about the moon? Vea has reminded me many times that the questions that the teachers ask are based on listening to children's questions and observing children's interactions. They are not random. They are premeditated and organized but also flexible and not necessarily always used in the context of real conversations. It depends on what happens.

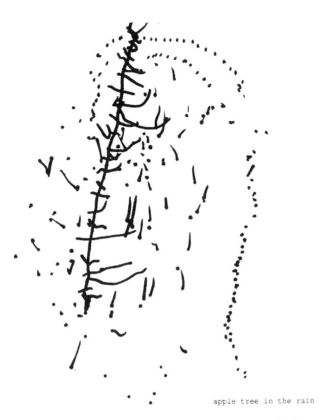

apple tree in the rain

FIGURE **6.3.** The Sun and the Apple Tree Are Friends, from the Diana School

In this project I see again the "pattern that connects"—the focus of the teachers on the relationships among elements as primary. Here the teachers are supporting 3- and 4-year-olds' spontaneous empathy for the elements of the world in which they live. Further, they are following children's thinking and children's theories in development about a special tree and its relationship to them as well as to the cosmos (see Figure 6.3).

I turn from the documentation to the door of the 3- and 4-year-olds' room, which is covered with the names of the children in the class in huge, oversized print. The letters and names almost shout the presence of these small children. As I step into the classroom, I meet the lively group attached to these names face-to-face.

Three or four boys and girls travel around the room building a story that seems based on large tubes, some big enough for them to get inside of, made out of plastic, cardboard, and Plexiglas. Their story, which I do not catch, moves with them, onto a low wooden platform in the corner on one side of the classroom.

A single, very little girl with dark hair and eyes stands at the light table holding red rose petals in one hand and transparent tissue paper in a range of warm hues in the other. Her face glows, illuminated by the light table. She talks softly to herself.

Four children sit around a square table in the middle of the room with a huge block of gray clay and sizable sycamore branches, taller than they are, stretching across the table between them. The children appear to be totally absorbed in attaching bits of clay to the branches. One of the teachers is observing the clay work, taking notes. At a nearby table, four children weave metal squares with holes and copper wire of several gauges into a big wire screen. A second teacher offers them encouragement and help when needed as she keeps an eye on the activity of the other children.

I join Kathleen, who has discovered a group of girls in the housekeeping area, which is tucked away under a draped fabric roof in the far corner of the room. On shelves we take note of a fantastic array of stuff for them to play with: china plates with blue flower patterns, tin molds to make tea cakes, canisters, nesting pots, silverware in a small organizer, tools to make pasta with, a scale to weigh food, a bassinet, a telephone, a makeup tray with a round hand mirror, and colored bottles of all shapes. A collection of perfume bottles and scarves decorates the floor. The girls sit on the floor, too, deep in conversation, trying on scarves, having a grand time.

I think to myself that this does not seem so different from life at home: busy, moving children working with each other and with materials to create worlds and stories. Some of it is being noticed and recorded by teachers, some of it is missed. Happiness and liveliness saturate the room.

We had noticed titles about leaves and sequences of close-up photographs of children exploring leaves on a board on the opposite side of the room. Before moving out of the classroom of the 3-year-olds, we study this piece of documentation. I translate for Kathleen, and she sketches.

The title, "The Language of Leaves," appears in a large font alongside a photograph of children immersed in leaves in the public gardens. The subtitles include "Theories," "Playing with Leaves," "Notes of Synthesis," and "Gifts to Families." We take time to read some of the children's theories on the life of leaves and glance at several of the teachers' handwritten notes hanging in plastic sleeves under the subtitles. We admire children's collages made of leaves and seeds, bark and twigs, on black squares of mat board. We leaf though the book hanging at the end of the sequence that features work of all the children in the class as well as teachers' reflections and comments. The book was given to families this school year at the winter holiday party.

This is a variation on the documentary style that these teachers used when I was here 9 years ago. What we see here is much simpler in format, less dense in text, more inviting, and clearer about the processes that are followed by both teacher and child during this kind of an investigation.

Again, I think of Carlina's words of yesterday morning. These teachers are asking very young children questions about their theories about life—the life of leaves, but their lives as well. The teachers are listening for the children's answers. "The answers" are evident here in both the words and the collage compositions of children. The thoughts of the teachers about the children's processes are included in a straightforward format at the conclusion of the sequence. A book that contains much more detail than the panels about the joint research is here for the more curious.

The Piazza

We move out into the piazza, where we find a hum of activity. Above our heads, clear plastic banners move gently in the breeze. A single word stands out on each, and each word is painted in a different color. As I read them out loud, I understand that together these words represent the rainbow of values that we heard Carlina speak of at Mills College last March: *Ascolto, Acoglienza, Valori, Responsibilità, Discussione, Scambio,*

Riunione, Participare—Listening, Welcome, Values, Responsibility, Discussion, Exchange, Meeting, Participation.

Four children are inside of the 4-foot-high, curved, sky-blue half-circles of wood that house most of the dress-ups for the whole school. We look in at what appears to be a mixed-aged group, but they hardly notice us. They are busy taking fanciful accessories off hooks and putting them on. One boy sits on the floor pulling the straps of red flippers around the back of his heels. A blond girl snaps a yellow life jacket on over a red, silky evening gown. Her companion smiles at us through green-lensed goggles, wearing a skirt over the back of her head like a veil. I wonder what is going to happen next, what stories might emerge among these children in this wild attire.

Several children play at the well-stocked store at one side of the piazza. A boy behind the counter gives two girls with shopping baskets cans of tomato paste and boxes of Barilla pasta. These items are marked with prices in single digits. He asks that they pay him in green, red, or yellow chips, which stand for 1s, 5s, or 10s. Then he might have to give them change. A teacher sits at a little distance observing the children, taking notes on what they do.

Isabella works with three children on the other side of the piazza. They are working with a branch that is balanced on a bench next to a big block of red clay. Isabella sits on a chair next to them with her notebook. At present, she is fully engaged in a discussion with them about what they are thinking of and how their plans are evolving. I can't tell exactly what the context is, but it looks as if they are studying plants and trees in the interior courtyard next to them. We will ask about this experience later when we have the opportunity.

The door to the courtyard opposite Isabella's group is open, and we step out into it. These interior courtyards are like secret gardens. Lush with ivy and Virginia creeper and violets in spring, these spaces embody the outdoors in the middle of the school. They serve as conduits for the natural light that floods the central piazza many days of the year. This design is repeated in theme and variation in many of the schools built during the 1970s in the municipality of Reggio Emilia. As I understand it, these plans were originated and developed by architects from Reggio. Further additions and ideas grew out of studies of existing school buildings and the patterns of movement and use of both children and teachers. Over the years, internationally recognized architect Tullio Zini, Vea's husband, has been a dear friend and supporter of the schools in Reggio. He has offered his help and ideas free of charge to the *pedagogisti,* teachers, and designers who have worked together on the evolution of the spaces.

The plan and the feel of the school are the opposite of most school designs all over the world. Often, schools feature long, windowless corridors that lead to rooms that are like separate boxes. That type of design affords little opportunity for teachers or children to build relationships with those in adjoining rooms or with life in the outside world. The architecture of the Diana School plainly reflects the approach to life and to school that this community lives: Human beings both learn and thrive in relationship to one another and to the complexities, beauties, and realities of real life.

I have found several architects whose ideas are both compelling and strikingly similar to the ideas about space and buildings in Reggio Emilia. One is Christopher Alexander, originally from England, now teaching and writing in Berkley, California.

Alexander (1979), in *The Timeless Way of Building,* insists that the spaces and places in which we live either bring out our best, most authentic, and wholehearted selves if they are what he calls "alive," or they actually oppress us if they are "dead." He believes that our liveliness and our thirst for life actually depend on living in places that are alive.

> Which places, which towns, which buildings, which rooms have that breath of sudden
> passion in them, which whispers to us, and lets us recall those moments when we were
> [most] ourselves. The connection between this quality in our own lives and the same
> quality in our surroundings is not just an analogy or a similarity. The fact is that one cre-
> ates the other. . . . Places which have this quality invite this quality to come to life in us.
> And when we have this quality in us we tend to make it come alive in the towns and
> buildings that we help to build. It is a self-supporting, self-sustaining, generating qual-
> ity. And we must seek it for our own sakes in our surroundings simply so that we our-
> selves can become alive. (pp. 53–54)

Alexander believes that no matter what our background, education, or culture, we recognize this quality by the way that we feel in spaces. He believes that
we are born with genetic imprints already in us to recognize what we need in space
in order to thrive.

He gives many examples in *The Timeless Way of Building* and its companion,
A Pattern Language (Alexander, 1977), of elements of architecture and design, which
he calls patterns, that, put together in different configurations in different cultures
throughout history, seem to generate the alive quality that he refers to.

Among the many patterns that he recommends for buildings are indoor sunlight; interior windows; filtered light; "common areas at the heart," small spaces within
larger ones, like alcoves and what he calls "children's caves" and "secret places"; work-
place enclosures; open shelves; doors with glass; flow-through rooms; sequences of
sitting spaces; and outdoor rooms. While reading Alexander's books, I was intrigued
to note how many of the patterns that he identifies are features of the schools in Reggio Emilia.

In fact, much of what Alexander writes about harmonizes with the way the Italian educators have thought about and developed their ideas about optimal school environments for young children. A passage in *The Timeless Way of Building,* in particular, rings with the truth of what life is like inside the schools in Reggio Emilia.

> In a building which is alive, there are no places which are way stations between mo-
> ments of living; every place is made in such a way that life can be fully savored there.
> Every square inch of it has some valuable purpose, and is able to support some moment
> of a person's life which is truly lived and for this reason every part of it is whole. (Alex-
> ander, 1979, p. 484)

The educators and the architects who have stayed close to the schools in Reggio Emilia have similar beliefs about the spaces that they construct for children, teachers, and families. Carlina Rinaldi (1998) writes:

> The scholastic institution, infant toddler center or preschool is viewed as a "living organ-
> ism" that pulses, changes, transforms, grows, and matures. . . . The relational qualities
> between the individual and his/her habitat are reciprocal, so that both the person and
> the environment are active and modify each other in turn. This is process oriented
> architecture. . . . An environment that is empathetic, that grasps the meaning of, but also
> gives meaning to the life of the people who inhabit it. (p. 118)

Today, standing in this sunlit courtyard, Kathleen and I can feel the pulse of this
place and the living reality of the theory of both Christopher Alexander and the Reggio educators and designers. Our gaze settles on the south wall, where child-sculpted

clay leaves, branches, and little animals made by the 5- and 6-year-old children twirl around the real vines and leaves that climb the wall. These sculpted leaves, which seem to move as they glisten in the light, are glazed in shades of olive, aqua, emerald, and lime. The wall seems even more alive with the sculpted leaves of the children intertwined among the climbing vines. This secret garden in the heart of the school sings with the voices of the children here: verdant, energetic, strong, healthy, growing (see Figure 6.4).

The Room of the 4- and 5-Year Olds

We move slowly back inside the piazza and toward Section B, the room of the 4- and 5-year-old-children. What sounds like Peruvian flute music pours out of this classroom, breathy and mysterious. Once inside, the room itself is shadowy, glimmering in low light. The main room is illuminated by an overhead projector, which is placed on a cart near the entrance to the room. The overhead is directed at a full-sized screen on the other side of the room. Two girls choose and arrange items from the bountiful collection on the top of a shelf that is parallel to the door. Here are intriguing selections that I have never thought of: crystals from chandeliers in a variety of colors, a family of sea horses, an assortment of different species of lacy coral, costume jewelry gem stones, pieces and parts of the innards of watches and clocks. The colors and silhouette shapes of the girls' compositions in light and shadow loom large on the screen and seem to orchestrate the changing scenery of the whole room (see Figure 6.5).

FIGURE **6.4.**   An Interior Courtyard at the Diana School

FIGURE **6.5.**   Classroom with Overhead Projector at the Diana School

This room is quieter than the 3-year-olds' room. We move through it, noticing another small group of children working with watercolors and roses on the light table on the other side of the overhead.

As we move into the room, we notice a series of documentary panels on the wall above the light table. It is composed in a similar style to "The Language of Leaves" in Section A. This piece, however, is about a jasmine plant that lives inside this classroom. It is entitled "The Life of a Jasmine."

The sequence begins with a bold title and a large photograph of a group of children surrounding the jasmine plant. The photograph is closely followed underneath by direct quotes of the children about the jasmine printed onto vellum. Subsequent panels inform us of their content through slightly smaller titles: "Fragrance," "Skin," and "The Dance of the Jasmine." These panels display photographs of children engrossed in the investigation of this plant; drawings and watercolors of leaves and blossoms; quotes of children's observations, comments, and theories about the life of the plant; and a last series of photographs of children dancing and twirling in space.

I read the comments of the teachers found at the end of the sequence out loud to Kathleen:

> Our wish is that the children desire to know things through an approach that goes beyond their first impressions and that, within the process of building their knowledge, they give form to it. They have sensitive antennae and a genetic attraction and capacity that corresponds to our desire. To make this possible, we have asked all the senses to participate in coming to know the jasmine that we have here in our midst in the section.

At a certain point we asked the children, "You have told the story of the jasmine in words and in drawings. Are there other ways that you could tell about it?" They said they thought that they could "play" it or dance it. Our hypothesis is that involving all their senses helps children both to construct a higher level of knowledge and to enter into dialogue with things that they encounter with curiosity, solidarity, and intensity.

"I like the way they use the word *solidarity,*" Kathleen says. "It is interesting that they say clearly right away that *solidarity* is what they are after. I haven't thought so much about that aspect of this work."

"I think that's one of the main ideas of the approach—for both children and adults to feel our connection with things in a deep way, to actually see it and say it and now, in this panel, to dance it," I say, thinking out loud.

We move on farther into the room and into the mini-*atelier,* since our time to observe is almost over. The door of the mini-*atelier* is open, and just outside two children paint at an easel. Their subject: field poppies bursting in papery bloom and bending their slender stems in their own improvisational dance.

A paint cart has been rolled outside and placed next to the children—one boy and one girl. The top shelf of the cart holds open jars of at least 24 colors, including many hues of red, pink, coral, and lavender. As I watch these 5-year-old children thoughtfully select and carefully render their impressions of the spring wildflowers, in bud, in bloom, and in the last stages of loosing their petals, I am reminded of "The Curtain" project.

In some ways, it is not surprising that children who come to school every day to meet experiences like the ones we are witnessing today thought of painting "beautiful, important things" for the curtain of the Ariosto Theater. It seems to follow that they might be led to envision something like a "ring of energy" in which every part of the universe is connected and emergent, for this is the truth of the life that they live and the very foundation of the philosophy that drives the schools they attend.

The Room of the 5- and 6-Year Olds

Though time is running out, Kathleen and I at least want to peek into Section C, the classroom of the 5- and 6-year-olds. By this time, many of the children have gone outside to play before lunch. In Section C, we find one of the teachers, Laura, still working with a boy who is transferring a small honeycomb-like drawing that he has made onto large, easel-size paper. He traces the image of his original drawing, which has been photocopied onto acetate, as it is projected onto the easel from an overhead projector. Laura explains that he will probably decide to paint this drawing once it is copied.

Next to them, an amazing collection of things fill the alcove of the room dedicated to construction. It looks like a stage set to me. Rainbow colors of acetate are laid out next to a "can" floor-light fixture that can be moved easily from place to place. Branches hang from the ceiling, suspended on transparent fishing wire. Other things—peacock feathers, chiffon scarves, leaves—are attached with clothespins to lines strung across the space. On the floor, blocks and tubes, animals and cones balance on one another in puzzle-like patterns. The low theater light on the floor, now covered with red acetate, causes this whole scene to throw an ephemeral, shadowy image, cast in red, onto the back wall.

Laura explains that, as teachers, they have observed children playing with light and construction for several years. The addition of various forms of light, as well as suspensions from the ceiling such as branches, are a result of their collective observations of children's actions and inclinations. During the last months they have gradually added more and more dimensions and layers to the construction area, giving, in turn, more and more possibility for drama and story to the children.

I am beginning to feel overwhelmed. This often happens to me when I return here. As "at home" as I feel, there are always brilliant new ideas evolving in the environment, in the thinking of the teachers, and in the work of the children. My feelings of being at ease at the beginning of the day in the 3- and 4-year-olds' room have transformed to something like disorientation and amazement.

Questions and Answers

It is time to gather in the *atelier,* and we are a little late already. Vea is answering a first question through the same interpreter she worked with during "The Curtain" presentation. The question is about organization and planning and how they do it. She shows us examples of organizational forms as she speaks:

> We use a number of different tools for organizing our work. We come up with yearly hypotheses based on projects that are continuing, new ideas we have and the children have, and research that we are involved in with other schools or other researchers. We formulate these ideas into a document that we call a declaration of intent.
>
> In addition to this, we have monthly and weekly hypotheses. We consider the context, the children, and the families. Given our context, we make certain projections. We project which groups of children might do what, which boys, which girls, what materials we will need, if we need to get anything that we don't have.

Another teacher asks a second question: What about the class-made books that go home? When are they made? Vea answers:

> We produce several different types of publications for different audiences: There are those that we call "research and study notebooks," which are important for documentation and professional development; the books that we make at the middle and the end of the year for families; and the publications that are directed to an audience outside the school that are published by Reggio Children.

I ask about the nature of the change in documentation style. Where did it originate? What are the new guidelines they use, if any? Vea smiles to herself as she begins to address this issue:

> Well, Malaguzzi used to complain that it took visitors 2 hours of craning their necks trying to read the small print in order to decipher what the children were doing and what we were observing in projects. We have been experimenting with new formats for documentation for a few years in different schools. The most recent things that you see here were done this year. We try to organize the work as a newspaper might, with a strong title—

like a headline. Then there are subtitles for the most important headings of the work that has been done; again, much like a newspaper.

We then try to present the work in a synthetic and understandable way so that the reader can get the impression of what we have done and how we have done it fairly quickly. We organize all the specific details of the project in what I described earlier as a research and study notebook. The process of making the books helps us a great deal. We can write our interpretations. We can ask colleagues to write theirs as well. If a parent or visitor is really interested, he or she can take the research notebook off the wall, sit down comfortably on a couch, and read it.

Another participant follows with a question about observation and how to begin. Vea responds:

The research that we have done recently on the work of the documenter has brought us to another level of observation, I think. The group of researchers from Harvard, led by Howard Gardner, that we collaborated with were very interested in the process of the documenter. We decided to organize a situation in which three teachers would observe the same group of children. Each of us would take notes on what we observed on an observation form we have developed that looks like this: with one column for what each child does and says, a column for the teacher's observations, and a last column for interpretation.

Each teacher's observation of the same situation was significantly different. We realize, even more than before, through documenting our own documentation in this way, that there is not something objective out there that we all see. We realize that documentation is first of all an interpretation. We see what we are ready to see. It is only through dialogue with others that we can overcome the excess of subjectivity that is inevitable. The notes that I take allow me to participate and to offer my interpretation to others. Through this we can begin to create a matrix through which we can begin to understand. It is not true that we see what happens. Slowly, we learn to see a little bit. Isabella, do you want to talk about this?

Isabella, who is sitting on the back of a chair on the other side of the table from Vea, begins to speak:

We are working with a group of 5-year-old children on something that they would like to leave the school as a memory when they graduate. It turns out that they feel a great solidarity with log left from a tree that was in the courtyard, from a tree that got sick and had to be removed. They want to connect it with the living tree that is there in what they have come to describe as a "bridge hug."

After some discussion, they decided that they wanted to build a clay bridge to this tree with something like their portraits on top. They made a model and then changed their minds. They now want the bridge to be transparent. They would then add pieces of clay and bark and even little pieces of glass to make the bridge shiny and sparkly. We spent 3 days taking the measurements. Now, we are starting to make another model.

I am realizing that I haven't yet really started learning how to listen to children. When the teachers asked me if I understood what they meant by listening, I said yes, but I did not understand. It is such a challenge to keep theory and practice together. After I observed and shared my notes with Vea, she helped me to realize that there were other more important things that were happening. Through my inexperience, I might have killed the project. Now, with the help of other colleagues, the project has its own life. I understand that this approach to listening takes a long time, and it is also endlessly interesting.

"Wow," Kathleen whispers in my ear.

"I know. The teachers are much more articulate about how they are evolving in their practice of documentation than they used to be. I understand that some of the work that Vea and Isabella just described will appear in *Making Learning Visible: Children as Individual and Group Learners,* the book that they have been working on with Howard Gardner and Project Zero at Harvard," I say softly. "I want to understand this evolution in documentation style better. The new style makes it easier to understand what happened. The teachers' roles and initial questions are evident. The projects themselves are not simpler, but the style of communication is clearer."

La Villetta

The weather is very hot, and our schedule is full and intense. All of us are showing signs of fatigue as well as excitement at the midpoint of our week. I catch the very last bus headed to La Villetta that departs from in front of the Astoria. I feel fortunate to catch a glimpse of the other school and some of the teachers with whom I worked during my 1991–1992 internship. I enjoy the drive out of the center of town, remembering my own bicycle route when I rode out to La Villetta during the winter and spring season. We pull up next to the side entrance to the school, and the last string of educators file off the bus.

Most of us head for the shade under the big trees in the back of the school to admire the fountains and small ponds that are part of the project of "The Amusement Park for the Birds" (see Forman & Gandini, 1994).

Today, welcome sprays of water splash our faces as we lean in to get a close look at a child-designed fountain made of umbrellas. I trail my fingers in the pond, trying to reach one of the little wooden boats afloat in this diminutive body of water. I notice that child-made wooden "feeding stations" for animals and birds have been added along the pond and in the trees since I was last here. These must be part of an ongoing project (see Figure 6.6).

We head inside, since we have a mere half-hour before the bus will return for us. I find Kathleen right away in the piazza, sketching the dress-up area made of curved yellow Plexiglas.

"I didn't get to draw the one at Diana, so I want to be sure to get the measurements and materials used in this one. And I want to list some of the dress-ups that we see here and the ones from this morning. Didn't you love the flippers?" Kathleen says over the top of her notebook.

I decide to go upstairs and try to talk with Giovanni Piazza before I do anything else. I climb the stairs, aware of the child-written numbers counting the steps

FIGURE **6.6.** Umbrella Fountains at La Villetta School

taped on each one as I ascend. At the second landing, an interior drawing of the school hangs large, featuring this very staircase and including the numbers that I am walking on. I know that this project started with a parent and child's excitement over their daily practice of counting these steps as they approached the classroom of the 5- and 6-year-old children.

At the very top of the stairs, I find a 5-foot-high undulating sculpture of summer made out of plaster and painted in vivid, curving stripes of color. I turn to the right and face the door, noting that my favorite Walt Whitman poem is still there. Giovanni is gathering his things to leave.

"*Ciao, cara!*" he says warmly.

He explains that he has an important meeting and is sorry that he has to go. I tell him how happy I am to be here and how many memories of this room and the time that I spent here I hold inside. We say that we will see each other again—the last night, if not before. I linger a moment after Giovanni leaves, taking in the details of this studio—the Plexi water table the size of a bathtub with extensive related waterworks built by Giovanni and the children; the generous rectangular table holding children's tall clay sculptures, still wet; the overflowing and beautifully organized materials; Giovanni's desk with computer, cameras, and books. A colleague tells me that she feels as if this room represents the creative mind of genius in three dimensions. She says that when she walks into this room, she breathes in the atmosphere made by "beautiful minds."

As I descend the stairs, I decide to tour the rooms in the brief time that I have left, focusing on any new forms of documentation that I find, curious after our discussion at the Diana School. In the classroom of the 5- and 6-year-olds on one big board I notice categories—Ongoing Experiences, Sharing from Home, and Projects. Under these titles there are photographs as well as sleeves holding conversations and comments of children. I imagine that this is a way to distinguish different types of experiences and to organize work-in-progress in a visible way for children, teachers, and parents.

In the classroom of the 4- and 5-year-olds on the floor below, I notice a large board with single photographs and titles naming many ongoing experiences. For example, under a photograph of children around the pond outside, the title reads "Amusement Park for the Birds;" under a photograph of children at the gym, a title reads "Visiting the Gym." The whole board must serve as a kind of index, from which parents, children, and visitors can get the feeling of the whole before they travel around the room and read chapter summaries on panels, or look at the research and study notebooks, which also hang here at La Villetta in every room.

I hear a call for us to come down. The bus is here. It is already time to go. I feel shortchanged and, at the same time, full to the brim. I am challenged and excited by all these new forms of making the ongoing experiences in the schools clearly visible and understandable. Vea's newspaper analogy is a good one. At both Diana and Villetta schools, the main experiences are evident right away in photographs and in headline-like titles. The teachers in each school have experimented with new forms of representing their work and invented their own solutions. I wonder whether and how these new ideas might help us clarify and communicate our work in the schools in St. Louis. I imagine Sergio's bees again. How can we be inspired by this idea of communicating more clearly, practically, and fully the ongoing work of children, teachers, and parents? What vehicles and systems can we create to further communication and dialogue among all parties?

A Meeting with the Parents

After a nap and a light supper, Kathleen and I feel refreshed and ready to attend a meeting with several parents of the schools. This will be an opportunity to hear a different perspective from that of the teachers, administrators, and *pedagogisti*. It will also give Kathleen a chance to connect with her constituency. We arrive in the designated room in the Astoria to find a relatively small group of people just beginning the meeting. One of the team of interpreters is here assisting, though most of the parents who are here speak English. Following are some of the comments from the evening. Paola Cagliari, a *pedagogista* here with the parents, begins:

> We believe that within the institutions of our schools we are involved in a kind of stubborn research for democracy. Our schools are founded on a culture of cooperation as a chosen value. We are deeply convinced that participation is a necessary value for the future of our community. We thought we would organize this evening around questions that you have.

The parents from the schools begin by introducing themselves and telling us what school they are from and what age child they have in school.

Kathleen asks a question: "What if there are children who are not getting along and the parents of these children begin to worry and wonder what to do?" Paola answers:

> Because friendship is such an important issue with the children, we might have a whole section meeting about friendship. We might discuss what strategies the children use to find friends. How can we adults, both parents and teachers, be a part of this experience of supporting friendships? In an exchange like this, we are offering many possibilities for dealing with possible problems and offering numerous points of view in this exchange of mutual support.

A parent adds to the thoughts of the *pedagogista*:

> It could be in a meeting such as this one that a parent who is worried about his or her child does not say anything. Nevertheless, this parent is feeling the solidarity of all the other parents and the teachers and, at the same time, is getting ideas about how to support his or her child.

Kathleen thanks them both. "There it is again," Kathleen says in a low voice after the conversation has moved on, "The word *solidarity*. Here it is in a different context completely. Here, I think *solidarity* means inclusiveness."

"That's true," I say, thinking about how solidarity with a jasmine plant compares to solidarity with fellow parents, thinking about democracy and the way that Carlina uses the word, thinking about the values on banners that hang from the ceiling at the Diana School—listening, participation, meeting, exchange, discussion, responsibility.

A participant asks about how the parents feel about documentation. Do they read it? Is it important to them? A mother who has not yet spoken leans forward and indicates that she would like to share her impressions.

> I am touched by the documentation. I find great pleasure, fun, amazement, and surprise when I read it. I feel the documentation starts a kind of circulation of communications. The teachers often meet with the parents to explain the context of what has happened. They also listen to the proposals of the parents. The teachers spend a lot of time with us as parents in section meetings so that we will understand the philosophy behind what is developing and learn how to follow what happens.

The discussion continues, and soon the hour or so that we have together is over. Several parents make concluding statements. This is one of the comments that I remember most clearly.

> I feel very proud to be a part of a system like this one. Every time that I feel that I am a protagonist in a situation with others, I feel happy. I am thrilled that my son is able to express the potential that he has inside himself with respect to the others around him. I think that we have experienced success with this dream of offering the best that is possible. It is education through the participation of all of us.

I remember the panel of parents who spoke to visiting educators at the College School in February. I think of the web of community among teachers, children, and parents in both places. With Kathleen sitting next to me in the midst of the Italian parents, I feel strands connecting the two communities now. All of us here tonight feel a grateful recognition of our common goals and our hope for the future in which our children will live.

DAY 5: A DAY OF REST AND REFLECTION

I wake up with what seems to be the full force of the cold Kathleen had when we left St. Louis. However, thankfully, she feels fine now. Since I feel that I really should rest, Kathleen will be on her own today. If I feel better this afternoon, I will visit Amelia in the Reggio Children office. She has offered to have a conversation with me reflecting on her work with the educators of the St. Louis–Reggio Collaborative. This morning Kathleen will attend a presentation on dress-ups given by Paola Strozzi, one of the teachers I worked with at the Diana School when I was here, and this afternoon she will visit an Infant–Toddler Center. We are divided into groups of 25 for the whole day today.

Dress-Ups

Kathleen is particularly interested in dress-ups. She has been working at the College School with Sally, who sewed costumes with the 3-year-olds this year, including Kathleen's son, John. Kathleen would like to offer her help to Jennifer as John moves into the Newport Room. Jennifer is also very interested in dramatic play and drama and would like to make it part of the declaration of intent of the class for the coming year. Jennifer plans to both alter and add to the classroom environment to enhance possibilities for dramatic play and to work with other teachers to follow the processes and strategies that children use in inventing stories and transforming themselves.

This morning, the presentation will take place in one of the small museums near the opera house and the Ariosto Theater. As far as I know, this will be a new experience for the participants—to view a presentation in an environment that is a part of the community rather than in one of the schools or the Hotel Astoria. The chance to move around to different locations gives us a greater sense of the whole city and a clear idea of the vital connections between the municipal schools and the community. I wish Kathleen well and return to sleep as she heads down for breakfast.

When she returns it is about 1:00 P.M., and I realize that I have slept the whole morning. "What was the presentation like?" I ask sleepily.

"It was so interesting!" Kathleen exudes excitement. "Paola started with slides of people from different cultures in costume, face paint, body paint. She said the whole impulse to 'become someone else' started thousands of years ago. She referred to Greek myths and the idea of metamorphosis. She talked about our current superheroes, who acquire special powers like the Greeks when they transform. I love how the educators here start with a historical, almost psychological, background. The presentations never seem to be just about early childhood."

"I wish I had felt well enough to come," I lament. "Where did she go with dress-ups after that?

"She showed images of very little children looking in mirrors, making faces, trying on hats to discover, as she said, 'who they could be, who they might be, who they want to be.' She talked about how we each put our identities to the test through childhood and adolescence, working hard to identify who we are. This makes so much sense to me in this bigger context of identity and experimentation. I mean that is what I did," Kathleen laughs. "It's not only play and not only trying different roles. Let me look at my notes. She said that this search for identity through choosing and assimilating different roles 'could be considered a narration—a narration in dialogue with others.'"

"That is a new way to think of the search for identity," I say.

"Next, Paola showed slides of dress-up areas in the schools. She said that the teachers and parents put a great deal of time and value into maintaining, washing, mending, updating, and presenting the dress-up clothing and accessories as well as maintaining the spaces. She explained that they wanted the spaces to be flexible, so that children could alternate between being actor and spectator. Lately, the teachers have been altering the environment with light images like the ones we saw at the Diana School yesterday. She continued with this idea of flexibility in the clothing and props— like a cape can be a parachute, a veil, a symbol of power. The conclusion was about the right of all children to have the time and place to experiment and to try on different 'selves.'"

"The historical and cultural perspective that Paola presents give us more background and substance to hang our experiences on from the past few days in the schools," I suggest.

"It really does," Kathleen agrees. "I have so many ideas now. I've been sketching room layouts like mad. I think I have an idea for how Jennifer could rearrange her room to facilitate some of this. I think she'll like it."

A Conversation with Amelia

By 4:00 I am feeling much better after sleeping most of the day. I get ready and walk the short distance to the office of Reggio Children at Piazza della Vittoria, 6. I climb the stone steps of this several-centuries-old building and enter the corridor that leads to Amelia's office. She greets me from behind her desk. "Where should we start? Why don't you just start asking me the questions that you have, and then we will just talk."

Louise: What has it been like for you to work with us in St. Louis over time—from 1994 to 2000 in three different schools?

Amelia: My working in St. Louis is connected to my stay in the States. I remember when you and I worked together in Reggio, and we started to think about the possibility of working in the United States. I was in Massachusetts in the fall of 1992, and you were in St. Louis. I remember that I went to St. Louis for the first time in spring 1993 with Lella Gandini and George Forman.

You were exploring things in your first year back in the United States, and I was also exploring things during my first year in the United States. I was in the middle of a transition myself. We were both in the middle of huge, important transitions personally and professionally. And I really didn't know about my future. I was outside of my context. In some way I left my roots in Italy.

Even so, I was attracted by the work in St. Louis and the idea that we might be able to work together. I really wanted to do something, and then a group of you in St. Louis asked and I accepted almost right away. I came back in 1994 to work with the three schools of the St. Louis–Reggio Collaborative.

I feel part of the history of your work in St. Louis. I think the roots of this experience need to be found also in our relationship that began in 1991 when you lived in Reggio. I feel that the experience working in St. Louis gave me the possibility to be a part of your history and to begin a new story where I could find other roots. Massachusetts, Washington, D. C., and St. Louis gave me the chance to feel part of a new circle of experience. I started to build a system of new roots under a new tree.

I needed those roots. I feel very thankful for your experience, because it gave me the possibility to build roots along the years. So I feel part of the history, part of the experience that we had together that for me was really essential. I feel part of the evolution and part of all the achievements. We had many goals and we struggled; and we fought, too, to achieve those goals. We wanted to go somewhere. We did not know where, but we wanted to go. To continue. I was researching along with you.

Louise: I remember my closeness to you in the beginning. I was so dependent on you when you would come. I somehow felt closer to you than I did to my colleagues in the St. Louis–Reggio Collaborative.

Amelia: I think that I was part of your dream. I was part of a sort of identity that you built in Reggio that you dreamt about and that you wanted to bring there. I think that it took a while for you to realize that you needed to find another identity. You had this dream about Reggio that was in a kind of cloud. You needed to find your feet firmly on the ground in your new place, in your new experience, and still keep your dream alive.

Louise: I can also remember when I began to feel the sense that we were coming together in our own way, that we in St. Louis were building strengths, using our own context and our experience to go deeper in our dialogue with the Reggio Approach. You were a resource for all of us in the St. Louis–Reggio Collaborative.

Amelia: In some way, this is another similarity we share. I, too, was trying to create a new context for myself and my work outside of Reggio Emilia. I still have a letter that Malaguzzi wrote to me in the fall of 1992. I had written him a sad letter in which I expressed the terrible loss that I felt being so far away from my context. He told me that I was in a stage in which I was building a new identity and creating a new life for myself. He said, "You will find new colleagues and new friends, and you will create something new." He also wrote, "Even if you are not aware of it, in this new life you will become a citizen of the world." I was struck by this.

When you began in St. Louis, your reference point was still in Reggio. You realized how much I was helping you with that. I think that you were also angry with yourself because you couldn't do things when I was not there. You had to begin to trust yourself and your colleagues in your new context. In the beginning, you were still using me as a channel for an experience that you fell in love with. This is a part of the strength of our relationship and our working together. But it needed to expand to the others, and it did.

There are different chapters in our history. Remember when Carlina came for the conference in 1997? There was a certain point when I realized that by using Carlina's way of looking at the schools, I could see things that I hadn't seen before. I noticed how many similarities the three St. Louis schools shared with the schools in Reggio. The most original one of the three was the St. Michael School. Maybe the fact that the St. Michael preschool is in a basement worked to our advantage in finding especially unique solutions to problems. But I felt a little bit of disappointment in my work. Maybe I had communicated too much of my style. Maybe I was not able to support you in creating an experience that was original.

Louise: Is that why you didn't return for 3 years? Maybe you thought we should have a little space and try on our own.

Amelia: I think I realized that I needed to distance myself a little. Maybe my presence was too strong, so I stepped back. It was pretty painful, because I was attached to the experience. Maybe it is like when your children leave home and you know that they have to find their own way.

Then when I came back last March, I was so happy that I could have flown everywhere. Because then I saw you. I saw what you had built yourselves. I saw the ways in which you had struggled with things. You had created your own collaborative way of solving problems and sharing. That was really a collaborative—a St. Louis–Reggio Collaborative, finally. You had found your own way of using the experience of Reggio as a reference point.

Louise: Before you mentioned Malaguzzi. I am curious. Could you say the most important thing that Malaguzzi taught you?

Amelia: One?

Louise: It doesn't have to be just one.

Amelia: So, let's see:

Do not give up.
Respect life.
Find dignity in yourself and your work.
Do not be satisfied about things; search continuously.
Use creativity as an aspect of your intelligence.
Be rigorous, professional, and serious about what you do.
Be aware of what you do; do not take things for granted.
Be flexible.
Learn how to listen and learn how to speak up.
Collaborate.
Find joy and pleasure in all aspects of your work.
Welcome emotions as part of your work and a part of your life.
Do not separate your life from your work.
Look at every situation as a whole, not in pieces.
Make a commitment to what you do.
Act on your beliefs.
Be spontaneous.
Follow your instincts.
Be positive and optimistic about life.
Know how to wonder, how to be amazed.
Accept who you are.
Be yourself.

Louise: But those things are the things that you bring to other people.

Amelia: Yes, because I think that I continue to feel responsible for what he taught me.

Louise: And we feel responsible for what you have taught us.

Amelia: It becomes a chain without an end!

Louise: I feel that this work is so expansive and much bigger than early childhood education. Especially in the United States, people are attracted to it almost like a fountain, a source of resurgence.

Amelia: Since the birth of Reggio Children, we have had 10,000 people from Italy and 58 other countries visit us on study tours. There is an increase in the number of ministers of education, policy makers, legislators, funders, and administrators from all over the world.

By this time, maybe we could say that Reggio offers these people from all over the globe a place where ideas can be exchanged. People come from around the world to visit us and understand us, but we think that they also come to understand themselves. At first, I don't think that I was so ready to understand the others or the differences among us. I had to learn a new language beyond English. Encounters with others requires openness, respect for differences, and exchange of ideas and knowledge.

I think that in Reggio we have learned to open our doors and to give value to the experiences that others bring in. I think that many of us feel that it is time for us as educators to take much more responsibility for what we do and to live in a context where new developments can begin that will maybe even make our continued life possible. Malaguzzi used to say that we need to be nostalgic about the future. It means to me that you should be optimistic and you should welcome everything that happens as part of a life journey. I think we need this attitude to continue.

Our time is up, and I thank Amelia for this opportunity to talk and remember together. I am so grateful to have had the chance to work with Amelia here in Reggio and in St. Louis over time alongside committed colleagues. Sometimes, it is hard to believe all that has transpired since I was here in 1991–1992. Since that time, every year the educators here have opened themselves up to the world in greater numbers as a place to meet, to find inspiration and hope, and to imagine the future. As I stroll home to the hotel, many ideas twirl in my head from this week rich with experiences and opportunities for dialogue in so many different contexts. The example of Reggio Emilia is as powerful a catalyst as I can imagine to cultivate, as Malaguzzi said, "nostalgia for the future."

DAY 6: NOSTALGIA FOR THE FUTURE

We awake hardly believing that the last day of our week has arrived. Thankfully, I feel much better. We will meet as a whole group back in the Hotel Astoria, where we started 5 days ago. Then, our afternoon is free. Tonight there will be a celebratory, goodbye dinner party in a cloisters on the other side of town, with music and typical regional food. Teachers from the schools we have visited as well as some of the parents and members of the community will join us.

This morning, as we settle into our seats in the large, now-familiar conference room, Amelia greets us once again. "Well, have you seen a lot? Have you learned a lot? Do you have more questions? We always hope that people will leave with more questions in their pockets than when they arrived. This morning we would like you to return to your dialogue groups. Why don't you talk about what you will take home with you—what insights, what thoughts, what questions. Then, like we did the first day, we can meet back here and share together."

Ideas to Take Home

When it is time to share, the facilitators speak from the podium one by one. The collective thoughts of the dialogue groups pour out almost like a litany of encouraging affirmations to carry around with us as we return home and move ahead within our own contexts. Jeanne begins and reminds us of the metaphor of the power bracelet. She says that among other beads representing key words and ideas, her group has added slow down; listen; rigor and depth; we know how to do this; we need to stay focused and persistent; we need to be secure in our commitment that anything difficult and worthwhile takes time.

Another group continues to add "bead thoughts" and questions to take home. We can't just live with this experience as some kind of dream we've had. We must read, discuss, think together, organize round tables. We have values. How can we best live our own country's values? Maybe we won't stop at a few questions. Perhaps we will go deeper.

And another string of thoughts follow. We want to let go of our frustrations and build on the positive. We need to listen for children's authentic questions. We want to treat every question with dignity and respect. We need to take the time to think and to process emotions. How can we create authentic environments? We need to start with white space, with physical emptiness. Successful experiences happen in all cultures. Most of these require genuine trust in oneself and in others.

As I listen, I think to myself that I hear many of the words and phrases that Amelia used yesterday in thinking about what Malaguzzi had taught her—find dignity in your work, find pleasure in work, think deeply, build on the positive, be persistent, do not give up. I envision a chain of qualities, of dispositions toward life and work that are catching on here, finding voice, continuing.

Our group creates a string of ideas in response to Sergio's directives the first day: "If you want to be like us, don't copy. We have never copied anyone. Be original." Can we recognize what is essential in this approach and within ourselves? What can grow out of acknowledged and celebrated essential ways of being? We speculate that some "copying" may be an attempt to embrace and experiment. We imagine that some "copying" is trying to find one's way in the dark. We are still trying to learn how to be original. We are trying to find our way to a holistic worldview in a fragmented, individualized society.

As we walk back to the hotel under the blooming trees, I remember Sergio's stories the first day and his use of imagery and metaphor. This kind of thinking reminds me of a group of educators in Portland, Oregon, who invented many metaphors for the Reggio Approach. They said that the whole approach was like:

> A web
> An opera; a symphony
> The solar system expanding
> The water cycle: Rain pools, water rises; it is changed by things around it,
>   and it changes things as it transforms
> A raindrop in a pond; the ripple effect
> Soup; more than a recipe; a community experience
> A summer tomato; inherent beauty; everything in one small thing

These ideas expressed in images defy copying and replication. They are not static; they are living systems, ever changing. These systems surround us. They are a part of us, and we are a part of them. They represent the world in a network of relationships that are evolving and constantly transforming, and we are inside the net. We cannot replicate what we, in essence, already are. The Buddhist image of the jeweled net of Indra comes to mind. Joanna Macy (1990) writes:

> [Indra's net] is a vision of reality structured very much like the holographic view of the universe, so that each being is at each node of the net, each jewel reflects all the others reflecting back and catching the reflection, just as systems theory sees that the part contains the whole. (p. 61)

To experience oneself in the world in this way is to shift one's view to a worldview, a universe view, a web-of-life view. Recognizing this view as one that fits with life and with the way we wish to live in school with children calls us not to copy but to embrace and to evolve from what we intuitively know to be true.

Reveries

Before walking with Kathleen to the party, which will begin at 8:00 P.M., I wander out of the hotel and across the piazza to sit at a table at a corner *caffe*. The pigeons fly down into the center of the open space and then swoop up to the roof of the *duomo*, wings flapping, cooing as they land. Swallows dip and sail on the soft evening air. The aroma of roasted espresso beans floats out of the *caffe* and into the piazza, which is filled with the echoing, full-bodied words of the Italian language.

A small boy runs on the cobblestones, back and forth, laughing. His mother strolls, talking alternately to him and to a friend at her side. A dog barks. The wheels of bicycles click and roll. A couple pedals by, holding hands as they ride. The leisure and quiet of evening descend. I think about how lucky I am to have had this week here in this place that I love, with Kathleen as my companion. We will take all of it back home with us, and we will digest it slowly. We will continue to share this experience with others from the St. Louis–Reggio Collaborative. We have a new network of friends from all over the United States.

I feel, somehow, that I have come full circle. I have come here with a parent who is a good friend, after almost 10 years have passed since I lived here with my family and worked as an intern at the Diana and La Villetta schools. I think of the 10 years of work with children, parents, and colleagues.

As I sit here, for some reason my mind travels to an experience that I once had many years ago in a career workshop. When asked what I really wanted to do in life, I answered that I wanted to make people cry—to move them to tears. I think I said this because I realized that I wanted to be engaged in work that is essential, that touches people, that touches me, that is about what matters. Reflecting this evening on both my career in education and the multitudes of educators who travel here from every corner and culture in the world, I think that this must be true for every one of us.

These schools for young children in the small city of Reggio Emilia, Italy, are like a beacon of hope for humanity—hope of a new way of living and a new way of being together, of an open way of learning and discovering who we truly are, not in isolation but in relationship to one another, not only as young children but as people everywhere.

Epilogue

Returning to finish this book in January of 2002 has given me the opportunity to revisit and to deeply appreciate the richness and complexity of our shared learning. It has also offered me a chance to consider the material from a new perspective, especially in the light of lingering questions that many of us in North America share. Some of the most difficult questions are about standards and assessment. Perhaps the most fundamental question is, How can we engage in constructive, emergent, vital work with children and at the same time ensure that they will meet mandated standards? Feeling that it would be valuable to think through this question in relationship to a specific project and with a group of teachers, I asked the Scent Project teachers at the St. Michael School if they would join me in dialogue.

Four of the teachers who launched the Scent Project agreed to meet with me to think together about several subjects in relation to one another: the Scent Project, the process of assessment, and the process of documentation. We decided together to read two chapters in *Making Learning Visible: Children as Individual and Group Learners* (Giudici, Rinaldi, & Krechevsky, 2001) in preparation for our meeting. We read "Documentation and Assessment: What Is the Relationship?" by Carlina Rinaldi (2001), and "Understanding Documentation Starts at Home," by Steve Seidel (2001). The chapters would serve as a common reference point for us. The major question that we wanted to address was: "Can we assess what the children learned in the Scent Project?"

Because we wanted to orchestrate a dialogue (described in Chapter 3), we met in the spirit of inquiry and with a shared eagerness to listen to each person's experience, intuitions, feelings, and thoughts on this subject. As a group we generated the sense of safety, energy, and possibility that Isaacs (1999) deems necessary to create a "container," or the psychological space in which dialogue can take place. We hoped that the conversation might take us somewhere new in our collective understanding of these issues as they relate directly to our everyday lives with children, parents, and one another.

We met in the St. Michael School studio from 1:00 to 3:00 P.M. on a school day early in January. The children in the classrooms were resting, supervised by other teachers that day. This is a designated meeting time for the teachers involved; they are accustomed to thinking together at this time of the day and week. I had asked them to reflect with me on subjects that we live with every day but rarely set aside 2 hours to talk about together. An edited version of our transcribed conversation follows, with some clarifying additions and changes made by the teachers. The flow and sequence of this transcript is faithful to the original dialogue.

Louise: One of the reasons that assessing the Scent Project is difficult in an American context is that, as far as I know, you did not begin your planning with a list of objectives to meet and skills to teach. You started with the idea that scent was a subject rich with possibilities for exploration and that, given meaningful experiences and provocations, children would probably develop ideas and theories in relation to scent and smelling.

Karen: If we begin with assessment of finite skills, that is different from beginning with the values that might drive a project. On page page 83 of *Making Learning Visible,* Carlina [Rinaldi, 2001] writes that through "representing their mental images" in various ways within a group context, children "modify and enrich their theories and conceptual maps." This seems to be a primary goal of the teachers in Reggio. That is huge. It isn't fragmented. We have to establish our values and big goals and then say, "OK, if this is the case, then we have a curriculum that is going to promote those values within a framework." Then you can make some assessment decisions, but they are based on a strong image of the child, not on making judgments about how Johnny is holding his pencil. In Italy they are aware of those skills, and they will work on them, but that is not what the teachers in Reggio are going to document. The givens are that everyone is different and everyone has his or her strengths and weaknesses.

Louise: During the fall of the year that I was interning in Reggio when I was at the Diana School, the children were making insects out of clay. What the whole thing was about, though, in the bigger context, was the interrelationship between trees and the insects, and the clay, and the ecology of the experience, and the group pursuit of uncovering ideas. They were not using clay to develop fine motor skills specifically. It seems like an upside-down thing that we in the United States tend to focus on the minutiae. We would put the fine motor skills at the top and then design activities to develop fine motor skills that often become meaningless. Instead, in Reggio, educators have a much bigger picture.

Karen: There are a lot of meaningful things for adults and children to pursue in school. In a meaningful context, learning skills fall into their proper place.

Melissa: You were talking about the whole ecological context that the learning was placed in. See, we would be thinking about, "OK, how many legs does the spider have?"

Chuck: Yes, context for learning. So much of the focus in the Reggio Approach is contextual. As Louise said, things get flipped for us. For example, we might walk around with our main context being, How do we judge children's drawings or how many legs does a spider have? So we think in this really reductive kind of way. That is our context as teachers. But the teachers' context in Italy is the children's experiences. The big context is always the children's experiences— walking through the piazza, the rain, the city. Using the rich context of the children's lives as a provocation for the development of thinking and the invention of ideas is more important than anything. There is a relationship between assessment and the contexts for learning. We only look at the context that we are familiar with. In Reggio, educators say learning always takes place in the children's lives, and they claim all of that and use it. For us that is more submerged.

Louise: In the Reggio schools *progettazione,* their projecting and imagining possibilities, I think teachers are thinking of deeper and deeper contexts within which to move themselves and the children—larger, deeper, more complex.

Chuck: The Scent Project was one of the first times that we were clear about going deeper with the context. We have done it before in many ways, but we went deeper still with the Scent Project. We collaborated and followed through together.

Karen: Maybe the Scent Project allowed us to do that because we were comfortable focusing on the big questions, ours and the children's. We trusted that important development in thinking and in skills would occur.

Melissa: In the "Understanding Documentation Starts at Home" chapter that you have been referring to, Steve Seidel [2001] writes, "In the United States the process of assessment is most often thought of as synonymous with evaluation and, in an American context, evaluation is a process of judgment, measuring or placing one work in relation to other works. Documentation is frequently seen as marks in a record book." [pp. 304–305]

Karen: When Amelia started talking about documentation, I realized that I had used that word strictly one way: Where someone would say, "We want you to document everything that this child does," meaning he or she is having a problem and you are supposed to document everything that that child does so that some help, some intervention can be offered for that child. Amelia was using the word in a completely different way. That was 1993. I had to switch my thinking.

Louise: And with the Scent Project I have a visualization of something like a spiral. Everyone's knowledge is going around together with every turn. You do one thing together, and then you go on to the next thing. It is really hard to pull apart what we are going to assess about what Pete knows in comparison to what someone else knows. The other thing that becomes confusing in an American context is that in the Scent Project we are not judging what the children know as being the "right" answer; instead, we are curious about their interpretations and theories.

   I think it is so important that we keep trying to articulate what this is all about, what the differences and similarities are between documentation and assessment, where we stand, and why we are doing what we are doing. When parents and visitors ask us about skill development, we think, "The children are learning to read and write and count in a meaningful context. What is the big deal?" But it is a big deal because it is certainly a different context that we are trying to create and at the same time satisfy the requirements and the expectations that are in our society. I guess this is a good thing. It is not that the Italian children aren't learning these skills.

Melissa: . . . or that they are that much smarter than American children.

Louise: They are exactly the same in terms of intelligence.

Melissa: I agree that it is really important to think about why we do what we do and to be able to articulate it. One day a visitor was observing here. We had taken the clay and put it on the block platform. The children were constructing a farm, and they needed mud for the pigs. She said to me, "I would never do that. We would not do farms. We would do trucks and we would only have the trucks out. Then we would do tractors." Think about it. How many different things can you do with just tractors?

Karen: She is missing how the children might make connections. You have all these trucks, but trucks do not exist in isolation.

Melissa: Then she said, "What you are doing is what I would do with my kids at home."

Karen: Maybe a more natural and complex environment *is* more homelike.

Louise: Do you think that teachers think that things will get lost and we won't be able to assess or that we won't be able to pick out what the child is learning at a certain point in time if things get too complicated?

Karen: In the beginning of working with this approach, I did feel like I threw the baby out with the bath water. I had to regain some balance. It really is a balance. When you are always looking at "How are his fine motor skills?" you are not thinking of the child as strong, rich, and full of potential, as the Reggio educators do. Let's be a little more positive and think of children as constantly learning every moment. They are making connections constantly. Have you read that book about brain development, *Magic Trees of the Mind* [Diamond & Hopson, 1998]? That is what is happening. This made sense to me when I taught kindergartners. They made incredible connections. The trees of the mind are growing and blooming.

Melissa: They were live oaks!

Karen: Absolutely. I said I learned to trust development when I taught kindergarten after I had taught the same children as 3- and 4-year-olds. I was worried, thinking, "Do they know their letters?" The kids who did not know all of them had somehow learned them over the summer, and it was not through drill and skill and moms with alphabet books. That is what teachers in Reggio know that we do not know—that you can trust development to take care of many of the issues.

Louise: I am thinking that everything we have just been talking about represents the image we have of the child but also the image of the human being as a person who is going to have this tree of knowledge inside him or her versus having to learn things in neat little segments or in isolation.

Melissa: Even when we started trying to work with the Reggio Approach, I remember thinking, "Just tell me what to do. Give me a formula." It is the way that we have learned in school. This is the formula, and you do it this way. There is no deviation up or down, back and forth, because this is the way you do it. Instead, in Reggio Emilia they approach most things saying, "Here is a problem, and let's see how we can solve it."

Karen: Yes. How can you, teacher as researcher, solve this problem of lack of parent involvement? How can you solve this problem that your block area is not engaging the children? How will you construct a meaningful context for learning with the children and then follow what happens? Teachers as researchers. That is a huge difference.

Chuck: What you all have been describing is amazing. On page 85 of *Making Learning Visible,* Carlina [Rinaldi, 2001] writes, "Doubt and uncertainty permeate the context; they are part of the 'documenter's context.' Herein lies true didactic freedom, of the child as well as the teacher. It lies in the space between the predictable and the unexpected, where the communicative relationship between the children's and the teachers' learning process is constructed." It is really about continually finding and creating contexts that will inspire new discoveries for the child and teacher.

Frances: I think that the traditional academic teachers cannot let go of the director's role. Those people have to make sure that most of the academic skills on the list are checked off. What I see is that the really incredible, unexpected things cannot be done then because teachers are so busy worrying about traditional skill building that has to happen by a certain age. We constantly stop ourselves short. What I hear from our peers from Italy is where they intervened and directed, where they didn't, and what skills and talents and negotiations among the children were involved. But they don't start with a checklist. The educators even negotiate on how they are going to reflect. They constantly refer to theory and practice and documents from other sources in order to assess what learning is going on. They participate in assessment constantly, but not in a checklist format.

Louise: Carlina calls assessment "deciding what to give value to."

Frances: And you immediately devalue learning by putting it in a checklist form. What I heard you saying was that skills are relative to conversation, experience, and relationship to whatever the knowledge base is. We are attempting to create contexts in which rich, dynamic, multifaceted learning takes place that can only happen in a group and because of the group. Documentation is about the process that a group of children experience and valuing what each individual brings to that experience.

In an American context, we don't look at the relationships first. Assessment in the United States focuses on one child in isolation. I think that it is useful for us to know and to share with parents that there are researchers who look at a 2- to 12-month period in a child's life and tell us what the norms are. At the same time, I think that we need to be careful not to be driven by these norms or to think that the academic norms represent the only kind of learning that is important. We need to continue to educate ourselves and the parents about creating a much richer and bigger picture of life in school.

Karen: It seems that standards are based on the idea that everyone is going to learn about the same thing at the same rate—same, same, same.

Louise: We have to come up with our own standards based on what we want to give value to. I think it should start with the priorities, the big ideas, and then work back. A friend of mine who is the director of a middle school just sent me Grant Wiggins and Jay McTighe's *Understanding by Design* (1998). It is written for high school and middle school teachers, but what they propose is exactly what we are talking about. They call it "backward design," determining what will foster enduring understanding and beginning with essential, open-ended, provocative questions that motivate students' and teachers' excitement, engagement, research, and thinking.

Karen: First, you have to figure out what you believe. If we believe that children are all different and if we believe that they all come to school with their own unique experience and interests and are eager to learn, then what do we have to do? What kind of school should we create for children? What do we want children to learn? How do adults support children's learning? What materials do we provide? What experiences?

Louise: What did you value about the Scent Project? What values did you start out with?

Frances: We wanted the children to understand that they had knowledge, that they could express that knowledge, that they could express the new knowledge that they were gaining.

Karen: We wanted them to experience transferring from one language to another, from one mode of experiencing to another. For example, when they drew smells and drew theories, then they could see and communicate ideas and think about them together.

Frances: We wanted them to know that they could exchange points of view and build on each other's points of view.

Chuck: And I think we wanted to explore something in which they had genuine connections that the adults had never given real value to.

Frances: What I wanted in that moment—I wanted to give more time to it. That word *project* meant that it was not done quickly. I did not want the children to say, "Done that. Now what?" To me, that is what that word *project* means—something that is such a gift that we spend time with it in that kind of exchange. There were things that happened, and we said, "Yes, we want this."

Karen: We had 5 months. The pressure of time was not on us. It was like a gift that we had C. C. here.

Frances: For me, C. C. was amazing because she lived out the right of a teacher. She had a natural way of being, and there was no pretense in any way. Smells were a part of her life, and she brought them in. Then she recognized the perception of scents in the community she was in and she proposed from there. She did not just introduce something because it was related to science; she pulled it out of her own life and her knowledge of her relationships and her community. She saw that she had something to offer that connected to who she was. Not only did she just bring it. She did not give the gift on her own; she asked us. She made proposals. She made herself responsible.

Chuck: At some point we knew what we had. It was big, and we said, "We have to pay attention to this." I had written maybe one or two things in my declaration of intent that year, and one of them was to look for and ask children for their theories. I remember thinking, "Where are the children's theories in this school? They think, they live here. They are here for hours and hours. There have to be places where we can find their theories."

Karen: And we needed to have practice ourselves in eliciting and drawing out children's theories.

Frances: This is an example of a time where one person's passion got everyone involved. Since then, we have had many more gifts from people in terms of what they could offer us as a viewpoint. We have finally shifted to really seeking out other people's viewpoints.

Louise: Can you say what you wanted the children to learn, what you checked afterward to see if they had learned? I get the sense that you were breaking new ground and opening the ceiling every time. That is maybe what confuses people? They say, "You mean you did not have goals and objectives?"

Karen: We wanted to research with the children, and we started with a list of questions that we generated together. I think that researching the answers became our goal.

Frances: We wanted to validate the fact that they know. These children know scent, and we wanted to illuminate what they know. As soon as we begin to share viewpoints about scent, we start to know more because we now know your perceptions and you know mine and on and on. If I care enough, if we care enough to find out, to listen, that is going to change our knowledge. If I wanted to give anything to a child, it would be the idea that there are few definitive answers, but that everything is worth spending time on if we decide to. If *we* decide, you know what I mean? The wheel would not be invented and the world would still be flat if we were satisfied with definitive answers. We really believe in the values and the strength and the power to construct. We believe in the possibility of co-constrution and the exchange of knowledge to illuminate what we understand.

Chuck: You know what it is like? The Scent Project is three-dimensional. In the Reggio schools, they come at so many things from so many points of view. If you look at a list of science standards or literacy standards, the conversation goes back to being one dimensional, or maybe *linear* is a better word. On page 87, Carlina [Rinaldi, 2001] says that documentation is "not aimed at giving the event objectivity but at expressing the meaning making effort." The Scent Project was about children and teachers making meaning together around the subject of scent—how we smell things, and what smells are, and where they are, and how they affect us. Both the children and the adults "made meaning" using language, conversation, gesture, invented games, drawing, theories.

Though we knew it before, we learned once again, through our dialogue, that these issues of standards, curriculum, assessment, and documentation remain challenging to put together, difficult to get our minds around, and infinitely complex. We struggled to try to put the American practice of assessment into some kind of relationship with the Reggio Emilio concept and practice of documentation. The central issue seems to be that, for us, and for many people, these ideas and practices do not overlap or fit together very well. It is hard to put them in the same equation. Trying to do so brings on the frustration that comes from attempting to put a round peg in a square hole. They just don't seem to belong to the same puzzle or the same system of thinking about learning, about life, or even about how we perceive reality. It is easy to get confused. Reading and rereading the interpretations of both Italian and American educator/researchers in *Making Learning Visible* [Giudici et al., 2001], as well as a collection of other authors whose books are stacked on my desk, has helped me to think about these things once again.

Much of the knowledge that grows from the kind of experiences that children, teachers, and parents share in Reggio Emilia and in our schools is difficult, if not impossible, to measure and quantify. I think of Judith Burton (2001) and her powerful words on this subject.

> Standards are not written to test how youngsters interweave myriad facts into constructions of important narratives, nor how they manipulate materials in the integration of knowledge and the imagination and mediate the world of self and relationship, or how they go beyond the familiar and test new possibilities. . . . Recognizing the complexity, multidimensionality, and variability that actually constitutes artistic learning and that resides at the heart of knowledge appears beyond the setters of standards and the writers of tests. (p. 42)

Judith Burton's thoughts on this subject remind me of Vea Vecchi's (2001) comments on "the falsification of indicators":

> It is self-evident that there are subjects and processes for which indicators are hardly applicable, such as those that are mostly connected to processes of deep expressive force (that do not involve simply problem solving), as well as those attitudes and concepts which are primarily *sown* in hopes that they will germinate in time. . . . In our opinion, it is this kind of learning that makes a difference to both children and to teachers, and more generally, the culture. This means an approach that involves constant attention to the quality of relationships and is thus difficult to verify by means of indicators, even sophisticated ones. In a sense, the language of relationships is one that we need to know how to speak ourselves in order to listen to it, understand it and assess it. (p. 212)

If we embrace the challenge of learning about children and ourselves through the Italian concept of documentation, we must begin to value the deeper, more complex knowledge of which both Burton and Vecchi speak. We must invent new ways to make all kinds of learning visible, including the "language of relationships." We must also begin to ask ourselves what *we* learned, all of us, during the course of our experiences, not only what the children learned. The adults and the children are involved in parallel and, at times, overlapping and intersecting research. They absolutely affect one anothers' learning as well as the course of how their co-research will proceed. The fact that American teachers may see knowledge, the child, and the teachers as separate, distinct entities, each of which has a niche, hinders our ability to embrace reality as a system of patterns and relationships in continual evolution.

In *Schools That Learn,* Peter Senge and colleagues (2000) predict that the "systems revolution," which asserts that "the fundamental nature of reality is relationships not things," will eventually work its way into our worldview, replacing Newtonian, mechanistic thinking and industrial age schools (pp. 52–53). "The systems revolution" takes its place among the ideas that Loris Malaguzzi gravitated toward in the work of thinkers such as Gregory Bateson (1979) and Maturana and Varela (1987). These are among the ideas that he courageously translated across disciplines into a pedagogy that has been in evolution ever since. In *The Web of Life,* Fritjof Capra (1996) explains systems thinking as follows:

> The ideas set forth by organismic biologists during the first half of the century helped give birth to a new way of thinking—"systems thinking"—in terms of connectedness, relationships, and context. According to the systems view, the essential properties of an organism, or living system, are properties of the whole which none of the parts have. These properties are destroyed when the system is dissected, either physically or theoretically, into isolated elements. . . . Systems thinking is "contextual," which is the opposite of analytical thinking. Analysis means taking something apart to understand it; systems thinking means putting it into the context of a larger whole. (pp. 29–30)

Our dialogue at the St. Michael School reveals our current understanding of assessment and documentation as two different worldviews: The first is analytical, reductionist, and decontextualized; the second is holistic, dynamic, and relational. It is hard to accept that these two approaches to learning and to the study of learning might be in opposition, but that is what it looks and feels like to us at this point. In many ways, we are trying to build bridges between two ways of living life in school. Both Karen and Frances suggest using standards and skill norms in discussions with parents, so that both teacher and parent can see, "in an American context," where the child is on a continuum. Karen says that she has learned to "trust development" and see the norms with more perspective and less concern. It has been our experience that engaged, motivated children in excited pursuit of meaning often travel way beyond standards appropriate to their age group. We know that some current thinking in the field of curriculum design, such as that of Grant Wiggins and his colleagues (Wiggins & McTighe), is similar to the Italian educators' thinking.

The worldview that frames much of our work in the schools of the St. Louis-Reggio Collaborative—in this case, the Scent Project—is not fragmented into pieces and parts. Rather, it is steeped in context and meaning making; it is whole, dynamic, and relational. If we are able to clearly articulate our values, our worldview, and our beliefs about the essential place of "making meaning" in our lives, and then demonstrate how this unfolds in the stories of children's and teachers' experiences, we will not only reach the parents of the children whom we teach; we will also begin to stand for and speak from, as Capra (1996) says, "a new vision of reality that is ecological" (p. 12). I am quite sure this is what the Italians mean when they say that in acting out our lives as teachers in this way, we are taking a political stance. We are standing for a way of being that is outside the norm, and that is ultimately crucial to the future of the planet.

Together, all of us have entered a new millennium, one that holds promise for us and one in which we face enormous global challenges. I carry with me a deep and profound hope, as I am certain we all do, that the wisdom of this small, vibrant city in the north of Italy will continue to have a huge effect on our thinking and our practice in education. I pray that it may also continue to inspire us to understand ourselves as part of a universe in which all parts are connected and linked to the past and to the future. I hope that in all parts of the world we might acknowledge ourselves as a piece of the Reggio children's vision of the "ring of energy" as we spin on this wild and precious planet in space.

References

Alexander, C. (1977). *A pattern language: Towns, buildings, construction.* New York: Oxford University Press.

Alexander, C. (1979). *The timeless way of building.* New York: Oxford University Press.

Apelman, M., & Johnson, H. (1984). Appendix 1. Stages in block building. In E. Hirsh (Ed.), *The block book* (rev. ed.). Washington, DC: National Association for the Education of Young Children.

Badiner, A. (Ed.). (1990). *Dharma Gaia: A harvest of essays in Buddhism and ecology.* Berkeley, CA: Parallax Press.

Bateson, G. (1979). *Mind and nature: A necessary unity.* New York: Bantam Books.

Berensohn, P. (1972). *Finding one's way with clay: Pinched pottery and the color of clay.* New York: Simon & Schuster.

Bohm, D. (1996). *On dialogue.* London and New York: Routledge.

Bruner, J. (2000). Citizens of the world, excerpt from speech on receiving honorary citizenship from the mayor and City Council of Reggio Emilia. In M. Davoli & G. Ferri (Eds.), *Reggio tutta: A guide to the city by the children* (pp. 122–123). Reggio Emilia, Italy: Reggio Children S.r.l.

Burton, J. (1991). Some basic considerations about "basic art." *Art Education, 44*(4), 34–41.

Burton, J. (2001). Lowenfeld: (An)other look. *Art Education, 54*(6), 33–42.

Cadwell, L. B. (1997). *Bringing Reggio Emilia home: An innovative approach to early childhood education.* New York: Teachers College Press.

Cadwell, L., Miller, S., & Strange, J. (1999). *Stories in clay.* Presentation given at the Martha Holding Jennings March Invitational, Columbus, Ohio.

Caine, R., & Caine, G. (1994). *Making connections: Teaching and the human brain.* Menlo Park, CA: Addison-Wesley.

Capra, F. (1996). *The web of life.* New York: Anchor Books.

Carson, R. (1956). *The sense of wonder.* New York: Harper & Row.

Ceppi, G., & Zini, M. (Eds.). (1998). *Children, spaces, and relations: Metaproject for an environment for young children.* Reggio Emilia, Italy: Reggio Children S.r.l.

Csikszentmihalyi, M. (1990). *Flow: The psychology of optimal experience.* New York: Harper-Perennial.

Dahlberg, G., Moss, P., & Pence, A. (1999). *Beyond quality in early childhood education and care: Postmodern perspectives.* London: Falmer.

Davoli, M., & Ferri, G. (Eds.). (2000). *Reggio tutta: A guide to the city by the children.* Reggio Emilia, Italy: Reggio Children S.r.l.

Department of Education, City of Reggio Emilia. (1990). *Cenni di storia* [An historical outline, data, and information]. Reggio Emilia, Italy: Center for Educational Research.

Diamond, M. C., & Hopson, J. (1998). *Magic trees of the mind: How to nurture your child's intelligence, creativity, and healthy emotions from birth to adolescence.* New York: Dutton.

Dreier, E. (1984). Blocks in the elementary school. In E. Hirsh (Ed.), *The block book* (rev. ed.). Washington, DC: National Association for the Education of Young Children.

Edwards, C. (1993). Partner, nurturer, and guide: The roles of the Reggio teacher in action. In C. Edwards, L. Gandini, & G. Forman (Eds.), *The hundred languages of children: The Reggio Emilia approach to early childhood education* (pp. 151-170). Norwood, NJ: Ablex.

Edwards, C., Gandini, L., & Forman, G. (Eds.). (1993). *The hundred languages of children: The Reggio Emilia approach to early childhood education.* Norwood, NJ: Ablex.

Edwards, C., Gandini, L., & Forman, G. (Eds.). (1998). *The hundred languages of children: The Reggio Emilia approach—advanced reflections* (2nd ed). Stamford, CT: Ablex.

Entsminger, V. (1994). *Teachers' perceptions of a pedagogic innovation: Barriers and mechanisms for successful implementation.* Unpublished doctoral dissertation, St. Louis University, St. Louis, MO.

Flinders, C. L. (1998). *At the root of this longing: Reconciling a spiritual hunger and a feminist thirst.* New York: HarperCollins.

Forman, G., & Gandini, L. (Eds.). (1994). *The amusement park for the birds* [video]. Amherst, MA: Performatics.

Fyfe, B. (1998). Questions for collaboration: Lessons from Reggio Emilia. *Canadian Children, 23*(1), 20-24.

Gambetti, A. (1997, April). *Presentation to parents of the St. Louis-Reggio collaborative,* St. Louis, MO.

Gallas, K. (1994). *The languages of learning: How children talk, write, dance, draw, and sing their understanding of the world.* New York: Teachers College Press.

Gallas, K. (1995). *Talking their way into science: Hearing children's questions and theories, responding with curricula.* New York: Teachers College Press.

Gardner, H. (2000). *The disciplined mind: Beyond facts and standard tests, the K-12 education every child deserves.* New York: Penguin Books.

Gandini, L. (1993). Fundamentals of the Reggio approach to early childhood education. *Young Children, 49,* 4-8.

Gardner, H. (2001). Final reflections: Making our learning visible. In C. Giudici, C. Rinaldi, & M. Krechevsky (Eds.), *Making learning visible: Children as individual and group learners* (pp. 337-340). Reggio Emilia, Italy: Reggio Children S.r.l.

Giudici, C., Rinaldi, C., & Krechevsky, M. (Eds.). (2001). *Making learning visible: Children as individual and group learners.* Reggio Emilia, Italy: Reggio Children S.r.l.

Hirsh, E. (Ed.). (1984). *The block book* (rev. ed.). Washington, DC: National Association for the Education of Young Children.

I Cento Linguaggi dei bambini: Narative del possible [The hundred languages of children: Narratives of the possible]. (1996). Reggio Emilia, Italy: Reggio Children S.r.l.

Isaacs, W. (1999). *Dialogue and the art of thinking together.* New York: Currency.

Katz, L. (1998). What can we learn from Reggio Emilia? In C. Edwards, L. Gandini, & G. Forman (Eds.), *The hundred languages of children: The Reggio Emilia approach—advanced reflections* (2nd ed.). Stamford, CT: Ablex.

Katz, L. G., & Ceasarone, B. (Eds.). (1994). *Reflections on the Reggio Emilia approach.* Urbana, IL: ERIC/EECE.

Kellogg, R., & O'Dell, S. (1967). *The psychology of children's art.* New York: Random House.

Kenny, V. (1998). *Gregory Bateson's notion of the sacred—What can it tell us about living constructively?* Manuscript submitted for publication; available at www.oikos.org/vinsacred.htm.

Kingston, K. (1999). *Clear your clutter with feng shui.* New York: Broadway Books.

Lewin, A. (1995). *The fundamentals of the Reggio approach.* Presentation to visiting delegation at the Model Early Learning Center, Washington, DC.

Lewis, A. (1998, fall). Student work: This focus for staff development leads to genuine collaboration. *National Staff Development Council Journal of Staff Development,* 24-27.

Lowenfeld, V. (1964). *Creative and mental growth.* New York: Macmillan.

Macy, J. (1990). The greening of the self. In A. Badiner (Ed.), *Dharma Gaia: A harvest of essays in Buddhism and ecology* (pp. 53–63). Berkeley, CA: Parallax Press.

Maturana, H., & Varela, F. (1987). *The tree of knowledge.* Boston, MA: Shambala.

Municipal infant-toddler centers and preschools of Reggio Emilia: Historical notes and general information. (2000). Reggio Emilia, Italy: Reggio Children S.r.l.

Pipher, M. (1996). *The shelter of each other.* New York: Putnam.

Rinaldi, C. (1992, January). *Corso d'aggiornamenti per nuovi insegnanti.* Address presented at seminars for new teachers, Reggio Emilia, Italy.

Rinaldi, C. (1998). The space of childhood. In G. Ceppi & M. Zini (Eds.), *Children, spaces, and relations: Metaproject for an environment for young children* (pp. 114–120). Reggio Emilia, Italy: Reggio Children S.r.l.

Rinaldi, C. (2000a). *The pedagogy of listening.* Address given to study tour in Reggio Emilia, Italy.

Rinaldi, C. (2000b). *Values and the Reggio Approach.* Address delivered at conference on research and documentation, Oakland, CA.

Rinaldi, C. (2001). Documentation and assessment: What is the relationship? In C. Giudici, C. Rinaldi, & M. Krechevsky (Eds.), *Making learning visible: Children as individual and group learners* (pp. 78–90). Reggio Emilia, Italy: Reggio Children S.r.l.

Robertson, S. (1963). *Rosegarden and labyrinth.* London: Routledge & Kegan Paul.

Sanders, S. R. (1991). Tokens of mystery. In *Secrets of the universe: Scenes from the journey home.* Boston, MA: Beacon Press.

Seidel, S. (2001). Understanding documentation starts at home. In C. Giudici, C. Rinaldi, & M. Krechevsky (Eds.), *Making learning visible: Children as individual and group learners* (pp. 304–311). Reggio Emilia, Italy: Reggio Children S.r.l.

Senge, P., Cambron-McCabe, N., Lucas, T., Smith, B., Dutton, J., & Kleiner, A. (2000). *Schools that learn.* New York: Currency.

Spaggiari, A. (2000). Introduction. In M. Davoli & G. Ferri (Eds.). *Reggio tutta: A guide to the city by the children.* Reggio Emilia, Italy: Reggio Children S.r.l.

Spaggiari, S. (1993). The community-teacher partnership in the governance of the schools. In C. Edwards, L. Gandini, & G. Forman (Eds.), *The hundred languages of children: The Reggio Emilia approach to early childhood education* (pp. 91–99). Norwood, NJ: Ablex.

Spaggiari, S. (2000). *Introductory address to the study tour.* Reggio Emilia, Italy.

Strozzi, P. (2000). *Presentation on dramatic play and identity.* Reggio Emilia, Italy.

The 10 best schools in the world, and what we can learn from them. (1991, December 2) *Newsweek,* pp. 50–59.

Thich Nhat Hanh. (2000). *The path of emancipation.* Berkeley, CA: Parallax Press.

Topal, C. W., & Gandini, L. (1999). *Beautiful stuff: Learning with found materials.* Worcester, MA: Davis.

Vecchi, V. (2001). The curiosity to understand. In C. Giudici, C. Rinaldi, & M. Krechevsky (Eds.), *Making learning visible: Children as individual and group learners* (pp. 158–212). Reggio Emilia, Italy: Reggio Children S.r.l.

Walsh, D. J. (1993, July/August). Art as socially constructed narrative: Implications for early childhood education. *Art Education Policy Review, 94*(6), 18–23.

Wheatley, M. & Kellner-Rogers, M. (1996). *A simpler way.* San Francisco, CA: Berrett Koehler.

Wiggins, G. & McTighe, J. (1998). *Understanding by design.* Alexandria, VA: Association for Supervision and Curriculum Development.

Index

Alexander, Christopher, 177-78
Alice and the Wire, 70
"Amusement Park for Birds, The," 24, 184, 186
Ariosto, Ludovico, 2
Ariosto Theater, 168-72, 181, 188
Assessment, 195-202
Atelier (studio), 3, 10, 60, 64, 81, 129, 153-54, 166
    at the College School, 16, 20, 22-24, 26, 33-40, 88, 106-7, 109-27, 132-36, 141-42, 160, 167
    at the Diana School, 107-9, 130, 173, 182
    outdoor, 137-41, 166-67
Atelierista (studio teacher), 3-4, 7-8, 10, 19, 30, 35, 82, 97, 142, 164
Avid Cinema, 39
Azzariti, Jennifer, 35, 97

Bateson, Gregory, 3, 130, 163, 169, 202
Berensohn, Paulus, 142
Big Bend Room, 20, 40, 62, 85, 112, 114, 121, 123, 125, 134
Block area, 36, 63, 85, 90, 93-95, 111, 136
Block Book, The (Apelman & Johnson), 95
Boiardo, Maria, 2
Bradshaw, Louise, 113
Bradshaw, Susan, 147
Breig-Allen, Cheryl, 7, 77, 82-83, 105
Bringing Reggio Emilia Home (Cadwell), 1-2, 4, 10-11, 16, 107, 140, 146
Bruner, Jerome, 3, 98, 163
Burrington, Barbara, 97
Burton, Judith, 131, 169, 201-2

Cadwell, Ashley, 7
Cagliari, Paola, 78, 186-87
Carson, Rachel, 131
Children, Spaces, and Relations (Ceppi & Zini), 106-7, 133
Ciari, Bruno, 3

Clay, 2, 13, 18, 44, 78, 105, 109-10, 121, 131-32, 136-46, 173, 175, 177, 179, 183, 185, 196
Clayton Schools' Family Center, 1, 7, 13, 58, 68, 79, 82-83, 86, 105, 111, 147
Clear Your Clutter with Feng Shui (Kingston), 115-16
Collage (newsletter), 46, 59
Collage, 4, 15, 18, 23, 82-84, 86, 105, 114, 121, 176
    materials for, 5-6, 20, 22-23, 35, 83, 118, 120, 126
College School, 1, 7, 10-11, 36, 45-46, 51, 53, 58-59, 61, 79, 85-86, 105, 113-14, 117-18, 147, 173-74, 188
    adoption of Reggio Approach, 24-25, 189-91
    atelier at, 16, 20, 22-24, 26, 33-40, 88, 106-7, 109-27, 132-36, 141-42, 160, 167
    day in, 12-41
    holiday party at, 46-49, 53-54, 59, 63
Community-Early Childhood Council, 173-74
Conference on Documentation and Research, 67, 78-79, 85
Csikszentmihalyi, Mihaly, 136
Culminating experience, 16, 105
Curriculum, 4, 24-25, 62, 113, 151, 158, 195-96, 201
"Curtain, The," 168-72, 181-82

Daily journal, 16, 18, 40, 46, 55, 59, 94, 111, 119
Danforth Foundation, 1, 6, 24
Declaration of intent, 33, 86-87, 90, 93, 111, 120-21, 152, 182, 188, 200
Devlin, Joyce, 87, 111, 113, 115, 119
Dewey, John, 3, 98, 163
Diana School, 8, 11, 24, 39, 47, 97-98, 102, 107-8, 130, 161, 168, 173-84, 186-89, 194, 196
    atelier at, 107-9, 130, 173, 182

Dieckhaus, Mary Jo, 83
Documentation, 3, 5, 8, 18, 22, 24, 32, 51,
    54-55, 59, 78, 81, 85, 87, 89-90, 93-95,
    97, 111-14, 146, 170, 174-76, 180,
    182-84, 186-87, 195-99, 201-2
"Documentation and Assessment" (Rinaldi),
    195
Domus Academy Research Center, 106
Dramatic play, 4, 95, 188
Drawing, 4, 23, 32, 94, 105, 113, 120-21,
    131, 134, 144, 155, 169
Dreier, Elizabeth, 95
Dress-ups, 177, 188-89

Edwards, Carolyn, 77
Engstrom, Lynette, 68
Erikson, Erik, 3

Fahlman, Penny, 162
Ferrario, Angela, 162
Finding One's Way with Clay (Berensohn),
    142
Forman, George, 189
Freinet, Celestin, 3
Fyfe, Brenda, 6, 8, 69, 89, 141, 147

Gallas, Karen, 25-26, 30
Gambetti, Amelia, 7-8, 15-16, 18-19, 34, 45,
    49, 51-52, 54-55, 57-58, 65-70, 74-79,
    86-87, 93, 102, 105-6, 162, 164-65,
    167, 188-93, 197
    in St. Louis, 79-85
Gandini, Lella, 189
Gardner, Howard, 6, 98, 183
Gateway Arch, 90, 102-5
Geismar Ryan, Lori, 7, 68-70, 77-78, 147
Geraldine E. Dodge Poetry Festival, 126
Goldhaber, Jeanne, 162, 164-65, 174
Graves, Judy, 68, 162, 164
"Gregory Bateson's Notion of the Sacred"
    (Kenny), 130
Guerra, Melissa, 7, 147, 152, 196-98
Guggenheim, Charles, 104

Harman, Danny, 112
Harman, Skyler, 7, 25-26, 30, 39
Hawkins, David, 3, 98
Hillman, Jennifer, 59, 61, 63-65, 93-94
Holiday party, at the College School, 46-49,
    53-54, 59, 63
Horse Chair, The, 71-72
Hundred Languages of Children, The
    (exhibit), 8-9, 57, 68-78, 86

Identity board, 13, 85-86, 89, 111
Innovative Teacher Project, 68
Insect Mural, 113-14
International Center for the Defense and
    Promotion of the Rights and Potential
    of All Children. *See* Reggio Children
Intimacy of Wire, The, 70-72, 74-78
Isaacs, Susan, 3
Isaacs, William, 98-99

Katz, Catherine, 7, 70
Katz, Lilian, 162, 164
Katzman, Mark, 83
Kenny, Vincent, 130, 159
Kingston, K., 116-17

"Language of Leaves, The," 176, 180
La Villetta Schol, 7-8, 11, 47, 115, 129,
    184-86, 194
Learning environment, 4-5, 106-8, 117-18,
    136, 145, 165-67, 177-78, 188-89
Lesch, John, 112
"Life of a Jasmine, The," 180-81
Light table, 36, 64, 76, 83, 118, 120-21,
    123-25, 132-34, 136, 175, 180
Little Prince (Saint-Exupery), 163
Lowenfeld, Victor, 169
Lyon, Susan, 68, 162

MacIntosh, Beth, 114-15
Magic Trees of the Mind (Diamond &
    Hopson), 198
Making Learning Visible (Giudici et al.),
    6, 184, 195-96, 198, 201
Malaguzzi, Loris, 3-4, 30, 58, 76, 97-98, 107,
    114, 168, 170-72, 182, 190-93, 202
Mandala shape, 144, 166, 172
Masek, John, 101-2
Masters, Dan, 109, 111-12, 137
Materials, in the classroom, 4, 10, 12, 20,
    34, 38, 44, 60, 76, 82, 89, 95, 106-7,
    109-10, 113-16, 132, 136, 151, 165-
    66, 182, 184. *See also* Collage, mate-
    rials for
    organization of, 5-6, 20-21, 37, 44-45,
    82, 117-26, 185
Maturana, Humberto, 3, 202
McBride, Elise, 121
Meninno, Isabella, 8, 173, 177, 183-84
Message center, 19-23, 32, 35-36, 89, 119,
    122
Meuth, Christi, 7, 19, 21, 23, 36, 39, 59, 62,
    85-90, 111

Miller Hovey, Sally, 7, 12, 14-15, 19, 21-23, 36, 39-40, 54, 63, 85-88, 90, 111, 137, 141-42, 188
Mills College, 3, 67-68, 85, 162, 167, 176
Mind and Nature (Bateson), 98
Mini-*atelier,* 20, 23, 32, 35-36, 83, 89, 119, 165, 181
Model Early Learning Center, 97
Montessori, Maria, 3, 98
Monticelli, Antonia, 78
Mori, Marina, 8, 130
Morrison, Sue, 7
Movement of Cooperative Education, 3
Moyers, Bill, 126
Municipal Infant-Toddler Centers and Preschools. *See* Reggio Emilia, preschools of

National Conference for Constructionist Teaching, 147
Neruda School, 115, 185
Newport Room, 31-32, 35-36, 38, 40, 60-62, 85, 87, 90, 94, 105, 111-13, 119, 134, 141, 188

Observation, of children, 19-23, 25-30, 32-33, 35-36, 88-89, 94-95, 97, 132, 141-45, 175, 177, 183-84
Observation notebook, 19-23

Painting, 2, 4, 112-14, 121, 131-32, 136, 144, 173, 181
Paper sculpture, 33-36, 110, 121
Parental involvement, 3-5, 10, 12-13, 16, 18, 20, 22-23, 33, 37-38, 43-66, 78, 82, 86, 89, 93-95, 99-100, 105, 114, 117-26, 132, 137, 186-89. *See also* Sprong, Kathleen
Parent Board, 14-15, 45, 50, 52, 59, 81, 173
Parent-Teacher Committee, 45-46, 48-51, 53-56, 60, 62-63, 66, 82, 120
Parent-Teacher Exchange evenings, 50-54, 59, 62, 64
Parent-teacher meetings, 15
Pattern Language, A (Alexander), 178
Pedagogical team, 3
Pedagogista (pedagogical coordinator), 5, 24, 78, 177, 186-87
Phillips, Jan, 6, 40, 54, 109, 111
Piaget, Jean, 3, 98
Piazza, Giovanni, 7-8, 129, 184-86
Picasso, Pablo, 72, 77
Pipher, Mary, 61

Plutarch, 163
PPTC. *See* Pre-Primary Parent-Teacher Committee
Pre-Primary Parent-Teacher Committee (PPTC), 82
Project Zero (Harvard), 6, 68
Project Zero protocol, 68-78, 147, 150
Protagonists, children as, 2, 4

Redler, Melanie, 115
Reggio Approach, 1, 8, 10-12, 21, 25, 33, 43, 59, 68, 82, 99, 108, 146-47, 150, 163, 190, 193, 196, 198
ideas of, 4-6
implementation at the College School, 24-25, 189-91
values of, 78-79, 110-11, 167, 176, 187
Reggio Children, 4, 7-8, 106, 161, 182, 188-89, 192
Reggio Emilia, 1, 8, 30, 44, 57, 104, 115, 172
history of, 2-3
internship in, 1, 7-8, 11, 44-45, 47, 56, 97-99, 115, 129, 161, 163, 173, 184, 189-90, 194, 196
preschools of, 2-7, 13, 21, 24, 34, 39, 43, 55, 58, 61, 76, 87, 98, 107-8, 112, 114, 117, 167, 177-78, 188, 191, 194, 196, 198, 201. *See also* Diana School; La Villetta School; Neruda School; Scuola Allende
study tours in, 10, 19, 125, 160-94
Reggio Tutta (Davoli & Ferri), 84, 104-5, 174
Ricco, Paola, 8, 161-62
Ridenour, Leanne, 59-60
Ridgway, Joni, 118-20, 126
Rinaldi, Carlina, 6-10, 58, 78-79, 107, 136, 159, 167-68, 172-73, 176, 178, 187, 190, 196, 199, 201
Roberts, Dorris, 86
Robertson, Seonaid, 140
Roland, Frances, 7, 77, 147, 198-200, 202
Rosegarden and Labyrinth (Robertson), 140

Scent Project, 146-59, 193-97, 199-200, 202
Schneider, Karen, 7, 81, 147, 152, 154-55, 196-200, 202
Schools That Learn (Senge et al.), 202
Schwall, Chuck, 7, 35-36, 69-72, 74-75, 77-78, 81-82, 112, 131-32, 147-49, 152-54, 158, 196, 198, 200-201

Scuola Allende, 165-67

Seibel, Kathy, 7, 25-26, 30, 39

Self-portraits, 23, 82-83, 85-90, 105

Sense of Wonder, The (Carson), 131

Shadow screen, 4, 76, 120, 123, 125, 133, 135, 179

Shearer, Terri, 59, 61

Shelter of Each Other, The (Pipher), 61

Shiva, 100

Shoptaugh, Sonya, 126

Simpler Way, A (Wheatley & Kellner-Rogers), 5

Smith, Luther Ely, 104

Snyder, Gary, 126

Soulard Market, 63, 90, 93-95

Spaggiari, Antonella, 104-5

Spaggiari, Sergio, 163-64, 167, 173, 186, 193

Sprong, Kathleen, 37, 59-60, 62-64, 120-26, 133, 160-63, 165, 168, 173-74, 176-82, 184, 186-89, 194

Standards, 195, 199, 201-2

St. Louis, 58, 67-68, 84, 93, 102-5

St. Louis-Reggio Collaborative, 1-2, 8, 10, 13, 20, 46, 49, 58-59, 65, 67-69, 78, 82, 85, 99, 105, 117, 126, 132, 147, 173, 186, 188, 190-91, 194, 202

history of, 6-8, 19

St. Louis-Reggio Collaborative Parent-Teacher Exchange, 50

St. Michael School, 1, 7, 13, 58, 79-82, 86, 105, 111-12, 146, 158, 191, 195, 202

Strange, Jennifer, 7, 16, 31-33, 39-40, 48, 54, 60, 90, 93-95, 102-4, 106, 111, 113, 119, 123-24, 137, 141-42, 147, 188-89

Strange, Michael, 121, 123-24, 137

Strozzi, Paola, 8, 188-89

Studio. *See Atelier*

Studio teacher. *See Atelierista*

Summer books, 55-56, 64, 66

Teachers

collaboration among, 10, 35, 67-100

as listeners, 25-30. *See also* Observation, of children

as researchers, 3, 5, 23, 26, 35-36, 69, 82, 93, 97, 198

"There Was a Child Went Forth" (Whitman), 129

Thich Nhat Hanh, 129

Timeless Way of Building, The (Alexander), 177-78

Tompkins, C. C., 146-48, 152, 154, 158, 200

Transcription, of children's conversations, 30-31, 39, 112, 148, 158

Tree of Knowledge (Maturana & Varela), 98

"Tree Project, The," 24

U.N. Committee on the Rights of Children, 161-62

Understanding by Design (Wiggins & McTighe), 199

"Understanding Documentation Starts at Home" (Seidel), 195, 197

Varela, F., 3, 202

Vecchi, Vea, 8, 30, 130-31, 159, 168-74, 177, 182-84, 186, 201-2

Vygotsky, Lev, 3, 98

Walters, Steve, 53, 59-60, 62-65

Web of Life, The (Capra), 202

Webster University, 6-8

Whitman, Walt, 129, 159, 185

Wiggins, Grant, 199, 202

Wilmes, Mary Jo, 113-14

Wind of the Fair, The, 70-71

Wyndham, Mark, 7, 31-33, 38-39, 54, 59-60, 62, 93-95, 111

Zini, Tullio, 177

About the Author

Louise Boyd Cadwell lives in St. Louis, Missouri, where she works as a studio teacher/researcher in all three schools of the St. Louis–Reggio Collaborative: the College School, the St. Michael School, and Clayton Schools' Family Center. She returned to St. Louis after a 1-year internship in the preschools of Reggio Emilia, Italy, where she studied with Italian educators to learn about the Reggio Approach to early childhood education. She continues to work with both Italian and American educators to invent vital new ways of living and learning in school in the United States. She received her Ph.D. in 1996 from the Union Institute. Her work as a teacher and researcher has focused on children's development through the arts and spoken and written language, particularly as children discover their place in the natural world.